BELFRY
HOCKEY

BELFRY
HOCKEY

*STRATEGIES TO TEACH THE
WORLD'S BEST ATHLETES*

DARRYL BELFRY
WITH SCOTT POWERS

TRIUMPH
B O O K S

Library of Congress Cataloging-in-Publication Data available upon request.

This book is available in quantity at special discounts for your group or organization. For further information, contact:
  Triumph Books LLC
  814 North Franklin Street
  Chicago, Illinois 60610
  www.triumphbooks.com

Printed in U.S.A.

ISBN: 978-1-62937-801-5

Photos courtesy of Darryl Belfry unless otherwise indicated.

Design by Sue Knopf
Page production by Preston Pisellini

I dedicate this book to my amazing wife, Ruth. You gave me the best gifts of my life: a true love partnership; our two children, Ella and Easton; and the permission to find my own path. That makes you the MVP of my life. Without you, there is no me.

CONTENTS

FOREWORD

WHEN DARRYL CALLED AND TOLD ME HE WANTED ME TO WRITE the foreword to his book, it was a huge honor for me. I know how successful he's been and how much his career has taken off in the last 10 years. I hold him in such high regard for what he's done for my career.

I began working with Darryl when I was nine years old. We worked together until I was 13 and moved away from home, first to Michigan and then Ontario. Darryl came to one of my games with the London Knights of the Ontario Hockey League when I was 17. I didn't have an agent at the time, but CAA was in town and wanted to meet with me. I invited Darryl to come with us. Sure enough, he sat right next to Pat Brisson, who is now my agent. He pitched Brisson his game plan with his video one-on-one work, breaking down players, and Brisson really loved it. I think that's where Darryl's growth really took off. He started working with guys like Sidney Crosby, Auston Matthews, Mathew Barzal, and myself, as well as some other CAA clients. Now he's regarded as one of the best guys in the world as far as skill development.

One thing I always liked about working with Darryl was that, while your coaches want you to play within the structure and certain things, Darryl always looked at the game differently, creating new ideas and talking through things that might work. When you're on the ice with him one-on-one, he's going through certain plays and situations and explaining how you can manipulate a defender and use your teammates. It was just so different from what you hear from anyone else. It's fun to look at the game in a different light.

I've spent a huge part of my career with Darryl—from the ages of nine to 13, when I first started working with him, to right after my time in the OHL, to now in the NHL with the Blackhawks. He helped me think differently and get not only my game to where it is now, but also my hockey sense. He helped me read and react to different defenses and learn things that can work in different situations.

The one thing Darryl could really do when we were younger is run a practice like no one else. He ran the best practices. They were always about two hours, and they would just go by so quick. You knew you were getting better out there. I can actually remember every Sunday morning my dad would drive 30 to 40 minutes to the rink in Fort Erie, Ontario. I would skate with the young kids from 7:30 AM to 9:00 AM. I'd then skate from 9:00 AM to 10:30 AM with kids my age and from 10:30 AM to noon with the older kids. I'd be on the ice for four and a half hours on Sunday mornings. Then, driving back, we'd start listening to the Buffalo Bills game on the radio. Can you imagine being on the ice that long today? It would be terrible, but his drills were fun. You knew your skills were getting better. You were working on different moves, deking goalies.

I've seen Darryl evolve over the years. At his Florida summer pro camp, you can tell he has more confidence going into it. Players want to be there. They know it's a good camp. You're going to get better and skate with good players, obviously, but you're also going to be learning from him. He definitely has more confidence and swagger. One thing I like about him as a teacher is it's not the same thing over and over again. You're always learning something new. You ask him about something, and he takes you through it in certain situations. In Florida this past year, after a practice, we were just working on something for 15 to 20 minutes. For me, it was about weight shift coming into the zone and how to be deceptive and get defenders thinking you're doing something other than what you're actually going to do.

Darryl knows my game now. He knows what's going to work and what's not going to work. It's about fine-tuning it and always trying to improve. Sometimes we take certain things from certain players. I really like the way Barzal skates, how he moves and hangs on to the puck, so we talk about certain things he does and what I can do similarly to be successful. It's never really predictable. It's an ongoing conversation about how to get better and how to pick up a little thing here or there to give yourself an advantage. He sends you three-game segments of your play and talks about certain plays and places on the ice. He'll say, "I'm just going to look into it and see what we can do more of, what we can gain on this play." It's cool he's thinking about it and putting his mind to figuring out something that works.

A few years ago, the Blackhawks were playing the Islanders at home. I hadn't scored for a bit and was going through a phase where everything I was shooting was high. Darryl said, "On the first shot of the game, I want you to come down and just shoot a blocker low a foot off the ice." Sure enough, I received a pass a minute and a half in, I shot a blocker low, and it went in. That's worth it right there. Little things like that don't sound like a big deal, but I probably wouldn't have known I was shooting high all the time. You don't get individual stuff like that from coaches. I wouldn't know I shot something like 15 of my last 20 high.

It's been cool to be involved with Darryl in the pro summit. I think we can grow it even bigger. I don't know what it's going to be or what the next step is, but I think we can keep building it. That's good for me, too. I love going down there and being able to skate with some of the best players in the league for five days and learn from them. It's a good situation for everyone. I didn't know Darryl was going to do anything like naming the camp the 88 Summit or having a T-shirt with my celebration on it. It's cool to see.

We have such a close relationship that we understand when the other might be frustrated about something or feel the other person is in the wrong. It's about working through those times and trying to figure out the best way to go about it to make me the best player.

He's been tough on me since I was a kid. I remember maybe my first or second game with him. We had a team called the Playmakers. I used to hang on to the puck a lot. I was probably what you would call a puckhog back then. I'd come down and try to go through everyone. I was getting through sometimes, but other times, I wasn't. He came to me and said, "Alright, if you try to go through a whole team again, you're going to sit on the bench the rest of the game." So, we were up something like 5–1 and I got the puck, went through the team, and ended up scoring. I came back to the bench and he said, "Nice; sit next to me the rest of the game." The whole last period I sat next to him on the bench. I scored a goal, but he wanted to get the message across. That really helped me develop my vision and playmaking, because before that all I wanted was to score goals.

For me, personally, I think there's another level to get to. How we go about it in the future is going to be pretty interesting. Darryl sending me segment stuff during the season is great, but in the summer I think we can work together more. Sometimes you just have to be happy with the way a career is going, right? But I don't know if that's really in our blood. It's like we're always searching for that next advantage—a way to shoot better, to be more efficient, to feel better on the ice, to create more time and space. If you give me time and space, I'm probably going to make a play, and that's the thing we're always searching for.

More than the coaching, I have a friendship with Darryl, and my parents do, too. He was a great hockey coach and he turned it into something else. I think if you ask anyone in the league, they would say they would want Darryl on their team. We're fortunate to work with him during the summers—even those he's signed with the Toronto Maple Leafs. Darryl's at the top of the game in skill development, for sure.

—*Patrick Kane*
Chicago Blackhawks winger and
three-time Stanley Cup champion
January 2020

INTRODUCTION

I DIDN'T DO MUCH READING IN HIGH SCHOOL. I WAS ADAMANTLY opposed to it, because I didn't like that other people were telling me what to read. But after high school, I realized I could pick up whatever I wanted to. So, I went on a reading tear. My first year out of high school I probably read upward of 60 books. Once I got started, I would just go, then that book led to another one, and then I was off to the bookstore and the books were picking me. A title would jump out at me, and that was my next book.

One quote that stood out to me during that time was all the difference I could make to the quality of my life would be in the quality of the books I was reading and the quality of the people I would meet. I really took that to heart and continued to be an avid reader for quite a long time. I also began to pay more attention to the people I was meeting and what their purpose was in my meeting them. There were people who would come into my world and, though I didn't know what the purpose was at the time, I was open to learning it. I would become a much better listener to what it was I was supposed to get from them. It was about the exchange of ideas.

My dad had a bunch of friends he would hang out with at our house. When I first left school and was in binge-reading mode, I wasn't working or going to school. I was just at home. I wasn't studying for school, but I was studying to try to figure out what it was I wanted to do. My dad's friends just could not get over the idea that my dad would allow me to stay at the house without having a job. My dad, at points, was also getting frustrated. He knew I was doing something, so I think he was a little bit more patient.

There was one day I remember when my uncle called the house and I answered the phone. It was around 9:00 AM. He said, "You're up?" I said, "I've been up since 7." He said, "I thought you slept all day." He basically thought I was lazy, and I was angry about that. The next time my dad and all his friends were in the garage, one of them said, "So, Darryl, what do you do all day?" "Well, I'm researching what I want to do." They were like, "What are you talking about? Researching? You just need to go get a job. I can't believe you're here." I said, "I'm not going to get a job to be a ham-and-egger like you." I don't know where that term came from, but it was the first thing that popped in my mind. I was angry and wanted to say the most hurtful thing I possibly could. Naturally, they asked what a ham-and-egger was as they laughed at me. I told them it's a guy who gets up at the exact same time every morning, has the exact same breakfast, leaves the house at the exact same time, drives the exact same way to work every single day, punches into work, does the exact same job with the same people for the next 30 years, punches out, drives the exact same way home, eats the exact same thing for dinner, and does it all every single day. That, to me, was torture. I explained to them I just couldn't live like that. If that's what going out and getting a job was like, there had to be a better way than that.

For the longest time, their joke was, *There goes the future ham-and-egger.* Of course, that provided a massive amount of motivation for me to become something different. My personality was oppositional. If you say I need to do something, then I was going to do the opposite. I had drawn my line in the sand that I wasn't going to be like them. I just wanted something different.

1

DEVELOPING ON-ICE PRESENCE

WHEN I GOT MY START AS A PERFORMANCE COACH, I WAS LIMITED in the way I could command a group. I quickly learned that developing an on-ice presence was a critical area for my own development. My lack of true presence was limiting the growth of the players I was trying to influence. It didn't take long to determine where my challenges and limitations were. For starters, not only was I young, but I looked even younger. I had no physical presence from either stature or hockey skill. The only projectable asset I could leverage was my passion. That's where I started. My starting point was to be mostly authoritative. I tried to demand the respect and attention of the group by being ultra-aggressive, loud, and animated in my approach. This is a stark departure from my personality, so naturally, I struggled with how to establish a more authentic presence. It became clear this was going to be a short-term approach, but I had to start somewhere. The issue was I was forcing players to give me their attention rather than commanding their attention through the quality of my approach and content. In an effort to improve, I embarked on what ended up becoming five stages of developing a presence.

The first stage was the sweat test push. It's creating a high level of energy to push the group to pass the sweat test. The sweat test is a hockey term coaches and parents use to evaluate a skate. After a skate, a player would remove their helmet and their mother would run a hand through their hair to see if there was sweat. That's the most basic way to evaluate whether an ice session had any value. Passing the sweat test is usually accomplished by manipulating the work-to-rest ratio and driving players like cattle, pushing and prodding them to perform at a high rate of speed. It's not necessarily doing things right, just doing things very fast. I spent most of my time when I was in this stage designing drills that were no more than 1:3 work-to-rest ratio. It was a sprint, and I was barking at them nonstop to move faster.

The ridiculousness of the sweat test push led me right into the second stage, which is where I adopted more of a showman's personality on the ice. I switched from relentless screaming and high energy to being more entertaining and pushing the group through positive energy. I went from a negative tone in pushing the sweat test to the opposite end of the spectrum, where I was more conscious of the show and how the whole ice moved. As you were watching from above, aesthetically, you'd see the ice move with ease. You knew we used the whole ice and the kids were up and down the ice sprinting. Now instead of being focused on work-to-rest ratio, I was concerned about ice utilization and rotations. I began to try to design more creative drills, assembly-line drills, where players did one part of the drill and then moved to another line to do the next part of the drill, and so on. I was managing the work-to-rest ratio that way and attempting to be creative with the way I managed the sheet. I wanted people to say, "This guy runs a good ice session and you know it because you can see how he manages the ice." The sessions became a production, with lots of moving parts coming on and off the stage with organization, timing, and ease.

The further I got into this process, the more I realized the first two stages were really all about me. They had nothing to do with the players. I didn't really enjoy the first two stages because I knew my impact was limited. For me to get to the next level, I needed to become more of a teacher. In the third stage, I sought to do that by adding more detailed teaching points and an emphasis on technical execution elements, while alternating between the sweat test and the showman. Stage three was about finding the detail inside the drill design while I was setting up the drills. I began looking to see technique differences in players, creating a skill focus inside the drill, and adding a detail that would address a skill deficiency.

The timing of the third stage was good, as it developed when I was working with a lot of different age groups and skill levels. I had developed a couple different ways I could approach the ice so I could take advantage of the learning opportunities that come from having to adapt to the ever-changing environments I was presented with in the fourth stage. I sought to use different tools for different reasons. This was the first time I wasn't teaching with a one-size-fits-all approach. I challenged myself to ask, *What type of group is this? Is this a group I need to push or need to look better aesthetically? Do they need more detail? Should I slow it down or speed it up?* I'd start off with a real push, move into more of an aesthetic ice-ballet look, add some detail, and finish with a push to make sure I was checking all the boxes in the end. The kids were learning something, it looked good from an audience perspective, and yet everyone was passing the sweat test. This stage started to feel like I was more in control and making key decisions about how to approach development.

The fifth and final stage wasn't something I was looking for; it just revealed itself. I was happy with the teaching pattern I was in, and I was getting good feedback from my clients. I had established more range and was constantly adding and combining different methods and drill sequences. However, the fifth stage started when I realized I could consistently influence the results in the athletes. I had the skill to adapt to my environment. Once I knew that, it was a real game-changer to focus on the content. It became less about the person in the show and more about the product.

It wasn't long before I could run any type of ice or a combination of stages to a given ice. We had the sweat test. We had the movement. We had ice management. Then, things turned again when we had elite ice. As I rapidly moved through my stages, I was also attracting more elite players, so we had to have elite ice, and it had to move in a certain way. In this stage, I felt I needed to do a lot of teaching to the parents. As part of the show, I would often narrate what was going on in order to educate the parents on what I was doing. I wasn't very comfortable with it, but I understood it was an important part of the process. I needed them to understand what I was doing because I was doing things so differently. As I shifted from the production to focusing on the content, it became more of a teaching progression, and I was able trust my results because I had discovered the impact of time.

In that discovery process, I had a moment that completely changed my perspective. A parent came up to me and said their son had transferred a skill I had taught him in a session to a game. He put it right in. I had no idea this was possible. However, once I realized players could be expected to utilize some of the skills immediately, it allowed me to trust the results even more. Up until that point, I viewed all development as a long-term process. All of a sudden, I realized players didn't need eight weeks to learn a skill. My details and progressions could lead to transfer right away. The natural question was how I could manage the speed of the learning rate.

The most difficult aspect of progressing through the five stages was wanting to still be authentic to myself. The struggle was I was becoming a different person when I was teaching than who I actually am. It wasn't real. I know I needed to do it that way because there really wasn't any reason for anyone to listen to me. I didn't have anything of much value going on. In order for there to be value, the players had to pass the sweat test. To do that, I had to push them. Because I was willing to create that push, I was building an audience. But then I needed to convert that audience into longtime clients, which could only happen from them coming to believe they could actually learn something from me. It was interesting as I attempted to shift from this alter ego to more of an authentic personality. It was quite a process.

I went through the five stages and ultimately found the truth in what I was doing. The truth was in the results. Once I knew I could produce the results, it settled my on-ice presence. I was able to say to players who skated with me, "If you listen, pay attention, and work hard here, you're going to learn something you'll be able to use. You'll become a better player because you came to me today—not eight weeks from now, but because you came today." That changed everything for me. I began a list of one-day transfer skills I could teach and then follow up for immediate feedback. This was a tremendous learning experience. I needed to develop myself to develop my presence. The more I became comfortable in the subject matter, the more I began to learn types of progressions that led to successful results.

When I first started as a young instructor from the ages of 17 to 25, I was shy and self-conscious. A lot of it was because I had never played, and here I was in a space that typically favored those who had played. I had zero experience. *You've got to listen to me.* Well, why did anyone need to listen to me? I was self-conscious about that for the longest time, which was a major problem. Once I became more comfortable with myself, I knew more about the subject matter and was producing results, I became more comfortable in my environment. It gave me the confidence and ability to execute without having other things on my mind.

During all of this, one of the most critical parts of my development was when I wanted to see how it would be for the viewer. I videotaped all my ice sessions for a few years so I could see what the audience was seeing. I was trying to see how the ice moved, how the sessions flowed, what errors I made in ice management, how long it took me to go from one drill to the next. Once I had more of an understanding of how to execute the ice, move the ice around, manage the time, and manage the reps, it became a lot easier for me.

I always felt like I had something to prove. At every ice time, I was trying to convince somebody I knew what I was doing. I would do that by executing the ice the best way I knew how. In the sweat test, it would be, *Look how hard I can make these kids skate.* That validated the money players spent to come to the ice time. As the players began returning, I became more comfortable they liked what they saw, and it gave me another opportunity to evolve.

However, to sustain my business, my focus was always the retention rate of the top players. I wanted the best players to come back more and more so that it would give me more opportunities to grow. I found it difficult to grow when I had ever-changing groups. If someone came once and left and then another person came once and left, it was more difficult for me to develop my skills. Even though I was doing the same amount of business, it wasn't the same business, because I wasn't getting any feedback from the audience. I needed that feedback and that opportunity to get more comfortable with people. The more often I had a core group, the faster I was able to grow and the easier it became for me to get comfortable interacting with those people.

The more knowledgeable I became, the more I was also able to field questions. People would have questions about my ideas. *Why are you doing this? What's your philosophy?* All those typical consumer questions. Early on, I didn't have a lot of good answers, and I wasn't all that confident in the answers I did have. As I became more confident and better researched, I was able to field more questions. From there, my confidence grew, people asked more questions, and more people began coming back. I was able to get into more exchanges where I could have better information to move to the next step or just understand what the next step was.

Even in just interacting with people, I'd be able to say, "Your son reminds me of this player who I worked with before, and these are the results we had." It created a story I could then back up through real experiences and successes. It gave me a sense of accomplishment for players to attribute their improved skill sets to the work they had done with me. That was critically important. I started to develop more of a range of expertise, which gave me the best opportunity then to continue to further the idea I wanted to become a teacher.

I didn't know what those five stages were in the outset. That's just how it evolved for me. I didn't know what the next stage was as much as I knew I had to progress to whatever that next stage was. I approached it with an open mind, and I was looking for clues to what that next level might be. As I was first going through it, I knew I didn't have a strong ice presence and needed to fake it before I made it. I had to *project* instead of *being*, and that's an interesting dynamic. There was a lot of posturing. It was attention-seeking. It was loud and boisterous, and anyone who knows me knows that's really not authentic to my personality. I always knew there was a small window in which could fool a group of people to come to me. Eventually, if I wasn't producing results, that fool-factor window would close, and I would lose those people. I couldn't afford to lose them, not just because I needed to sustain my business. That was important, but it was less important than getting the feedback. I wanted the feedback. The longer I was trying to expand the fool-factor window, the less likely I was going to be able to hold those people. I knew I continually had to move away from posturing. That was such a long process, because I just didn't know how to do it. There was a lot of experimenting. A lot of it was changing my on-ice personality and self-evaluation. I would try to project myself a certain way and then evaluate it. I did a lot of videotaping of my ice sessions to see if I came at it in a different way, what the result would be.

When I went through my initial reading binge, I read a lot about the value of modeling people who had success, so I endeavored to experiment in modeling. I would go around and watch coaches who were well-respected in my area. I would watch how they managed their ice times. I wanted to see what stages they were in and see if someone was at a different level than me. That was a difficult process. Most people were stuck in the sweat test, doing the same things I was doing. The approaches weren't all that varied. There weren't a lot of people coming at it from a different perspective. This also motivated me to evolve, because there is no future for me in being the same. I have to be different and better. What I wanted was to be myself and still be able to produce a better result using a different method than everyone else. It seemed forced because it just wasn't me. I was struggling with modeling, and I ended up moving away from it. I started using a more introspective method. I stopped paying attention to how other people were running their ices, because it wasn't taking me where I wanted to go. It wasn't leading me closer to what I wanted; it was actually taking me further away, because my objective was to produce better results differently, and modeling someone else was leading me to produce the same or worse results in what appeared on the surface to be the same approach. I've come to understand that in trying to copy someone else's approach, I was missing a lot of information. I didn't know what I didn't know. I didn't share the same background knowledge or the same experiences as these coaches, so I had no chance of fully modeling them. The best I could hope for was to be a dumbed-down version of someone who was producing results at a rate I was trying to exceed. It didn't take long for me to abandon modeling.

Varying my personality and changing who I was for the group was also an interesting part of the process. I went through four levels of that. I could vary whether I was the taskmaster, the court jester, the facilitator, or the teacher. It's like talking to someone with an accent. I find if someone who has an accent talks to me for an extended period of time, I'll begin almost mimicking or adopting that accent, in a way. I would do it subconsciously, not intentionally, but it was a way for me to feel a greater connection. It created this chameleon effect when I was speaking to people. That's how I was when I was experimenting with varying my personality for the group and then using each of these elements—the taskmaster, the court jester, the facilitator, and the teacher. In a single ice session, I wanted to be able to use all four of those personas in a different way and for different reasons.

I found once I started combining two or more of those elements I was able to set up my peaks in a training practice. I was able to build toward a peak, and that allowed me permission to spend time teaching or adding details. It allowed me to slow down for a certain amount of time before I ramped it back up again. I wasn't straight teaching for an hour, because that would be too slow. I needed to add these different elements. I was consciously aware of how I was projecting my on-ice presence.

There are three elements that are important to creating different looks inside a single ice session. One is the push-pace-drive-energy element. You have to manipulate pace in different ways, such as through work-to-rest ratio, going from 1:4 to 1:2. When they go quicker, you can build pace. I could drive the pace and energy without having to project myself and be cattle-prodding the whole time. I could do it by structuring my drill set. I could have the work-to-rest ratio be the driver. Sometimes I could come out pushing pace through the ease of the skills' execution. I could evaluate the group and make decisions about what skills these players were learning and how easy it was for them to execute those skills. If the skill was easy for the group to execute, I could push the pace with that. The elements I added—a puck, passing, pressure—would have an effect on the pace. I needed to understand how I could push pace without having to scream at the top of my lungs.

Then there's the matter of effort versus learning: How much effort can I put into pushing the kids to their maximum energy expenditure while still maintaining a learning element? If you push a player to his max heart rate and he's constantly performing at the highest level of effort, it's going to create a lot of tension in his body. It's difficult to be athletic or learn at that pace. You have to back it up a little, to not quite maximum level, to add those details, then switch back and forth from adding a detail at a reasonable pace, pushing the pace, coming back and adding another detail, and then pushing the pace again. The balance between effort and learning was a way of pushing the pace and driving energy.

The third element is practice peaks. I noticed when I was the taskmaster everyone was at one speed, so it was difficult to show the ice was moving at a high rate. If people are moving at different speeds, that aesthetically allows the ice to look better. But if it's playing out at one speed, it's difficult to have any real effect. What we wanted to do was have more of a buildup. It started with a blistering pace and easy skill level, allowing them to perform at a high rate, and then I'd manipulate the work-to-rest ratio to reflect the ease of skill. If it was something easy, we could work out a 1:4, 1:2, or 1:1 ratio. But if it was something we were really trying to teach, we could back it up and provide opportunity for reflection. That would be like 1:4

or 1:6 work-to-rest ratio. I was growing more conscious of how I was setting my drill design and building my sessions.

Within practice peaks is the concept of energy spikes. This is a major tool that helped me when I was trying to become more of a teacher. I could feel when the ice session was starting to get too teacher-oriented. It was too detailed and was sucking the energy out of the skates. What I needed to do was stay on task and stay inside that teaching, but add energy spikes. One way to add an energy spike is to create competition. If I was building an ice session and I could feel the energy getting lower, I would switch to a drill that was competitive inside the skill set I was working on.

For example, if I was working on tight turns, I would be very teacher-oriented in terms of how focused I was on details and expanding the work-to-rest ratios so the players could focus on learning those skills. If I then felt the energy slowing down, I would pivot to a more competitive drill in the middle of the teaching sequence to spike the energy. Another way to create energy spikes is to run continuous drill sequences, where the drill execution links one repetition to the next. Continuous drills are excellent because the continuous nature of the drill can drive the pace. If I want the pace to be high, we design a drill that is short duration with a short line, to the degree the route of a single player moved across multiple zones would be the degree the energy of the group would be lowered. To spike the energy, the continuous drill would be in one zone with a line of three-to-four players moving through. The next progression to continuous drills is multiple puck assembly-line drills. The assembly line shortens each player's route, and the multiple pucks determine the frequency of movement which carries the energy. Once I had that energy spike, it was easier to go back into the teaching.

The next part is that you want to lead from behind. You want the group pushing itself. If you viewed the group as if you were a dogsled operator, you're managing the speed, but you're facilitating, driving, directing. You're not carrying the energy; the energy is carried by the group. That just allowed me to become more of a manager of the development. The best part of leading from behind is it's less directed by the instructor and more by the athlete. When the athletes are ready to move on to the next step, they can show it by their level of capacity. You can see they're ready, so you can then pivot and move to the next progression. The progression for when you're leading from behind is related more to the athlete's execution quality and not based on a program you've presented with times. The skill instructor's ultimate goal in managing the ice is to get to a lead-from-behind role. Once you get there, that's a sweet spot to really teach and make a big impact.

2

FINDING MY VOICE

ONE OF THE MORE INTERESTING PROCESSES I WENT THROUGH while learning to teach was developing what I call my voice. There were three elements to that process. The first was managing my emotions while training an individual or a group. The second was managing my tone and how I verbalized my instructions to the players. The third was managing the vehicle I used to deliver the message or how I engaged the listener.

My introduction to finding my voice was learning to manage my emotions. My mentor, Bud Chenard, kept telling me it was important to manage my emotions and find a way to push the players. This was especially true when I was in the sweat-test ice sessions. Managing my emotions would be a key to evolving out of that stage. The theory was to flip the whole thing backward. When I was happy and things were going well, that was when I should push the players to the next level of speed and execution quality. And when things were not going well or I was unhappy with the effort, execution quality, or consistency, that was the time to support them with more patience and direct teaching. Early on in my teaching, I wore my emotions on my sleeve. You could always tell whether or not I was happy with the way the ice was going.

I remember having a conversation with Bud in which he said when you think the effort level is low or the attention to detail is not there, that's not the time to show your displeasure with them. That's the time you need to be more supportive. You have to be more creative in your approach to get them on the right track. If you just react in a negative way to a negative play or net-negative outcomes, you're just perpetuating the problem. You're not problem-solving.

The same is true when things are going well. When you have developmental momentum and everything's snapping along, you don't want to show you're overly happy because you're inadvertently creating an artificial ceiling. Your attitude toward the players' performance will suggest achievement and complacency. You want your attitude to suggest elevating and pushing to another level. When you like the execution, push for more speed. When you like the speed, push for execution detail. When you like the speed and the execution, add another skill or variable to test those factors in a different way. Continually push their limits.

When I liked what was going on, I tried to be stern. I started with an attitude that the execution wasn't good enough, and I began harping on small details. To set the tone, I started with skills I knew the group could do well, then started driving details and demanding speed and execution. I wanted to test different ways I could push them. It was more for my development initially than theirs.

When it was going well, I tried to learn what I could do to make it better. When it was going badly, I tried to take the emotion out of it to the point that I wasn't showing how unhappy I was. I'd take that time to be more supportive and creative in my approach to try to right the ship. Maybe I'd walk it back a step and build the skill a little more deliberately or look for ways I could manipulate the pace. Instead of bringing the group in and saying I was unhappy with the pace, I would mix in a drill that sparked the pace. It's similar to what I talked about with developing presence. I would focus on the buildup, create an energy spike, add competition, create another practice peak, come up with an easier skill set, delay the work-to-rest ratio or whatever I could do to encourage those players to build the pace I was seeking. Once I had it, I could start pushing again. If it was the actual skill execution I was displeased with, I would go back a few steps in the progression, build it more deliberately, and add pace with each progression.

The second element was managing my tone and how I was manufacturing intensity or shaping the environment. In order to manufacture intensity, I would use voice inflections. I would start to slow my wording down to create an environment or create energy. The process required a lot of feedback. I had to really work on it with bigger groups and learn how to use those different techniques to my advantage. A lot of it was trial and error. I found the hardest thing to do was manufacture intensity without being overly boisterous or using a push sweat test approach, like a drill sergeant screaming at the players. I wanted to get away from that and manage the intensity through voice inflection. I would quiet my voice so I could create a greater sense of attention to detail. I'd create consistencies in my techniques so I could train the players that whatever state I was in would be the mode we'd go in terms of attention to detail, pace, and intensity.

The third element was shaping the environment. This took a lot of time and was a big challenge for me. There are two things to keep in mind when you're shaping an environment. You're either creating a set of permissions or you're creating pressure. The permissions for players are permission to fail, permission to slow down, permission to trust themselves, and permission to push themselves. There is a whole set of permissions, and which permissions you're trying to push depends on where you are in the development process.

Early on, I wanted an environment where it was cool to fail. I wanted the players to feel like failing was part of the development process. I would go out of my way to create that permission. One of the things I did was train at a high pace. If you weren't on the edge of being out of control where you were falling, then you weren't at the right spot. If you were executing it at just a high enough pace to hold your edge comfortably in the change of direction or in the turn, then you were not at the level I wanted to be. I wanted you to be questioning with each foot you put down whether or not your edge was going to hold. This dovetailed perfectly with the sweat test, because it was a great way to drive pace.

The challenge is permissions to fail are different with each player based on personality and skill set. The challenge became to personalize the permission and challenge the outer edges of failure within each player. I had to teach myself how to find the permissions for different kids. Players started to fail spectacularly and more regularly as I began to focus on it, and creating those fails is one of the ways I was able to shape the environment for failure. I did all the demonstrations, and I could create failures in permission through the demonstrations. If I wanted to push the envelope, I would create failure in my demonstration so the players could see what it looked like. I'd say, "This is how hard I want you to go. See how I'm on the edge? You can look out of control. I almost fell, see how wobbly I am?" I started to get really good at illustrating that and then, in the next demonstration, overcoming it. There was a real process in learning how to utilize the demonstrations to create the failure permissions.

Then there's permission to slow down. When players are training, we're often trying to push them to perform at this high rate, but it's difficult to learn new details at the highest speed. So you often have to create permissions to slow down to acquire the detail and then speed it back up again. Creating those permissions was an important process. This took me a long time to understand. I didn't know that players couldn't easily acquire new skills at maximum energy output. Once I learned that, the perspective change was critical to the way I utilized permissions.

Sometimes players don't realize how well they're doing something because they can't see it for themselves. They can only feel what's going on. That's often uncomfortable in the learning process. If they're learning something new, it's not going to feel good. It's going to feel awkward and different. Even though the execution could be good, it's not going to feel right to them. So you're seeing they're on the right track, but in their mind as they're going through it, it still feels awkward. They have some tentativeness as they're pushing forward. You need to respect your responsibility as a teacher to create permission for them to trust themselves. This is where our use of video became important. We could illustrate on video how technically sound their execution was. Even though the players were feeling awkward and clunky, they were able to see what you were teaching on video. That gives them trust in themselves and trust we're moving in the right direction, even though it doesn't feel great at that time.

Once they've acquired the new skill and start to feel better with it, we need to push them to that next level. How much faster can we execute it? What can we add to it? It's about creating permission to continue to evolve this skill after they've achieved the minimum standard of execution. Those permissions are important in shaping the environment.

The other aspect that goes with shaping environment is creating pressure. We're sometimes looking to add pressure. You add pressure by reducing the amount of time and space available to the player or by inserting competition, whether it's even competition or stacking the deck against them. We'd add pressure by including more stimulus. That's where the multiple pucks idea came from: adding pressure to an otherwise normal skill execution where they had to handle a puck by handling two pucks. Can you handle two pucks with the same grace, ease, speed, and quality of execution?

Sometimes I'm trying to alleviate pressure. I'm trying to create a pressurized environment and then teach them how to alleviate the pressure in that environment. There are ways to accomplish that even when there's heavy pressure on you from a physical perspective. You may have two opponents chasing you down. It could be a situation where you use deception to turn people's feet. You make it look like you're going into small space to draw the pressure and then you play off the heels of the opponent to get into open space. The players learn how to alleviate that pressure rather than just satisfying it. We're not taking the pressure away. We're teaching coping mechanisms and skilled responses when the pressure is on.

The next two parts are important. As I'm trying to create a vehicle to deliver the message and engage the listener, I'm also trying to create relatability and be more connected to the listener. Part of that is the language I'm using. What words am I using in terms of vocabulary? Is it appropriate for the group? Sometimes one of the things I did for relatability was coin new terms. That reshapes the meaning or creates a greater focus for the meaning, and that would help them capture and understand the ideas better. It's very similar to how creating nicknames for people can dramatically improve relatability and personal identity among a group—the same concept I found to be true with coining terms. It creates an identity to the skill and relatability which improves retention.

Another aspect of relatability is energy, depending on the age of the group. Sometimes you have to possess a lot of energy because the group is younger. They respond to energy they can feel. I would manipulate that energy through my body language in demonstrations. When the players were in drills, instead of standing and observing them, I would be in the drill mirroring them as they went. That creates a level of energy and puts me inside the rep, which is excellent body language to create relatability for the player and feel like we're in it together. You can pull a lot of intensity from a player by doing that.

The other thing I learned early on, and this continues to be a difficult thing for me, is that sarcasm is the enemy. The worst coach to players is the sarcastic coach. Very few players in my experience respond favorably to sarcasm. Even though that type of humor can be funny in a social environment, there isn't much of a place for it on the ice. I've tried to find a place for it because sometimes that's my natural way of finding humor in things, but it's the enemy in a development environment. It's a real mood-killer. It has a way of alienating players more than it does pulling them together. Even when humor does goes off without a hitch, it still has a limited effect. It's just not worth it for the risk involved.

Another important part of relatability is the demonstrations. There is a visual aspect to relatability, and it's important to be able to show what you're doing. It also sometimes creates that teacher failure. Sometimes you're doing a skill that is incredibly difficult, and in having a teacher failure inside of that demonstration, there's a relatability and acknowledgement between the student and teacher about how difficult that skill is to execute.

In the beginning, one of the worst things about me was I couldn't skate or handle the puck. In the end, it turned out to be one of the best things, because I was so ultra-focused on my own demonstrations and learning to execute the skills at a strong competency level, so the players had a good visual to work with. I started to leverage that to create relatability inside the teacher failure. Those demonstrations are an invaluable way of creating relatability with the athlete and being able to deliver the message.

When engaging the listener, I find there are three elements to manage: the success rate, the teaching approach, and the type of content you are sharing. These elements create decisions and motivations for the athletes and determine whether they're going to continue to stay engaged in the process because they're motivated by the content, by the way you're working the approach, and by manipulating the success rate in a way that creates challenges for them. Regardless of the way you manipulate these three elements, they're all critical in engaging the listener.

There are a handful of important aspects inherent in managing the success rate. One is the use of failure. I use failure to push players to a point where they can feel they may need to get better and that there's another level. You're just stretching them out. There's a higher level of failure present than they're accustomed to because you're stretching the capacity of the skill. I also use failure for humility. Often, if a player is moving along well in the development process, he or she has a ton of motive, a ton of momentum. The player's feeling fantastic because everything is just flowing, and it feels easy. That's a great time to generate a high failure rate to create humility and sharpen the focus on what that next level is. *Hey, you've come this far; it's great. You look like a million dollars here in this particular skill set. Now let's push it.* In pushing it, you create that humility because the success rate plummets and the player's back in a build mode. I use it to refocus. Sometimes players can get sloppy in the execution of something because they have a high proficiency in it. They know they can execute the skill at a high rate. I use failure in those instances to refocus them on details they're skipping through or becoming nonchalant about.

I'll also use failure to create conflict. Sometimes I want to manage the athlete's mental state and create conflict so I can build a success. I'm trying to build confidence in a player. Confidence is really a series of successes. The more confidence you have, the more likely you are to achieve more successful things at a higher rate. When you're losing your confidence, that means failures are coming up more and more and the successes are more infrequent. What I try to do is create a conflict in the athlete. We'll work something that has high success/high failure rate and creates a conflict. It puts me in a position where I can start to build because the players are conflicted. They don't understand why they're not able to perform a skill. That puts me in the driver's seat in terms of being able to start the building process toward that next level.

I will manufacture the conflict and also use it to create emotion in celebrating breakthroughs. I can predict where the players will have the highest level of success, so I can manage their emotions by putting them in spots where they'll struggle and spike them in opportunities where they'll be successful. I can celebrate that success so they feel a sense of accomplishment. I can manage and be in control of those emotions by the way I manage that success rate. Using failure is an important element of a variety of different teaching skills. For me, it's the stretch, humility, refocus, creating conflict, and creating emotion. Those five elements are important in failure.

Now, I also use success to stretch, but we are at a point where the player has built enough emotional equity to take risks. You use this success rate to get the player in a mental state where he or she is prepared to start risking more failure. You can use success to build that. You can also create a boldness to try something new because the players are feeling good about themselves. You've created that invincibility. They're thinking, *Wow, today's my day.* Okay, well, if today's your day, this is a great opportunity to embark upon something that's a lot more difficult. You use success to build momentum. This helps manage the players' emotions. To get that series of successes, you're putting them in a mental state to where they're ready to go.

You can also use success to reshape mood. I can pivot from using failure to create that conflict or establish humility to start working toward a success and managing the mood. You sometimes want the players in a roller coaster. You want them to be feeling the highs of the high and then drop them and have them feel the lows of the low. I can manage that by using the content and by the pace. By the progressions I'm using, I can put them on that roller coaster and then get them on the climb. They start climbing up the hill and start to feel good about themselves, then I take them only so far, drop them right off the cliff, and they bottom out. Then we create another climb. Those are the peaking processes. You can use the peaking process for development by managing this success rate. Managing success rate is a major part of how I manage my ice time. I'm constantly aware of the players' state, where we are in that emotional level. I know when the right time is to push the players, to start stretching them. How much equity do we have in this player so he or she has the confidence to risk going to the next level? Those are all important things.

To manage their state, sometimes you need to just capture players' attention. A lot of times I'll start a session by putting them in a state where they look like they've never played hockey before. They look like they've never skated before. You create the feeling that this is going to be a real struggle. That captures their attention right away. Using success rate to manage their mental state is what allows me to engage the listener.

The second element involved in engaging the listener is my teaching approach. Where the player is in his or her state, where he or she has developed mentally, all those factors weigh into whether I'm doing a deliberate practice. Is this a methodical build? Is this a serious Type A personality player where we're going to start at the beginning and deliberately build one piece after the next? Some players don't respond well to deliberate practices. You have to hide the technical elements inside of fun. Sometimes even with Type A personalities, I try to hide the highly technical skills inside of fun activities so they're unaware they're learning. Then, at some point, I'll show them, *Hey, you weren't aware of this, but you were actually learning this interesting concept along the way.* It's great for a lot of younger players. Getting their attention through failure is another approach—creating a challenge and then pushing them through.

Once I had the knowledge that I could create a skill inside an hour that the player could use, I could begin creating challenges for them. I was also challenging myself. If I bit off too much for the hour I had this player, he or she wouldn't be able to to achieve the level of confidence in this new skill to use it the next day. How much should I bite off so by the end of the session they're feeling good about it? That's a real process. There's a lot of trial and error. Every player is different. There are a lot of things that go into those considerations, which are largely experience-based. It's an interesting approach because you're taking on the challenge as the teacher that this player will learn this skill to the level he or she can use it tomorrow, and the player is embracing the challenge he or she didn't realize would be this difficult. Thus, the player becomes ultra-focused through the initial failure component.

The third element is the content you use. What exactly are you teaching them? How relevant is it to their game? How game-specific are the things you're using? How personal is the content? Are you able to articulate or illustrate to the athlete what the relevance is? Is the player in a place where he or she has the capacity to start talking about where the skill will fit? I love it when players say, "Hey, that's a great skill, I could see myself using that in this situation." Often thats situation is one I haven't considered before, but it gives me insight into the way they're thinking. That creates context for them and engages them. If the player knows you are embarking on a process that's going to improve specifically something highly personal to their game, it speaks directly to something they know they have to work on. You can then position yourself in a beautiful spot to push that athlete, because they're going to be ultra-motivated. They know what path you're taking them on. They're trusting it more because they know you have the insight of what's relevant and specific to them.

Sometimes we pick elements the player has a hard time identifying in his or her own game, so we lose them in terms of motivation and engagement. It's up to you, the teacher, to show them the game-specific relevance and the personal aspect if they can't see it for themselves. You can go on the ice with some players and show them anything, and they'll immediately start thinking about how they can use it in their own game. You don't even need to do it, but it's almost fun to try to pick things that are a challenge for them to figure out how to use in their game. Those players are different. But not every player is like that. Some players need to be explicitly shown. It's up to you to read your audience and create that connection with them through the content.

Being connected to the athlete is another important aspect of engagement. There are a few different facets of it. Does your approach match the listener? Does the way you're approaching the development match how the listener learns? Does the content match the athletes' needs? If it doesn't match their needs, you're automatically going to be disconnected. They're going to say, "I don't know how this fits in my game." They're going to have questions about you and the relevance of the ice time, and that's going to directly affect their engagement and motivation. Also consider—does the success rate match the motivation? When they're motivated, are you choosing the appropriate success rate? Is this a time when you can break them down, drop them off a cliff, start them with a low level of failure and start building them up? Or are they in a poor mental state where they aren't going to absorb that well? Are you better off going down a road where you build them up first, get their mental state in a spot where you have some good momentum, and then stretch them by altering the success rate? With celebrating success, you're putting the players in a situation wherein when they do achieve this success, you join in that success and acknowledge it, because that's your equity to stretch them. You want to be building equity all the time. It can be small steps where you're just building little successes along the way, but you're celebrating each one of them because you're going to ultimately leverage that equity to stretch them into the next goal. How connected you are is a critical component to the engagement process.

3

CONFIDENCE SOURCE

The hardest part about creating authenticity in your teaching style is finding your confidence source. Where is it? What is it that leads you to believe you can actually do it?

There really isn't a substitute for building confidence; it is genuinely a process. Early on, I taught without the confidence I could do what I had set out to. I had a bunch of players looking at me like, *Teach me something*, and I didn't know if I could do it. The only way you can build confidence is by putting one foot in front of the other, throwing some ideas against the wall, and finding a way to get it started.

You then have to be mindful of what's going on and read the athlete. The major skill that comes from becoming a confident teacher is an awareness of what's going on, not only with you, but how your approach is being received by the athlete. The athlete can express understanding in a variety of ways. He can repeat what you're saying verbally, confirming he understands what you're trying to do. She can express it back to you athletically. Sometimes, you'll see confusion across their face. There are times you want to create confusion; you want them to feel uncomfortable with what they're doing.

There's just a whole myriad of information you're collecting when you throw something out there for the players to learn. You're trying to collect that information to make decisions about what to do going forward. It's incredibly difficult to be an effective teacher when you lack confidence. The limiting factor is it impacts your instinct. You're second-guessing. You're not fluid. You're mechanical. It impacts your ability to have a natural flow in what you're presenting. You lack that ability to step forward confidently in a new direction or trust what you're seeing.

The process of building confidence is difficult. Just when I felt like I had acquired enough confidence to trust the direction I was going, I would be presented with another challenge of a player I had difficulty reading. There are a lot of kids you can read easily. Their facial expressions, the way in which they express themselves athletically, they're predictable, and you can read what their level of understanding is, which makes it easier to push the next thing forward.

When you're trying to manage the success rates in particular, you need to have an accurate picture of the players' perception of what it is they're doing. Their perception is going to impact their ability to perform. You need them to feel uncomfortable, yet you need to get them to understand what you're moving toward—that they're making progress even though it doesn't feel like it. You want to have an accurate gauge of what's going on. There are kids who are difficult to read, and they have difficulty in their response to failure. Their reaction to failure is to get angry, or it creates a lot of tension in them. They get down on themselves and they don't know you're taking them down a path to create improvement. Every time you go into a failure rate, they shut down or they have a problem staying focused. That makes it difficult to make any meaningful gains. You run into these situations where each kid's reaction is different. Trying to manage all of that can be daunting. It took a long time to build confidence, and I still have situations where I'm just not all that confident I'm in a good space to read the situation and trust my instincts on what to do next.

The confidence source comes from three different areas. The first one is the ability to read the situation accurately. If you can read the situation well, that allows you to be confident enough to move forward. But if you don't trust you're reading the situation accurately immediately, that's going to affect your teaching confidence—and then you have to trust your response instinct. Once you've read the situation or read the player, then you trust in your response instinct of what to do in the next part of the sequence. The third area is your actual teaching ability. When you know what you're about to take on next with the player, you have the ability to set up the progression the right way, so he or she will be able to acquire the skill.

All three of those things are important, and each one of them will impact your own personal confidence in what you're doing. If you lack confidence, it's going to be difficult to deliver the material authentically. Players can pick up on that, and that was difficult and is still difficult for me because I'm an open book with my emotions. I still have a hard time managing them. Players can read weak spots. If I'm trying to put on a poker face, that creates little problems in terms of the authenticity of how I'm presenting myself to the athlete. All those factors weigh into the speed at which the player's going to acquire skills. Your confidence in your ability to pull this off is paramount and can fast-forward or delay the development of your athlete.

To help build confidence in reading a situation and a player, I love to review video beforehand to gain a knowledge of the athlete before we even start. That allows me to predict what their capacities are going to before we even get on the ice. It's an important element for me, particularly in new situations where I don't know the person and how he or she is going to react. The benefit of the research is being able to anticipate how players are going to react at least athletically, what their capacities are going to be, and where the limitations are going to be. I'll be able to have a fair understanding of that before we even start.

Then there's the element of being able to read the players personally. How do they respond? What's their reaction going to be? Is it different when I challenge them or when they fail? How do they respond to success? All those things are important. Being able to accurately read three initial pieces of information is going to help guide me through the development process and create better teaching situations: the skill, the player's reaction, and my interpretation of what's really going on.

Being confident I'm reading the situation properly is important. I like trusting my response. Having a feel for what to do next is critical, because if you're trying to do it from a personal perspective, where you're trying to learn as much from the athlete about where to go next, that impacts the pacing. For example, if I was teaching a player a particular skill and I got to a certain part of the development and there was a skill gap, understanding then what areas of the player's skill set I could leverage best to be able to pull this new skill set into is crucial.

Every player has certain projectable assets. They're solid areas of the player's skill. When you're attacking something new or trying to change a bad habit, it's easier to attach that new skill to one of the player's existing assets. That asset becomes a vehicle to acquire the new skill, because players understand the assets they're more familiar with. That's what allows you to fast-forward the development and give them confidence to to push forward. Did I read the player's asset right? Was I able to attach the right asset to the right skill?

As a broad example, let's say the player is a good skater, and the skill I'm trying to influence is his or her ability to shoot. In order to affect the player's shooting, I would leverage the player's skating ability. I would focus on his or her footwork as an area to be leveraged. The player feels comfortable with his or her skating. Even though the shot is something we're trying to influence that is foreign to them, I would create familiarity inside the player's asset base, which is skating inside the shooting movements. Then, I'd leverage that to influence his or her willingness to go through the process of learning the new shooting mechanics.

What about if it's the reverse? Let's say the player is not a good skater. Let's say the player has good, quick hands, but his or her skating is not that strong—not leverageable—and I'm still trying to influence a player's shot. Well, then I would come at it from a hands perspective. That's where you want to connect the shot to the player's best asset, his or her hands, which allows the player feel more comfortable while I'm trying to create so many uncomfortable movements. The skating is going to feel awkward. The shot itself is going to feel awkward. So, I need to create some familiarity and leverage that top asset. Again, trusting my instinct about which asset I'm going to attach to this skill is going to be critical to the outcome. It's going to either fast-forward the development or slow it down and create even more problems. Having a feel for where I am in that process, trusting my instinct about what I'm trying to influence with the player, is important.

Every time you start a process of development for a skill, and particularly when time is of the essence, I want to maximize my impact and the number of skill takeaways the player could use the next day. That creates a lot of pressure, because I need to be able to engage in a development process in this one hour that will allow the player to have a functional enough knowledge of that skill to feel comfortable using it the next day. I've got to make sure I'm taking the appropriate risk and giving myself enough time to build it so the player has that takeaway. There are a lot of risks in development. There is a risk I bite off more than I can chew and put myself in a spot where it would be difficult to create that ultimate takeaway in which the player can actually use the skill. I need to make sure I have calculated it properly and made the right decisions about how I can create the accelerators.

Attaching an asset to the skill is an accelerator that allows me to create the familiarity and trust I need for the player to be open to going through that development process. There are going to be hurdles we have to overcome, but ultimately it's about knowing I've made the right choices to achieve the result we're looking for. A lot of equity has to be built to create risk. You want to build up relationship and ancillary skills around what you're trying to tackle. Every skill we're trying to work on has ancillary skills that support or potentially support it. The risk involved in attacking that skill is associated with the amount and quality of ancillary skills available to support the development. If those ancillary skills aren't there, then I would have to take less risk in the development process.

My ability as a teacher to create a logical and natural progression for the development process is associated with the risks of development and making sure I understand players' capacities fully. I need to know their restrictions so I can create a development path that allows them to achieve the takeaway when the session is over. I need the confidence to read the situation properly, read the player properly, and to trust my instincts about what I can leverage. That allows me to forge forward. I also need to trust my teaching ability and the logical and natural progression I've selected to go down. I need to have built up enough equity to feel comfortable in taking the risk toward development and share that equity in the risk with the athlete.

All of this is why, as a teacher, it's difficult to build confidence. There are a lot of ways this process can go sideways, a lot of ways you can put yourself in a spot where the player just can't acquire the skill because you picked the wrong progression. So, it's really not the player's fault; it's yours, because you've chosen a poor path. Now you've got a frustrated athlete who's trying to acquire the skill, but because you've misread the situation, your instincts about the development are off and then you pick the wrong teaching progression. In the end, the player's not going to acquire the skill no matter how talented he or she is because you've selected the wrong approach for their development. Once you make that decision, it's critical that you have all three of these pieces in place. If you don't, then you run the risk of having a frustrated player, and we don't want that. We want to have a player who, after every ice session, feels a sense of accomplishment—and that's directly related to your confidence.

4

PREPARATION

LEARNING HOW TO PREPARE FOR TRAINING SESSIONS FOR MY athletes was quite a process for me. It took a lot of time to develop how I could arm myself with the most information so I could be effective and trust my instincts. I had to put in the work before spending time with the athlete.

Some of this work can be done before meeting the athlete, if you've never met him or her. Some of it you learn on the fly, and then the preparation comes from leveraging the experience you've had with other players. That allows you to read situations and act quickly. You can't really learn experience. My preparation is threefold: 1. I get to know as much about the players as I can; 2. I figure out how they learn; 3. I then decide where I want to start.

I know where I want to end. I understand skill progressions and have it in my head where we are starting, what that sequence is going to be, and what the continuum is inside that skill set sequence. Then, it's a matter of identifying quickly where the player needs to start in that continuum and being able to plot their individual plan from there. A lot of it happens in the moment, but at the same time it's not off-the-cuff. By being well-prepared, I'm then just identifying where the information is inside the previous preparation, and that allows me to make good decisions going forward.

There are three things I need to know about the player. The first is his or her skill assets. I have to understand what this player does well, what's projectable, and how stable the projectable elements are to build on.

The second is I need to know how the player thinks—his or her personal game structure. I need to understand how my player processes the game because that's going to impact how we approach certain skills. I can't counter the way a player thinks. If the skill package isn't connected to the way the player thinks, it's going to impact the logic of skill acquisition. You want to give the player as much of a big-picture context as you can. This is why a player's personal game structure is so important, because it illuminates his or her decision-making mechanisms.

Then, I need to know any development restrictions a player might have that are going to impact the acquisition phase of the skills from a physical perspective. This is a major part of my philosophy. I believe in working with the player's existing assets and using that as my starting point. It creates so many advantages when you do it that way. It is gasoline in the development process.

What is a projectable asset? It is a skill the player has that you can build on. For example, the player has outstanding crossovers. That means he is going to have a capacity to change speeds and have a reasonable functional ability to produce power on the outside edge. That would be different than a player whose main asset is skating in a straight line, which is more inside-edge oriented. I could get into a lot more change of direction work with the player who has good outside edges and can cross his feet. That gives me a lot of directions I can go in terms of how I can use that to set up other pieces I want. If I was trying to impact the player's ability to carry speed through a turn, I would be able to leverage the crossover and the outside edge to put him in a good posture inside the turn because he is used to having good posture inside the crossover. I would use the crossover to establish the body position I want on the outside edge, and I would use that as part of what I was trying to do inside of that change of direction. How do I stitch what I'm trying to work on with what his asset actually is? Those are the leverages and key parts I'm trying to process as we're ultimately trying to add those two things together.

With the skill expression element, let's say we're trying to work on a player establishing better body position. I have three players in a group. The first player is 6'2", 210 pounds, not really fleet of foot but has tremendous power and upper-body strength—just a real powerhouse type player. The second player is a 5'8" speedster with excellent skating ability who has good strength inside his core but isn't very strong. This is a guy who is on the ice, not in the ice. The third player is much more gangly, 6'2" but about 160 pounds. He's tall and long but not heavy or strong; he's just underdeveloped physically. I'm trying to get each one of them to learn how to establish better body position for puck protection. All three of them have different skill expression elements I have to keep in mind.

The powerhouse player is not going to learn how to get body position in the exact same way as the 5'8" speedster. They're going to come at it very differently. And even though the first and third players are the same height, they don't have the same assets, so I can't teach them to get body position the same way. Now, establishing body position still has the same properties. You will use all kinds of tactics to get the position they're trying to perfect that are ultimately the same. You still want to have your hips through the opponent's hands. You want to get in front. But how each player gets there is very different and the assets we use with each of them will be very different. That has to be expressed and kept in mind as I'm making the adjustments for each player. It has to be personalized. It's got to fit the assets of that player. There may be some situations where a player has to come at getting that body position from a different perspective than how they think.

I have a real interesting story about teaching players how they think: the spider versus the bull. This was a concept I created alongside Hayley Wickenheiser when I was working with her. Hayley is a first-ballot Hall of Famer and is widely considered the greatest female player ever to play the game. I started working with her prior to the Vancouver Olympics. When I watched her game while doing my research on her, I noticed she was very much a bull in how she was acquiring the puck. She would literally hunt the puck down, steal it from whomever, win loose puck races—all that kind of stuff to get the puck. It just didn't matter where the puck was, she was a heat-seeking missile trying to go get it. As a singular approach, that's restricting. It's difficult to create offense from that mindset, and there are lots of times in a game where by hustling and over-pressuring the puck you can put yourself out of position to get what we would call more favorable offensive pucks.

Here's a player who's tremendously gifted offensively and has achieved a high level of success, but with each year that goes by the capacity to create offense from chasing the puck around like a bull becomes harder. We wanted to change her mindset in certain situations to become more of a spider. The analogy I used was a spider web. If she could envision herself as the center of the spider web, and all threads would come back to the middle, everywhere she went she was just in a great position. She would get a lot more favorable pucks and would be easier for her teammates to play with because she would be available more consistently rather than over-supporting the puck.

There were times where Hayley's teammate would have full possession of the puck in the corner, and she would over-support and get right over there to the puck—almost looking for a handoff. The problem is when Hayley's teammate has the puck, she's being checked by someone. Now Hayley's coming over and she's drawing her own check, and we have a situation where what was really a one-on-one in the corner has become two-on-two in the corner. Hayley inadvertently reduced the amount of space her teammate had to work. Offensively, she's being counterproductive. She's working hard. She's a bull in a china shop. She might actually come up with this puck, but she's got to navigate her way through a small space with four people, making it much more difficult on herself. Here's what the spider would do instead: when your team has a puck in the corner, you allow that one-on-one to happen and you move to the next best puck-support position. Where is it? Is it above the puck, even with the puck, below the puck? There are lots of decisions to be made quickly; how can she decide? Well, that's going to be based on what she wants to do next.

I would study Team Canada to systemically understand its game. Every team has spots in the offensive zone they want their players to adhere to. I wanted to have Hayley moving into those spots so it created a predictability for her linemates to find her, in concert with the system of the Canadian team. In certain situations, being a bull creates a disadvantage and it's better to have a spider mentality.

Now, you can't be a spider all the time, either, because there are times we need to go get a puck. It's a 25/75 race. There's a 25 percent chance you're going to win the race, 75 percent chance you're going to lose it. That's a situation where you need to apply pressure inside that race and dictate your opponent's escape route, which impacts your ability to make the next play in puck separation. Even though you're going to lose the first race, you're trying to influence your opponent's ability to make the next play. That's a situation where you don't want to be passive. You don't want to be a spider lying in wait. You need to force the issue. But when your teammate has clear control of the puck, you want to support the player in a spot where you become accessible to receive the puck.

In the NHL, perhaps the best player who does this is Boston Bruins center Patrice Bergeron. He just might be the easiest player to play with in the NHL. He's just always available. He always gives you an out. He puts himself in great position by reading the situation to weigh acquiring the puck off the pass versus takeaway acquisitions.

What we do know is to be a skilled player, you want to value pucks acquired off the pass. You want to acquire them two-thirds of the time. If you have acquired 10 pucks by loose puck or forced turnovers in a game, then we need you to be getting 30 pucks off the pass. We know offensive players need the puck off the pass more frequently. It creates more favorable offensive situations. We don't want them failing to get loose pucks, because they need to be competitive. There are times in a given game or shift you have to be a bull and a spider, but you have to recognize when to do what.

That was a major aspect of understanding play patterns or Hayley's personal game structure, how she was getting the puck and putting herself in better positions so she could leverage her offensive ability by reshaping how she was thinking about a given play. That's an example of influencing how a player thinks and maybe reshaping some of their perspectives.

There are other players who just don't really get engaged. They get accused of being non-competitive when really they're just over-using their spider instincts of being available. It's not that they're not engaged; they're just sitting in space. Now, it's great when we have full possession of the puck and you just find these little seams to slide into. That's fantastic. But when we don't have the puck, we need you to force the issue and pressure the puck. You need to force turnovers. Being able to switch back and forth between being a spider and being a bull, that's the challenge.

What are the unsuccessful patterns the player has? It's interesting to ask this question once I've done the research. *Do you realize you get the puck on your backhand in the corner 10 times a game, but your positive play percentage is 30 percent, and of that 30 percent, only 10 percent of those are leading directly to a shot?* Here's a high-frequency event with a very low success rate, and you're not converting those into any chances to score. This is an automatic pattern that occurs often, which is a bad script for the player. My goal is bubble this up to the surface so the player becomes aware of the issue and we can start problem-solving together. What types of plays can reshape this in your mind? We add different levels of awareness to this particular situation that allow you to then influence this more positively.

You see this in players who have been playing the game for some time. You get a third-year NHL player who's been playing hockey for 20 years, and over those 20 years he's developed play patterns and a personal game structure that have been effective for him, allowed him to achieve the success he has. Some of the patterns he's aware of, and some he's not; he just does it automatically. Over time, it went from conscious to unconscious and now it is just an instinctual read. There are also negative patterns he does constantly he's not aware of, and they lead him down a path to have negative results. Bubbling this up to the surface and seeing what these players are actually aware of inside their game is a fascinating process. I need to have that conversation with them to get a sense of how they think and whether what they're doing is conscious or unconscious.

The third thing I need to know about a player is his or her development restrictions. Another good story I have as it relates to movement restrictions involves Matt Ellis. He started in Detroit, went to L.A., and ended up in Buffalo. He's just a wonderful player and guy who out-worked and out-prepared his opponent to find his way into 400 games in the NHL. He was an undrafted player, wasn't highly touted for his talent. When I met him, he was captain in AHL

Grand Rapids and was looking to improve his skating to the point where he could skate at the NHL level.

Matt was incredibly strong. He could basically lift 500 pounds any which way he wanted. But that power and strength weren't translating into his skating—that was his movement capacity issue. There were guys who were significantly less powerful who were able to produce power in their skating more effectively than Matt and were therefore better skaters. How is it this player has this tremendous asset he's able to use so powerfully off the ice, but when he gets on the ice it's really not transferring? It was about where his weight was distributed in his skates. He was constantly on his heels. He was never really forward. He didn't have a positive shin angle. He was literally fighting against himself all the time. Our objective was to then push him forward so he could get the weight in a better position on his skates, leverage that into power and, ultimately, skate more effectively.

For Matt, it was about having more edge control in that posture so he could learn how to access the power he had. I remember talking to his trainer. I was so intrigued by Matt, because I could see his power and people were telling me he's legendary in the gym— like it's almost a rite of passage to get to the NHL to train with him off the ice. You think you work hard, and then you watch him train and realize how hard you really have to work. He was really like the gold standard of preparation off the ice and how he took care of his body. Then to see he had these restrictions on the ice, that was a fascinating process for me.

There are all kinds of sources of restriction, injury history aside. Many players just don't have good mobility in their hips or dorsiflexion in their ankles; they have a poor core, their lower back is weak. All that creates restrictions, and those restrictions are not things you can overcome in an hour's ice session. These are things that need to be addressed in the gym. I don't know anything about the gym, so I need to talk to their strength coaches and say, 'Hey, here's what I see.' I send the strength coach a video and have them impact those movement capacity issues, so that when I work with the player again, those issues have been addressed and they're more capable of acquiring skills.

What do I do when a player has these movement capacity issues? Let's say the player has really tight hips. He or she has no ability to pivot because of the restriction. As a result, I can't use an open pivot. I can't just say, 'Well, okay, that's it, go see your trainer and come back and see me in six months after you've fixed these issues.' I need to establish bridge skills. A bridge skill is something that buys time for a trainer to influence the player's strength and conditioning for that particular skill. It's not a direct improvement; it's like an ancillary improvement of the thing we're trying to influence. We want to ultimately do both the ancillary problem-solving and the direct problem-solving at the same time. But we can't address the direct issue until the player improves his or her movement capacity.

On the surface, you might look at it and say, 'All the players restricted here are tight in their hips and just can't move—this is a big problem.' But I look at it as a depth of skill opportunity, because now we can build all the ancillary skills. We can create a level of capacity on the ice for the players to compete and then wait for the physical capacity to catch up. Then, we have both. Sometimes we're just trying to create a tactical opportunity so the player has enough leverage to perform.

One of the better examples is body position. It's such an important aspect of hockey and something we're constantly working on. How each player gets into and utilizes those body positions differs widely. One of the skills we've used as a bridge skill for body position is what we call the Kane Push. It's a skill I named after Patrick Kane because he used this a lot—still uses it—in situations he felt like he was going to be overpowered. He'd establish a position directly in front of the guy who was trying to check him. It would disable the player's ability to hit him. One of the things you want to do as it relates to body position is establish these positions early. You can't always cut in front of somebody because the spacing might not be there. The bridge skill here would be to anticipate and establish body position. You position yourself off the wall if that player is starting to encroach that space prior to getting the puck so that when you get it, you have already built the escape route to turn into. Bridge skills are about leveraging the mind and how you can anticipate where the play is going to be in order to overcome a physical restriction.

The other bridge skill we use a lot is influencing the defender's feet. If you're skating up the boards with the puck and the defender has his feet pointed toward you like a heat-seeking missile coming to make contact, you're in a difficult position to defend yourself. Every second that goes by that player is continuing to take away more space. What we want to do is this: as the player is coming toward you, you come off the boards toward him. When you do that, the defender will turn his feet parallel to the boards. As long as the defender's feet are parallel to yours, he's no longer taking away any space. It's harder for him to make contact, so you effectively disable it. In a situation where you would be grossly overpowered, you have taken control of the defender's ability to close space, which is a bridge skill that allows you then to learn how to manipulate the defender's feet. By doing that, you've now protected yourself in a situation where normally you just adapt to eat that contact.

When you develop the physical capacity to absorb that contact or maybe even reverse hit and feel more comfortable in those contact situations because you've addressed that strength issue, you can use the Kane Push. You put yourself in an early body position, influence the defender's feet, and you can also use the reverse hit. Now you have three skills you could use because we worked on these bridge skills, which allowed you to survive when you weren't physically able to compete properly. The bridge skills buy some time for you to build the desired skill. You have three assets you can then leverage to move to the next spot.

Another way to work through development restrictions is by using technical leverage points. These are scaffolding assets. Scaffolding is the ability to stack one thing on top of the other. Let's take the example of body positioning. Once we have good body position and we've learned how to use the Kane Push effectively, we can scaffold those skills into a change in speed. We can also scaffold them into puck protection. We can scaffold them into manipulating, forcing switches, or changing checks. Part of the solution to development restrictions comes back to leveraging the players' assets and building these bridge skills which allow them to compete at a time they probably shouldn't be able to. Scaffolding those assets into other aspects then turns a development restriction into a depth of skill opportunity.

The next part of my preparation process is to learn how the players learn. In a new situation where I'm just meeting the player for the first time, I've done my homework on researching his game, know where we want to go, and know what his restrictions are. Now, I need to understand how he learns. These are initial probing situations where I'm going to test the player right away for his response to failure. How is he going to respond? What strategies does he use to overcome failure? How does he shape failure in his mind? What's his attitude toward it? Is this a challenge? Is it a problem? Does he get angry or frustrated? What's his response to failure? That's going to tell me how much failure I can use in the early part of the development process.

What's the player's response to success? Does he get content with success? Is he looking to use success as an accelerator in other things? What's his reaction to it? What happens when I start manufacturing problems? Let's take the player down a road where he's able to achieve high levels of success and then see what happens when I manufacture a problem. That all tells me how the player learns. That is directly related in large part to his response to failure, his response to success, and what happens when a manufacturer creates unexpected problems inside the development.

Normally, you would think of learning as visual, kinesthetic, or verbal. The truth of the matter is all learning is brain learning and all learning in hockey is at its core an athletic expression. Regardless of how a player takes the information in, its output is always an athletic expression. It's less important how he learns, because it's all brain learning. More important is his response to failure, success, or manufactured problems. In the end, I'm going to have to be able to produce an athletic expression, and a lot of times that's going to be related to the player's willingness to learn—what his mindset is in key moments. I'm going to want to be able to have control over that. That's why I need to understand how he learns.

The last piece is the progression. I know the first drill I'm going to use. I know where I'm ultimately going, and I know where I'm starting. What I don't know is exactly how I'm going to get there. Every player is very different.

This is of one of the differences between coaching and teaching.

Coaching is very much a plan. It's got time management elements to it. When coaches design their practice, they meticulously lay it all out. They've got a warm-up, then key elements they're trying to work on, then some systemic things they're doing. It's all time-sensitive. They know how much time they want to spend on each component, and that requires pacing. How much speed the practice is going to have, how much energy expenditure they want the players to have— that's coaching.

Teaching is very much a progression sequence. We don't really know where it's going to go or how the players are going to respond. We don't know how fast they're going to learn. I can't say, 'Well, this is going to take five minutes.' I don't know if it will take five minutes. It could take two minutes; it could take ten minutes. I don't know until we get in there and start putting the progression together. It's less contingent upon time and planning. I don't know how long it's going to take to build. I just know that's part of the progression sequence and we're going to work on it until the player gets it. Then we're able to move on to the next part of the progression.

This started early on for me. When I first started coaching, I would pre-plan all my drills. I would draw them all out and color-coordinate them. It was all very neat. The description of the drill was all written at the bottom. I had this elaborate flip chart process. I would discuss the drill with the players and then I would flip it over so then the next one would be revealed. It was a fantastic system for me…up until the day I forgot the flip chart at home.

I got to the rink and remember being in pure panic mode with my mentor. 'Bud, oh my god, I forgot my plan at home. I don't know what I'm going to do.' I remember most of it, but you know now I'm going to have to draw it. I'm trouble; I don't have my plan. I'm not feeling very comfortable. He said, 'Do you know where you want to start?' I said yes. 'Do you know where you want to end?' 'Yes.' He said, 'Well, why don't you just get started and then read the athletes, just watch how they're responding and then you'll see something you either like or don't like and just build a drill for that and away you go.'

That's exactly what I did. I got started on my warm-up drill, kind of knew where I wanted to end up, and then I was relating everything back to where my end goal was. That's how I was picking the next topic I wanted to work on. That, to me, was a game-changer. It changed everything because I realized I didn't need the flip chart; I needed to read the athlete more effectively. I was probably more effective in that practice as a teacher than I was when I was more prepared from a coaching perspective. At that time, I was coaching kids who were in Peewee, so none of it was really coaching—all of it is teaching at that level.

Now, if I had been coaching midget AAA, where there's a lot of coaching involved, maybe this wouldn't have been as effective. I would have needed to be more concerned about pacing, energy expenditure, systematic parts, and all those factors. But once I forgot the flip chart and had worked off, basically, feel, I noticed I was more effective. The players' capacity to learn spiked because of my new ability to focus on those things. That was on the progression part of the process, rather than the time management part or how much pre-planning I had done. The progression was based on the athletes' capacity. That was critical. Now, I operate exclusively off feel.

We'll get to teaching progressions later in the book and how the skill continuum works. The next step for me was to really learn about those things so I could be effective at reading the athletes and knowing exactly what needed to come next.

HAYLEY WICKENHEISER
on Darryl Belfry

Hayley Wickenheiser was Hayley Wickenheiser by the time she arrived to Darryl Belfry.

She had already proven herself as one of the greatest women's hockey players. She wasn't content with that, though. She sought to take her game to a whole other level.

An obstacle in doing that was the playing structure of Team Canada. It confined her. She wanted to play freely and creatively. The goal was for her and Belfry to figure out a way to do what her coaches sought, but also be able to play the way she wanted.

"I just needed someone to implement it within the system I was playing on the national team because not all of the players or the coaching staff saw the game the way I did and Darryl did," said Wickenheiser, who was inducted into the Hockey Hall of Fame in 2019. "It's like how can we do this, but can we still make you a part within the system? In a way, we kind of came together. We challenged a lot of things we were doing at the national team level. Some were received, some weren't.

"It was a way to play the game better and elevate the game. More of a creative way, less of a 'this is the way

it's always been done, this is the way it'll continue to be done way' and more of a free way. The whole premise of what I was trying to do is to play with more freedom and not be so boxed in by a system, which happens to a lot of players on a lot of teams. It was no different than what I was experiencing within the national team. I was always a dominant player, but I wanted to feel more dominant and free and do it in a way that I could bring my teammates along with me."

Belfry identified through his research that Wickenheiser played like a bull on the ice. She was aggressive and dominant. That worked sometimes, but not always. Belfry believed there was a better way to go about it that would benefit her and her teammates. And so, Wickenheiser was introduced to the spider.

"The analogy was to go from a bull to a spider," she said. "You lug the puck as a bull, and as a spider everything comes to you and through you. I think that's where his Spider stick brand came from, actually, was this bull-to-spider philosophy. It really challenged me to change my game, to continue to make other people around me better and more effective, which then in turn would also make me a more effective player.

"It definitely was an adjustment. There were times I would default back to the old pattern of forcing a play instead of going away from the puck and coming back to it or letting it happen. It took some time. We used a lot of video feedback, talked a lot about having goals for every game. Like, how many quality shot attempts do you want to get, or offensive entries inside the dot line?

How many plays can you extend? When the puck touches your stick, will it die or does it keep going on? What I did with Darryl is we created really tangible goals that I could measure at the end of game.... Quite honestly, a lot of coaches and teammates I was playing with didn't really get it or understand it, but I seemed to be playing well and producing, and that's all that mattered. But to try to explain it, both Darryl and I were quite ahead of the game at many points. It was more of a solo project between him and I at times."

Belfry and Wickenheiser were on their own figurative team then and now they're literally teammates, as both work in development for the Toronto Maple Leafs. Their on-ice relationship has gotten stronger, too.

"When we work together with the Leafs, when I'm on the ice with him, it's very seamless in what we're doing," Wickenheiser said. *"Often he'll make a comment or I'll make a comment, and we'll kind of nod. Sometimes we don't even have to speak. We just look at each other and we know what we're trying to do. That's over 10 years working together and getting to know someone really well. I really respect him."*

TESTIMONIAL

PAT BRISSON
on Darryl Belfry

Player agent Pat Brisson was spending time with his client Patrick Kane during the 2010 Winter Olympics. Kane was preparing for an upcoming game and looking over notes Darryl Belfry had sent him.

Brisson expressed an interest in seeing what the notes were.

"I sat with Pat one night and he showed me kind of a text from Darryl about his breakdown of how the opponent was playing, how he should attack the game in certain ways," said Brisson, who is the co-head of CAA hockey. "He happened to be pretty much right on. It was very accurate in his approach. I felt how comfortable Pat was with Darryl. For me, it was very important, especially with a such a great player as Patrick Kane, who I call the Picasso of hockey, he's so creative, he's so unique, for him to work so closely to someone like Darryl, it brought instant credibility.

"I started looking at his trends and how he approached his teaching. Talking to him, I saw that he wasn't just talking like a normal coach. He was definitely in favor of trying new things. He just had a special approach. He's very articulate in his view. It was the way his message was transferring to Patrick and other players, but also to me as I was trying to understand what he was doing. I was sold immediately."

Brisson was fascinated by what Belfry was teaching. It was something he didn't see elsewhere.

"Just things like in the offensive zone how to create space for yourself, how to spin off the wall, things I just don't think 10 years ago we were as open-minded about," Brisson said. *"We were very traditionalist in our game. He was a pioneer, so to speak, in doing skill sessions.*

"It was like using your left side vs. your right side in this occasion or spinning off here with your head up on that side of your stick opened this way, things like that I found interesting. If you're a skilled player or someone who can really learn, you can definitely benefit from it."

Brisson being sold on Belfry meant more high-end NHL clientele for Belfry. The way Brisson saw it was if Belfry could influence his player's performance, that could in turn impact the bottom line of the future contract he'd be negotiating. Put simply, better players, better contracts. With that, Brisson has made an effort to steer his clients in Belfry's direction.

"At the end of the day, it translates into quality, into better shot attempts, into better results," Brisson said. *"Therefore, the better results translate to hopefully better salaries and confidence and so on and so forth. In today's game, you've got to look at all these little things, whether it's the skating, the off-ice, the mental approach. Darryl touches both. I think he touches a lot on the mental side of things and very much so on the analytics on how to translate your skills into better odds of performing. You try a certain*

thing a certain way, maybe seven out of ten times it's going to work if you do it this way or do it that way.

"He's also very passionate. I see Darryl as a teacher also. If Darryl wasn't a skill coach, I could see him as a teacher in school. I could see him like having a class in history or something like that. He's got that approach."

5

ACCOUNTABILITY

My perspective on accountability changed the day I realized there are levels to this game, in terms of capacity and skill expression, and levels to teaching.

When we're in the teaching environment, the teacher is ultimately responsible for the students' learning. Initially, I thought the onus was on the student to come in with a good attitude—a desire to learn, to put their best foot forward, to be a good listener, and to take responsibility for their own learning. In a perfect world, that's absolutely right; those players are easy to work with and we all love working with them.

But my thinking on that evolved. I learned that as the teacher, I share responsibility. I can come in with a good attitude toward the development of this player and be prepared for the skills I'm trying to teach. I'm responsible for the development path we're taking. I'm responsible for understanding or influencing failure versus success rates. I'm responsible for all of that. Once I started to realize, *Well, wait a minute, I'm responsible for quite a bit here*, I started to think about this as 50-50 relationship. The player has a responsibility to come to the rink and share 50 percent of the learning responsibility. I also share 50 percent of the learning responsibility.

I reached a new level as a teacher once I learned I could influence a player's skill in a very short period of time. My level of understanding about accountability had to advance along with that realization. If the player does not acquire the skill by the end of the day and isn't able to use it the next day, then I'm the reason for that.

What I found is it's not entirely true that the player shares responsibility. I can influence a player's attitude, so ultimately the buck stops with me. Once I shifted my mentality to take accountability if the player didn't learn, it created a ton of opportunity for me to grow. It was one of the best growth opportunities I ever really had. It impacted how serious I was toward each player, my level of dedication, and how responsible I was for each of them to achieve some level of success.

As part of this process, I started videotaping practice. I was trying to understand my practice progression from the start to the end. I would analyze all of my demonstrations. Was the demonstration exactly the way I wanted this skill to be executed? Did I have all the details? Was my elbow in the right spot? Was my weight on the right part of my skate? Was the puck in the place I wanted it? Did I have my head in the right place? Did I show different details from different angles?

I also examined the reps. How many reps did each player get? Did I remember who the first player in line was so they had an equal amount of reps, or did I just change what I wanted to change? Was the player on the back half of that rep sequence always losing a rep each time? What was the real work-to-rest ratio?

Initially, I had the work-to-rest ratio attached exclusively to when the drill started. I knew I had four corners working; every player in each corner would start the drill when it was their turn, and I would work my way around each corner. That creates a work-to-rest ratio of 1:3. Once they got going, I would spike the energy by having the players in opposite corners go at the same time. That makes the work-to-rest ratio 1:1. That made a ton of sense to me until I started videotaping practice. Then I realized the work-to-rest ratio really also included the time it took to set up that next drill. So, how long did it take me to do the demonstration? How long did it take me to do describe what it was we were doing? How long did it take for the players to actually get started? Even though the work-to-rest ratio once the drill started was 1:1, it could have taken me two or three minutes to get a five-minute drill set up. Now it's a seven-minute drill. That has to be factored in.

I also had to think about time management. How fast was I between my transitions? What was the total time for the actual drill? Did I transition from the drill at the appropriate time? In other words, how efficient was I in the learning process? Did a functional amount of the group understand what we were doing, and were they competent after two or three reps? Did I know they were ready to move on after three reps and we didn't move on until five? If so, I had added two more reps I could have attached to the next progression. Those are the types of things I was interested in.

I also looked at pacing. How was I pacing the skill acquisition between stretching and perfecting them? Again, I'm manipulating the players' success and failure rates. In the first few reps, the player is acquiring the skill. When we get to a point where we're executing at a high rate, that's the perfecting part. Now it's time to add another element to stretch their capacity. Are they able to carry that skill into the next progression?

It could be as simple as teaching stick-handling, and while I'm teaching stick-handling, I also want them to have a good rotation in their upper body. Once I start with the basic stick-handling motion, I start adding the upper-body movement. What's going on with their lower body? Is their lower body weight transfer good? Now they have to bring the weight transfer, stick-handling, and upper-body rotation together. Once they've acquired that, I'm going to focus on what their eyes are doing. What is their head doing during this time? Are they able to stay true to all the elements I've been building? If they can't do that when I add the next layer, it's a false positive. They can do the skill when they're focused on it, but they can't do it when they're not. That's not true learning. I have to push it into the subconscious, and it should be able to carry forward. If it's not carrying forward, that impacts the pacing of the skill acquisition.

Peaking is another aspect of skill acquisition for which I'm accountable. I need to make sure this skill is moving toward a game-like execution. I need to be building this toward a peak. How many peaks have I been able to build inside of this structure? Did I do the right progressions? What else could I have done? My pacing was good, my peaks were good, the time management was on point, but did I do the right progressions? Was the progression effective? Did they learn it quickly because of the progressions I chose?

What about my player interactions? How many times did I speak to each player? Was I so much in correction mode I did not really address the positive things they were doing? That impacts their feeling toward the skill. If they're always being corrected, that's a positive, but it's also a negative because I'm not reinforcing when they're in the perfecting stage and they're not feeling like they've made progress. It's like one step forward, two steps back. So where's the development momentum for that player if I'm not interacting with him or her properly and personalizing the experience?

When I was going through the practice video, these were the things I was interested in—because somewhere along the way, if the player did not acquire the skill by the end of the practice and was not able to use that skill the next day, the accountability fell on me. There would obviously be something inside this process I missed or didn't do properly. Maybe I made judgment errors or progression errors, or maybe the interaction I had broke down somewhere along the line. If I'm really honest with myself, I can see where that problem happened. By tracing it back, I could see where I missed key cues that would have moved the process along at a better rate, or I realized if I'd spent more time on a key area, that would have allowed them to acquire the skill. Instead, I didn't afford enough time in the perfecting stage for the player to really understand and get a feel for the skill. When I tried to stack something on top of it, it just wasn't able to support it and we weren't able to move along at the right pace.

However, skill acquisition is not about the speed at which you're acquiring it. It's more about the precision with which you're acquiring. You want the player to leave with the skill. If you only focus on speed, you're possibly going to miss something or shave reps that are important. This is where trusting the feel is so important. It's manipulating the success rates, understanding where the player is mentally and which reads I have on the player that told me this was the best time to be able to push this program along. Then, I ask myself what were some of the other factors from a technical teaching perspective I may have missed?

A key component for my development was assuming a failure to acquire the skill is always my fault, not the player's. I did more reflection on my own performance, which then fast-forwarded my actual overall ability. It allowed me to raise my level of standards in my performance with the players. I became more conscious of my process while in the teaching environment. When I was on the ice, I would be evaluating the pacing and the way I was creating my demonstrations. How do I know the demonstration was good? Well, I'm going to get the feedback from the players even if they don't say they don't understand—either the look on their face says they don't understand or it becomes apparent when they first start the actual skill.

Sometimes I want to create that conflict. I want it to be a little ambiguous or go through the demonstration fast and challenge the player to share the responsibility. Sometimes I actually want to create a problem to encourage an interaction with the players. That creates dialogue and helps us build more of a relationship. It's not always about trying to make it perfect. A lot of times in order to get it right, you want to make it wrong first and create problems that weren't already there or you didn't really need to as part of the process. This could be the first time I'm dealing with the player, or the player might already be comfortable with me. I need to create these problems to encourage dialogue, because I don't want to have any assumptions. Once assumptions start building up, that is a real limiting factor for the player.

There are levels of accountability, and that's a reflection of skill trainers' real skill set and the level of players they're dealing with. Their effectiveness with those players is reflected in what their expectations are. If they're saying the players aren't smart enough or skilled enough to acquire the skills, that's a reflection of their own skill level. They just haven't gotten far enough through the levels to assume it's all their fault if it doesn't go right. Once I understood that was a critical piece to opening up the next level of my development, I started to really take it seriously.

6

FEEL-BASED LEARNING

EARLY ON IN MY COACHING AND TEACHING CAREER, I NEVER PAID too much attention to how people learned. The only thing I really knew was there are three primary mechanisms to how people learn: audio, visual, or kinesthetic. The way I approached teaching after I learned that was making sure I included every opportunity for those inputs to be used inside my teaching. If I did that, I thought I'd cover all the bases. Along the way, the difference in learning styles would pop up frequently.

For example, in a given drill, I would want one of the better players on the ice to do the demonstration. I'd say, 'You're going to go up here, turn there, turn here, go over there, and then do this and finish with a shot. You got it?' The player would look at me like, 'No, I don't have it.' I would explain it to him again, and he would say, 'I need to see it first.' Then I would walk him through it, and that would finally allow him to do it.

That became an eye-opener. I started to pay attention to which kids were more or less interested in going first. Some wanted to see it first or get a couple of reps in first. I knew there was something going on there; I just didn't know what.

One of the things I did later on in my group settings was try to make it as easy as possible for kids to go first. I wanted there to be more of a battle for kids to go first. I noticed a lot of times I would go to a line and say, 'Okay, you guys ready?" There'd be one kid who pushed to the front, and every other kid was trying to find their way to the back of the line. They just didn't want to go first. I wanted kids to be excited to go first. I wanted to flip this.

I had to be more responsible for the conditions I was creating that made it easier for kids to go first. One of the things I would say is the player who goes first has every opportunity to make all the mistakes, because there's no expectation he's going to do it right. If you're a kid who doesn't understand what we're doing, then the best place to be is first because I'm going to talk you through it. However, after you've seen it a couple times, well, now I'm expecting you to do it perfectly because you've had every opportunity to see it.

I tried to do a variety of different things in group settings to make it easier and more comfortable for players to go first. It's not uncommon to see that situation where everyone is literally battling to get to the back of the line. It could be because of their confidence, learning style, where they think they fit in the group, their level of understanding, or what they feel like the repercussions would be if they weren't successful—that their teammates could look down on them or they would feel embarrassed. I wanted to get through that.

The first time I had to become aware of the importance of learning styles was when I had a career day of five hours of ice time, each hour a private lesson with an NHL player. It was one of those days I had circled on my calendar. The stars had aligned so that those players wanted to work with me on that given day. In the days and months that followed, I watched these five sessions over and over again because I wanted to relish the idea that this was possible, that this had happened, and I wanted to find ways I could be more effective inside those hours. It was a special day, and I wanted to do my due diligence. As I watched these ice sessions, I noticed there was a distinct difference in how each player approached it. Three of the five players were elite, top-end NHL players, and the other two guys were good NHL players. They weren't bad by any means; they were guys who would play in the league for 10 years. But you could see the three elite NHL players did things differently than the other two in their approach to learning. As I picked up on this, I started to be ultra-sensitive to it. I was working with some junior players who weren't on their way to the NHL and wanted to see if they had similar learning traits.

This is where feel-based learning started for me. I understood that audio learning, visual learning, and kinesthetic learning are all brain learning in the end. But ultimately, all three of the learning inputs have to be expressed athletically. So no matter how you're taking in the information, it has to go through some conversion process to ultimately end up as a physical kinesthetic expression. When I understood that, I started to pay attention to how players would go through this conversion process of taking what I was saying or showing them and expressing it athletically.

One of the things these players did that was unique was to make all their corrections before the first repetition. I would explain a drill as follows: "I need you to take the puck from the corner, get up to the hash mark, weight shift inside out to load up the outside leg, then cross over toward the middle of the ice, making sure you keep the puck coming last. Then, I need you to continue to use that weight shift to load up that crossover, and once you get to the dot I want you to use some type of a deception and shoot the puck." I would then walk them through it. While I was doing that, I'd look back and see the elite players just standing there. But while they were standing there, they'd be going through a visualization process mirroring what

I was doing but using small movements. I would come back and ask if they understood, and they would say, "Yes, I just have a question about this particular part." They would ask about their hands, or how to keep the puck back, or where their shoulders should be, or about the weight shift. They'd have all these different questions about the execution. Then, as I explained it to them, they would either have follow-up questions, or they would stand in place and show me a small rep of the movement. I would either answer yes or no or demonstrate whatever the correction would be. They were making all those movement corrections before they would even start the drill. When they started, they would just be looking for confirmation as to whether or not that was exactly what I wanted.

They had done all the corrections before the first rep, which to me was absolutely fascinating. It was very different than the other players. Mid-level NHL players did not approach it that way. They were elongating their learning. Their approach was more of what I termed rep-based learning. Some learners are feel-based and others are more rep-based. I would explain the drill to the rep-based learners, and they would go and do it—incorrectly. They would ask, "Is that what you want?" I'd say, "No, I need you to do this way." They'd go right away and do it again. They would have to do all the corrections after the rep was completed. Sometimes, they would lose their place in the corrections and we'd be back at the beginning. It was like tug-of-war. It was a frustrating process, and I found it difficult to manage the success rate because the players would start to get frustrated about the little things they weren't able to do. So I started showing these players the video and say, "This is what I'm seeing, and this is the correction." They'd try to do the drill again, but these players are reliant on me to tell them what to do. With them, it's all external corrections. There was nothing really going on internally in terms of their awareness of what their bodies are doing.

It took a long time and these players acknowledged it was going to be frustrating.

In feel-based learning, players approach the drills with an acute awareness of what their bodies are doing. They're doing internal corrections before they even start. They want to feel the movement so they can get a feel profile of how their body is supposed to move. Then, they match that up with what you're saying you want from them. Once they have that, they try to replicate that feeling inside the movement. They would come back and their feedback would be feel-oriented. "Oh, I feel off balance. I feel a little bit weird. I feel strong in that position." All the adjectives they used to describe the way their body was moving were feel-oriented.

I quickly started paying attention to this, and I now believe learning style is a major separator among elite players. One of the challenges I had with both groups of players was that I had no idea how the exercise felt to them. I only knew what it looked like, which was my only way of judging whether it was right or wrong. The players, when they're doing the actual exercise, have no idea what it looks like. Their exclusive way of understanding it is only how it feels, so we immediately have a communication problem. It's like we were speaking different languages, so we needed a common medium.

That's when I started to bring out the video. We would tape every session. (Before we had iPads, we would use the flip camera.) I wanted to be able to confirm for the player that he was doing the right thing or that I was making the right correction, because a lot of times they would say, "Oh, that feels weird." When the correction felt weird, they were more hesitant to go down that path. But with a visual, I could show them where they were in terms of angles of movement—how much faster or overall more efficient the whole movement was. If I didn't have that visual to be able to compare, the players would feel nervous about making a change because it felt weird to them. They'd prefer to go to a more comfortable movement pattern. It might feel better, but movement-wise, it's not correct, it's not efficient, and it's not going to lead them down a good path. The reason the movement felt weird is because they're changing a bad habit.

As I started going through this process with more elite NHL players, I realized how much more they were willing to seek to understand. First, they weren't just listening and doing. They were trying to understand and internalize what was going on. They would say, "I could see that working in this game situation." They would talk through it all, just trying to understand how the body's supposed to move, what it's supposed to feel like, what the anticipated benefits are, where the efficiency is.

The truth of the matter is when you're working with movement, you're trying to make changes. The more I can get the body to move naturally—the joints moving in proper order, moving from one foot to the other smoothly, athletically being more forward, having the upper body aligned or leading the lower body—all those things that make the body move more efficiently. Once moving more efficiently feels better to the athlete, they'll start to adopt the correction.

The next question became, *Can you teach someone who is not naturally feel-based to have a more acute understanding of his body?* These players may not get to the level the top-end guys are, but can they develop better than they have? The answer is yes, of course they can. I started to educate myself more. I would ask players how they felt in a movement and listen to how they described their body awareness. I was collecting more information because I wanted to know if they felt good. If the way these players understand how the movement of a skill is expressed is incorrect, that means they're in a poor movement pattern their body has adopted and is expressing as truth. That's why it feels comfortable even though it's not correct. In the process of changing, it's going to feel weird for a while until the players hit the timing correctly, and then suddenly it will just feel way better than what they had previously been doing.

That was the start of the process of educating the player. The feel-based player needed to be convinced how changing the movement pattern in a certain way would influence his ability to move more efficiently. I had to be able to illustrate those anticipated benefits. The player who wasn't coming at it from an overly feel-oriented perspective needed to be educated as well on how it's supposed to feel easy. There's a reason the skill is clumsy; it's because the joints aren't firing in the proper order

What I started to do was really analyze the pre-rep routine the top players were using and what commonalities they shared. There were some subtle differences, but for the most part they were pretty similar in what they were doing prior to starting. I would teach players who weren't as inclined to start this way to adopt this pre-rep routine. For example, I would say, "In this situation, I need your knee to be forward beyond your toecap. We need to establish the shin angle at a particular degree. In order to get that in the right degree, you should feel the laces on your skates digging into the top of your ankle. That's how you would know you're in the right position." I would have them gradually push their knee forward toward the ice and tell me when they felt the laces biting into their ankle. I'd then review the clip and show them the angle, then draw it to show it was at 55 degrees, pretty close to where we want to be. So when they felt the laces on their ankle, that's how they knew they were in the right position. If they didn't feel it, that means they've lifted the degree of that shin angle, putting themselves in a less effective position. That's the feel cue.

If I wanted to teach them to turn and I needed the upper body to initiate the movement, I would say to them, "When you turn, you feel tension in your core because you're turning. If you don't feel tension in your core that means you've probably turned in one piece. We want you to turn in two pieces, initiated by the upper body and followed by the lower body, so that the lower body is using the torque the upper body is creating to help create more efficiency or speed in the actual movement." That's what we're after.

Those steps were important to create a feel-based feedback structure in which I could describe what it was specifically I wanted the players to feel so they could have a more heightened awareness of those feelings. What inevitably would start to happen is once they got into the movement, they would start to feel other things. They'd feel tension in other places. Other elements of their body started to feel differently because they were creating more awareness outside of what I was specifically working on, which to me was a good sign we were moving in the right direction.

I wanted use more feel-based questions when I was talking to players to elicit feedback. When I asked, "How did that feel?" I wanted to hear, "Oh yeah, I felt weird; it felt different." Well, weird and different are good, and I could confirm to them that if it felt different or weird, that means we're on the right track. If it feels the same, that means we're probably closer to the old habit and we're not making any positive impact.

I also wanted to confirm the feel on video. Depending on the player and their acuity for level of feel, I was interested in showing them on the video that they were on the right track—that the angles and the movement principles we were trying to influence were moving in the right direction, even though it didn't feel very good. That would fast-forward the development because then they were more willing to stay in that uncomfortable stage. When people say "you've got to feel comfortable being uncomfortable," this is exactly what they mean. This is how it's being expressed. It feels weird because that's when change is occurring. Your body is reacting to a movement pattern you've done over and over again for however many years. Even though it's incorrect, it's familiar, and the body has adopted it as truth. But as soon as you begin go the process of change, it's going to feel weird until you get to a point where you hit it just right. You're educating the body that this movement is way easier, more effective, more efficient, and as a result I feel good. This is the movement I want to do. Then, the old habit starts to feel weird, and now you're training your body to move toward more movement efficiency principles. But in doing that, you have to constantly show the athletes they're moving in the right direction; otherwise, they're going to have anxiety about it not feeling right. You have to have confirmation, and that's why the video medium is so important when teaching.

The thing about movement efficiency is when the body moves as it's supposed to—the joints fire in the proper order, you're in the proper position—your movement is going to feel easy. I can't tell you the number of times I've been teaching someone to shoot the puck, and when they shoot with an incorrect body movement and technique, it leads to over-shooting, or difficulty shooting, or using all their energy to shoot. It's a hard process, and they can feel how much tension it takes to execute that shot. When it's the opposite, when your body moves the way it's supposed to move, even though you're shooting the puck at a hard pace, it's easy to shoot. It feels easy when it comes off, smooth and fluid. From a teaching perspective, we're looking to move them toward the highest expression of skill, which is fluidity. It's not tension; it's fluidity. They can mistake familiarity for fluidity, but there's a difference. There is a process of learning which usually requires them to feel uncomfortable, and I have to constantly reassure them they're moving closer to fluidity and further away from familiarity.

There is a key to sustaining that movement change. When I implement the changes and we get to the end of the ice session and they're moving the way I want and they can feel those changes, how long is it going to take them to regress back to what felt more familiar? How long does it take for the old habit to return? Depending on your ability to educate the player to have a more acute feel for that movement change, if they have enough reps inside that fluidity to feel the difference, you have a chance to create a sustained movement change. If the new way feels better than the old way, they'll adopt it and won't look back. The better and more acute the feel is, the more possible it is for them to be able to sustain that movement change.

When we're impacting movement, we must also consider that the specific movement change is going to impact other movements within the sequence. It's important to understand how that movement impacts everything else, because that can also create complications in terms of the feel. The player can be focused on things inside the movement chain that feel different but are not specifically targeting the actual movement we want. We have to be aware of the whole system, how the whole thing moves. If we're only focused on one piece, other pieces in the movement chain can influence how that player feels, and that's going to affect their learning.

One of the simplest chain reactions we have is when a player is skating, the movement should occur from the largest joint to the smallest joint in sequence. The hip initiates the movement, the knee continues the movement, and the ankle finishes the movement. If you get full extension through the ankle, the muscle group and the joints are fully extended, then the body automatically snaps back. It's like an elastic band. It snaps all the way out at the very end and comes back in. For example, if the knee joint starts the movement and precludes the hip from going, you're now having to force the movement power and it reduces the body's to move properly. You want to have that chain reaction move in the most fluid way possible.

The movement sequence starters are also important. For example, on a tight turn, the movement starters are that your head turns and you move the puck—then that initiates the chain reaction of your shoulders coming around, your hips coming around, and ultimately your legs coming around into that turn. By turning your head and moving the puck, you're then repositioning your body over top of your inside leg outside edge. Now you've put yourself in a good spot to start the sequence, especially if you're shifting angles in a good spot going forward.

Puck placement in movement is critical because it can either drag you down or it can escalate what you're doing. That's why the upper body moving first is so important, because the puck can be a cue. For example, on a turn, it's way easier to put the puck in the new direction first and your body will just follow it. If you want to use a tight turn, you put the puck tighter to your body and your body will naturally move in a tighter radius.

Automation also impacts movement. There are certain automated movements players have adopted over the years that you're trying to bring to the surface and fix. But ultimately, you have to throw it back into the subconscious. Once you've impacted this movement pattern, you have to hide it in other parts of a sequence. You're putting something before it and you're putting something after it so the body will automate through that movement.

The true test comes when the players are focused on other things and they're not consciously aware of the changes you're trying to make. They're not necessarily feeling the movement; it's now automated. What are the principles the movement which is occurring? Is it closer to the new movement, or is it closer to familiarity? That's what will determine whether or not that feel movement pattern you used has a chance to create sustainable movement change.

TESTIMONIAL

LARS ELLER
on Darryl Belfry

Details have always been important to Lars Eller and his game. He can't do much with generalities.

In coming to Darryl Belfry for help, Eller found someone who talked a different way than most of the coaches he had come across in hockey. The hockey language and terms were different, but it was also much more detailed. That especially attracted Eller.

"Darryl, like myself, is extremely detailed with everything he does," Eller said. "Just for example, he always brings out the iPads and films every single rep you're doing on the ice. When we're doing stuff, normally coaches will just tell you, they'll draw up a drill and then go like, do this to the best of your ability, do this as good as you can. With Darryl, he'll explain how he wants you to do something specifically, where he wants the puck to be on your stick, where he wants your feet to be.

"If you find out, oh, I'm having trouble doing this. Why can't I do it the way I want to do it or how can I do it better? You'll go back and look at the video in slow motion, and Darry will actually look and see stuff that I didn't realize myself. It's like, you can't do this 90-degree turn here because all your weight in on your left foot. You got to get your right foot down on the ice to make this turn. You

can't do this because all your weight is here, you're stuck. Simple stuff like that, little very detailed stuff like that."

Eller also learned how specific parts of his body are connected to other parts and how his game can be dictated by that.

"Wherever you want to go with your feet, your upper body has to lead that movement," Eller said. "You want to move the puck where you want to skate. First you got to move the puck, then your hands will follow and then your upper body will follow and eventually your lower body will follow. A lot of little details that can make a difference in the game. Because at the NHL level, everybody has talent. Everybody has skill. To get a separation from being a good to a very good player or from being a very good player to an elite player, some nights the differences aren't very big. He can help you utilize your skills to the best of your ability. He has a unique talent for that."

Belfry helped Eller in that separation and assisted in making him a consistent NHL player.

"Darryl, for sure, put some stuff in my game that I didn't have before and have a better understanding of how to use my skills better and assets," Eller said. "I always had that, but maybe didn't know to use them better than I would. He helped me take my game to the next level. There was a lot he helped change. Changing my feet on shots, changing the angle when I shoot and my general footwork when I was skating. I used to be skating in straight lines all the time. When I first got into the league 10 years ago, the coaches would just preach skate as hard

as you can down the line, chip it or skate around him. To be successful at that point 10 years ago, you had to be stronger or faster to beat guys one-on-one. One of the things Darryl taught me was the crossover. Instead of skating in a line, I could cross over and manipulate the defenseman. You could put the defenseman in positions that are favorable to you."

7

DEVELOPMENT IS PERSONAL

ONE OF THE MOST IMPORTANT THINGS I LEARNED IS THERE'S A big difference between teaching and coaching. Those two terms often get blended into the same meaning. There is an assumption that when you are coaching, you are teaching. There are elements to coaching that are teaching-based, sure, but teaching, in and of itself, is very different.

Coaching is the management of assets inside of a group. It's managing the achievement gap and trying to minimize the amount of exposures you have from a competitive perspective by buoying up the bottom of the group. There's a large focus in coaching on the middle and the bottom of the group to make sure they're undergoing improvement. The goal is for them to become functional as assets of the team. There's often an effort in coaching to reduce the athlete to just playing it simple and focusing on their strengths. From a coaching perspective, it's about contribution. You want to maximize contribution while minimizing exposure to risk. That's the way you manage the achievement gap.

Teaching is very different. It's personal. In a teaching environment, you're teaching almost exclusively to the top. When I first started, I was teaching to NHL winger Nathan Horton. He was my best player, so I focused on teaching him. The approach was very much *lead, follow, or get out of the way.* From a group perspective, when you're teaching, you're trying to create a drag effect. There's an elite player who is pacing the group's learning, and if that top player is learning, then everyone else gets dragged along that same path. But if the top players in that group aren't being challenged, then they're not having the opportunity to learn new things and the pacing of the group goes down toward the middle or even the bottom. When that happens, you're going to slow down the development process. Our focus was always to teach to the top, and then we want to get that bottom player to chase me as we're teaching the top player. What I mean by that is we want him to be so engaged in what's going on that he's chasing me for more information.

For example, when we'd get on the ice, I would immediately challenge the best player. I'd put him in an awkward position where it would be difficult for him to be successful right away. That captures his attention. Now he's trying to battle to get the skill under control. We try to focus on that player to get him started. Then we purposely leave him alone, let him try to figure things out on his own, and go to the other end of the rink and start working with other players. Eventually, that player starts to come around and starts chasing you to engage with him to set him on the right path. That's how you know you're doing an effective job of teaching to the top. Some of the top players have enough ancillary skills that they can leverage one skill against the other and can start to figure it out on their own. They'll come to you and say, "Hey, is this it?" They already know they've captured it. They just want to let you know they've figured it out already and they're going to need a better challenge than that. Focusing on getting the top to create the drag effect for the rest of the players then sets the development pace for the entire group.

Like coaches, in a teaching situation we are also trying to manage the achievement gap, but it's very different. The way we manage the achievement gap is we attempt to level the playing field by making sure it's a new skill set for everyone. If the top player is challenged, then every other player is also challenged. Everyone is now learning, even the best player. They start at the same level in their understanding of the skill. They don't all have the same level of background knowledge, depth of skill, and ancillary skills that would allow the best player to learn at a faster rate, but they've leveled the playing field. You tighten the progressions to make it easier for the lesser-skilled players. You want to make it easier for them to stay with the development process, even though at some point they're going to run into a skill gap that precludes them from pushing forward at the same rate as a better player. The better player has more depth of skill to continue along the pace, but at least initially you can capture everyone's attention by putting them all on equal footing.

The other thing we do is try to change the environment. We do that by managing the competition. For example, let's say you're a middle-level player for your group. We would put you in a competitive situation against someone you're better than. That allows you to work the skill and build confidence in it. You have acquired the skill; now it's a matter of perfecting it against someone you can impose your will on and start challenging yourself. Then, we'd work you against someone who's better than you, which makes you have to execute at a higher rate with better purpose, better timing, etc. You're constantly changing your environment, working with people who aren't as good and then working with people who are better, and the competition then drives the risk. Your risk level is going to go up against someone you're better than. But when you go against someone who's better than you, your risk level is naturally going to drop. You're going to use fewer skills. You're going to only try to use your best ones because you're trying to fend off someone who's better. Manipulating those changes of environment is an effective tool in managing the achievement gap and teaching players how to how to utilize that to the best of their ability.

I know small games are all the rage right now. There's this idea that if you do small-area games, the game will teach, and there is some truth to that. I also think it can fail to have any effect on the achievement gap. What I mean is if you're on a regular team and you do a three-on-three cross-ice game, the best players on the team are going to be the best players in that game. Unless you've done something to level the playing field—maybe introducing a new skill everyone has to learn and apply inside that game—the achievement gap will remain the same. My argument against only doing smaller games is that they have a role in the development process, but they are not the development process. I often see people think games are the teacher, and that does nothing to give a fair competitive opportunity for those who are playing in it unless you help manage it. The achievement gap is an important element as it relates to a teaching environment, and manipulating those aspects is critical.

When you're doing your progressions and you end with the game, which includes skill elements you've been working on all practice, now you've got something. Then, you could demand what's been done in the practice be done in the game. Kids have to manufacture those moments to apply those skills. That's different than just playing on raw skill and ability, which we often do. You have to drop the puck and let them play. When we do that, the best kids have the most advanced skill set—they are the fastest, the biggest, the strongest, and so they can freely impose their will, be more creative, have the puck more often, generate their scoring chances, read off other good players. They have low levels of stress because they're better, so they have more opportunity to take risks as it relates to development than when they're matched up against someone who's better. If there's no other context than just playing three-on-three, there's nothing happening to influence the achievement gap. We want to be able to manipulate that to improve the players' ability to perform and use those games in a teaching environment, which then allows them to influence their skill set and become more capable. An important aspect of teaching is managing the development and achievement gap. If we're not actively managing the achievement gap, then we're just going to perpetuate it, and that's not really teaching.

Coaching is managing assets. You want the players to just leverage the top end of their skill or recognize a situation in which they're over-matched and start minimizing the risk. Teaching is a completely different approach, where you want players to apply the skill with varying degrees of competition and understand how to manage themselves in those different competitive environments. That, in turn, allows them to start leveraging skills and building higher degrees of capacity to get the skill to where they could use it against higher levels of competition, thus putting them in a spot where they're improving or closing the achievement gap.

One of the other things we're trying to do in a teaching environment is read off the athletes and run with a player's skill expression. If a player has a slightly different way they're expressing the skill, you're going to run with that. For example, I tell the players to protect the puck against a defender, and every kid is just putting his back to the defender and doing a traditional puck protection, and then you see one kid who uses an offensive stick check. This player is protecting the puck and he leaves the puck to check or lifts the stick of the defensive player and makes his next move because the stick has been moved out of the way. That's an excellent skill expression that's unique to the group inside this puck protection drill. We would then run with that. In a teaching environment, you would stop it right away and say, "Hey, I just saw a really cool thing. Jack just did this. I want to now incorporate that in." We would then do a drill on stick checks and come back to the puck protection plays piece. The players would do their traditional back-to-the-defender puck protection but then also look for an offensive stick check. That encourages and embraces the exploration of the skill and self-discovery.

Back in the drill, you might see something else—maybe instead of putting their back to the defender, somebody puts themselves sideways. Now that player can beat the defender to reach for the puck and then spin off the check to get into open space. That's different than a player using his back to defend. You now have an offensive stick check with this additional side-shoulder protection. I would stop the drill and say, "Jane just did this really cool skill expression as it relates to puck protection, so let's embrace that and start moving toward those things." That's what I mean by reading and running with skill expression. Players will always add something a little different that's still in the same family of development, and you'll want to run with those elements.

When you embrace individual elements in the teaching process and incorporate them, it engages the students. Now they're all thinking creatively. They're all looking for their own expression of this skill to contribute to the whole group, and as a result, the whole group's learning. It's a fascinating process to run with skill development. That's what I mean when I say teaching is personal. In a coaching environment, you're not necessarily going to embrace that. You might look at it whether it was effective and led to a chance. You might congratulate the player for his effectiveness, but you're not going to stop the whole drill and add that to the development process because you only have a few more minutes and then you're on to the next drill. With teaching, there's no time limitation. You have all the time in the world to explore adding different elements. It's a totally different attitude.

In embracing exploration, it's important to consider what's easier from a mindset perspective. Is it easier to correct a bad habit or teach a new skill? If you asked a bunch of players, they would all say it's easier to learn a new skill. Changing a bad habit is difficult to do. It's painstaking. It's frustrating at times. There are a lot of negative emotions that come with breaking a bad habit. What I try to do is shape the skill development so that every skill, even the bad habit, is viewed as a new skill. Rather than break an old habit, we're going to replace the bad habit with a new skill and set the player up from a from a mindset perspective to again try to take more risks in their own individual development. That allows the experience to be much more personalized because the players feel like they're learning a new skill.

In a teaching environment, I'm interested in players' training habits. What are they doing inside the training environment? We want them to look for work—add another rep. If they experienced a bad rep—maybe they mishandled the puck, fell, or made a bad pass—they would immediately go again because they don't want to lose that rep. In a coaching environment, players only have so many times to go. If they miss it, they miss it, and we're on to the next guy. Teaching is looking for work. You want to make sure your quality control is high.

Once you have a good functional understanding of what the original drill capacity is and players are on their way to perfecting this skill inside of the expectations, you're then looking to add skills to it. Add a little deception, add some change of speed, add a different skill as it relates to the puck—whatever the case may be, you're going to really want to get all the corrections done before you engage in the development because you don't want to waste a rep. If players are focused on their training habits, they want to understand first, get all the corrections, and get a feel for what they're doing, and then the first rep is a real repetition.

Our game of hockey is built on transition, so you want to add the next piece that would go on the very end of the skill you're working on or envision what that might be. If it's a shot, for example, you might shoot and then track the puck for puck recovery, because as soon as it releases off your stick you're now on defense until your team recovers the puck. You're in transition, so now you're jumping to that loose puck wherever it might be. Sometimes that takes the form of a continuation drill, where you have to shoot, go get another puck, and pass to the next guy. That starts the same sequence but going the other way, making it a continuous flow. Sometimes those transitions are built into drills, but a lot of times they're not. As a player, you have to find ways to add those continuations in. As part of the teaching environment, we have to train our players to have good training habits. These training habits are important as it relates to every player taking personal responsibility for his or her own development.

In personal development, we often find players' best asset is also the first source of restriction in their game. We want to focus on expanding the asset base and minimizing any negative effects of their best asset. For example, if you're physically more mature than most players you play against, you're going to rely on being physical and using your body in different ways. The best part about that is you can physically hang onto the puck. You can feel good about getting around the rink. The bad part is because you're relying on that physicality, it's difficult to want to add layers to that. Or maybe you're really fast; the fact that you have a lot of speed means you probably try to play at top speed more often. You're not going to develop changes of speed or you're not going to develop as much as it relates to timing. You might get there too early too often. In development we're constantly looking to maximize a player's assets but also guard against the best part being the worst and provide more depth of opportunity, so the player does not have to carry the burden of their best asset.

You may already be familiar with Anatoly Tarasov's concept of the three skill speeds in hockey—speed of hand, speed of skating, and speed of mind. There is also a fourth skill speed—perception of speed. You might be able to skate fast, understand conceptually where you need to be, and have great hands, but what's really important is the fourth skill speed, your perception of speed. Everyone, when they're playing, is viewing the game as being played at a certain speed. The perception of that speed for each individual person is different. The top player, for example, sees the game being played at a very slow pace, crystal-clear. The weakest player on the ice feels like it's going 90 miles an hour, in a blur. The game is going the speed that it's going, but the perception of speed is different for each player, and that's why that's an important skill speed to continue to develop. I don't know that we do enough development as it relates to skill speed.

For the longest time, I could group my clients into three different buckets. The first would be players who were trying to make the NHL. They were right on the cusp and coming to me to try to get that last push to get them over the hump and into the NHL. The second bucket would be players already in the NHL and changing roles. Maybe they got traded or their role on their current team is going to be different. Maybe their age is reducing their effectiveness at a certain style and they have to adjust. The third bucket would be the top players in the game. They're seeking me out to build a room onto the house, to understand a specific area of the ice in which they can become better. They're looking to create inside of that.

For players who are trying to make it into the league, what's really important is translatable skill: how much you can keep by going from one level to the next. If you're moving from the OHL directly into the NHL, for example, there are some parts of your game that make you successful at the OHL level you'll be able to keep when you go to the NHL, but there are also specific habits that are going to be difficult to transfer. Some of it can be kept, some of it needs to be replaced, and some of it has to evolve. This part of your game has to be manipulated so that it evolves and becomes much more effective. Maybe it needs more layers or more context, more speed, more strength, but it could survive if it evolved. A lot of this is dependent on the mind evolving first, and that's the difficult part for this group because they've gotten this far doing things a certain way. Now they're on the cusp of making it, and in order to make it they're going to have to make more changes. They're reluctant because there's a fear that if they try to make these changes and it doesn't work out, they'll regret knocking themselves backward when they were right there. It's a fascinating group to work with, because once they can overcome that lower appetite for change and start making some meaningful changes, they can really take off quickly and understand where their competitive advantages are so they can leverage them and ultimately reach their goal.

My favorite player I ever worked with from the second bucket was Drew Stafford. At the time, he was with Buffalo and had performed well, with a 30-goal season at one point. The Buffalo team was undergoing some massive changes, and Drew's game was being changed and the role he was playing was getting phased out. He needed to find a way to hold on to his identity while going through these changes. It was a fascinating experience to go through with Drew to carry some of the stuff that made him successful in one part of his role, but then realizing he's not playing top-line minutes with top players and he's not in offensive situations as often. We needed him to still be able to execute, still make plays, still generate chances, but also to be effective in the role he was going to play with his assets. But what were those? What could he keep? What things are going to have to evolve? It's a great process.

The third bucket, the players looking to innovate, have the highest appetite for change. They have the most capacity and the most equity with their coaching staff to carry a lot more risk in terms of how they play. They're able to look critically at different areas of their game that are ineffective or not as effective as they should be. They can ask the questions and start building new pathways to greater levels of success. Sometimes it's just rebuilding an area of the ice that's consistently not as effective as it should be. We throw out some new ideas to buoy it up or find new skill expressions in high-frequency areas that will offer them more options to generate. Sometimes it's taking an elite skill they have and trying to add more layers to it or disguise it or evolve it to become even better. Obviously that innovative group is the easiest group to work with because those players are highly motivated to make those changes. They know they've got to continue to evolve.

In player development, the goal really is to break the rules. We don't want all players to play the same way under the same set of rules. In coaching, you definitely do. You want every player to adhere to a system, style of play, systematic responsibilities. There are all kinds of movement restrictions to make sure there's uniformity and predictability within a group. But when you're working with someone individually, we actually want them to break the rules inside of skill expression. That doesn't mean break the rules as to how they're being coached; not at all. It's a different expression of breaking the rules. For example, under-handling is a big buzzword right now for most coaches, skill instructors, and players alike. They're talking about how they can under-handle the puck. If everyone learns to handle the puck the same way, then where's the advantage? There is none. Top-performing players don't want to be under-handling, as it pulls some skill sets down to the median. You want to find ways to make it appear as though you're going to under-handle and then use a handle in a certain context to disguise what it is you're going to do.

Another rule we can learn to break involves body contact. The rule is if you know you're getting hit, then you should get close to the walls to take that contact. You don't want play five feet off the wall because that's the danger area where you're going to be most at risk to get hurt, which is true. However, the rule we want to follow is to start in space so we can initiate contact instead of being in a situation where we're accepting the contact. We're going to come and meet the contact or we're going to change the contact point to make it less effective. We're going to get into space or spin off or bait the guy to come in for contact and roll off that check. We're looking to try to break those rules whenever we can because that's what creates the uniqueness of the athlete. Each player has a different way to express the skill, and because it's different it becomes a competitive advantage. As long as what they're trying to do is in concert with good movement principles and good hockey play in general, it can be really effective.

We also want to empower the athletes into their success rates. We work off the 8 out of 10 principle. If you can do something 8 out of 10 times in the NHL, that makes you ultra-elite. Most players are operating anywhere between 4 and 6, somewhere around 50 percent. If we can go 8 out of 10, we're immediately putting ourselves in an elite bracket. So, we have to acknowledge failure. When you're coaching, you aren't motivated to acknowledge failure. There's no such thing as a good turnover. Coaches don't want to turn any pucks over that lead to chances because that's how you lose hockey games, and that's 100 percent true. But when you're teaching, it's different. We acknowledge there are going to be two mistakes and we're going to give ourselves permission for those two mistakes in exchange for the other eight. We are going to trust our results. The development process is so important as it relates to acknowledging and manipulating success rates. We want our players to play with a free mind and not be worried about making mistakes. The way we mitigate that is we acknowledge the possibility of mistakes. Hopefully, there are going to be mistakes 2 times out of 10. But the 8 other times, we're going to do it really well, and that will give us an opportunity to trust our results.

TESTIMONIAL

JASON SPEZZA
on Darryl Belfry

Jason Spezza had gotten so used to playing a certain way with the Ottawa Senators. He was there for 11 seasons, and there was little reason to change things up. He was successful doing it his way.

But when he was traded to the Dallas Stars in 2014, Spezza discovered what he was doing in Ottawa wasn't going to translate as easily as he hoped to his new team. In particular, he found himself with the puck less in Dallas, meaning he was less effective.

Spezza recognized he needed to alter something. He just wasn't sure what. So, he called Darryl Belfry.

"I was having a hard time transitioning," Spezza said. "I had been in one spot for a real long time. I felt like I had more to give in Dallas. I was just feeling like I wasn't getting the puck as much as I was used to, just kind of different things. I felt maybe by approaching Darryl to see if he had some ideas. We had some great talks early on. There was a lot of back-and-forth early. Once he got know what I was looking for, watching my game a little bit more closely, it was extremely helpful."

What Belfry and Spezza pinpointed was Spezza wasn't getting the puck as much from his defensemen. He was accustomed to playing with a lot of the same defensemen in Ottawa, and they were just in sync. In Dallas, Spezza had talented defensemen around him. The problem was they didn't have that background knowledge or experience together.

Belfry went through Spezza's games, focused on his patterns and his defensemen's patterns, and began explaining to Spezza how and where he could get the puck more.

"For me, it was a lot of where I was just putting myself to get the puck," Spezza said. "I had kind of played with the same system and structure for a long time. In Dallas, I wasn't getting the puck from the defensemen through the middle of the dots as much. That became a big focus of just getting into the dot lane and being in the middle of the ice. I find when you play with the same guys for such a long period of time, it's easy, because guys know where you like getting the puck and you know when they like to give the puck. It just kind of happens and you find yourself in the right spot. I went to a team with a lot of talent, but I was just having a hard time getting the same amount of touches as I was getting normally. He really helped dive into that."

Spezza transferred Belfry's advice into the games and had a different second half of the season with the Stars. He ended up with 60-plus points again.

"For me, my relationship with Darryl was most beneficial when I first went to Dallas," Spezza said. "He really helped me transition from team to team. I'm really thankful I got in touch with him at that point because he did a great job

of helping me acclimate to my new surroundings. I don't think I would have been as successful in my first few years in Dallas without having Darryl's input."

From Spezza's perspective, it's been fascinating to see Belfry work with different players, like himself, John Tavares, and Auston Matthews, and achieve success across the board.

"[Tavares, Matthews, and I] all came from different spots…and we all used Darryl and all had success individually with him. I think now having the ability to work with him with a team, I think it makes the buy-in more prevalent. We all believe in him. He's got our ears. And I think that can help the group when you see a bunch of guys believe in somebody, I think it makes it a lot easier for him to come on the ice and gain the respect right away."

8

TRIPLE HELIX: BACKGROUND KNOWLEDGE

I KNEW RIGHT AWAY WHEN I STARTED TEACHING I'D TO NEED TO develop a process, some way I could correlate what I was doing with the results. My entire career, I've been refining my process and trying to find different ways I could produce and, more importantly, predict results.

I went on my reading binge right after I finished high school, and one of the first books I read was *Principle-Centered Leadership* by Stephen Covey. I originally read it because I sought better time management principles and wanted to become a better leader. Years later, the single thing that continues to come back to me is a passage about the law of the farm. Essentially, the law of the farm is that there's no cramming in farming. Farming has a specific process and important timing elements. It has a sequence of events that are important in order to produce the desired result. If you shortcut the process in some way or eliminate one of the elements necessary to grow of the crop, you're not going to yield the desired results. Over the years, I've continued to come back to this law of the farm as my base premise of how I want to operate as a teacher. I don't want to shortcut the process. If the player is learning the right skill at the right time in the right order in the right sequence, I'm going to be able to leverage that into a higher degree of training-to-game transfer. A higher degree of transfer of play is really the name of my game. I need the player to be able to learn the skill and apply it at the right time.

The other influence that left a mark on me was a documentary on Yellowstone National Park. The park's biologists had some challenges balancing their ecosystem and were trying to figure out how to restore it. What they did was introduce wolves to the park. But what they didn't realize was by introducing the wolves, they were not only succeeding in their original intent, but they were also doing a better job controlling the elk who were eating all the vegetation. The wolves then actually impacted the rivers, as well. Other plant and animal life at Yellowstone National Park were able to thrive now because the presence of the wolves. What I got out of that was how one change can have a ripple effect on multiple components, which is an important part of the skill development process. I took that to heart. I started to incorporate the knowledge that if I could make an impact on one area of a player's skill set, it could have an impact globally on all other aspects of his or her game. It's been a real game-changer for me. Prior to that, I understood the impact of frequency—that if something was occurring at a high rate it was an important aspect, especially if I could influence the success rate and create a global impact on the player's game. Now, as I'm trying to add other skills to a player's skill set, I'm conscious of how that impacts other aspects of their game.

Another documentary, *The Biggest Little Farm*, also confirmed what I was doing from a skill development perspective as a direct parallel. It's about a couple who decided to buy a farm. Their idea was to create an old-school, natural way of farming. In doing so, they ran into all kinds of different challenges. They had a mentor who understood how to set the farm up. His vision was a diverse farm where one thing would impact others, and the more diverse the farm was, the more it would run itself at some point because it would have checks and balances in nature. One of the challenges they kept running into was different pests. For example, the better they grew their fruit trees, the more they attracted snails. Then the snails attracted birds. They were basically ruining these strong fruit trees. They viewed pests as unnecessary and needing to be eliminated. They also built a strong chicken farm which was yielding a ton of eggs, which they would sell. But coyotes would break into the farm and kill the chickens. With the fruit trees, they realized ducks eat snails, so they introduced the ducks to the fruit tree area to eat the snails, which had a positive impact on every aspect of developing the fruit trees. They just needed the checks and balances. The same was true with the coyotes. They needed to better protect the chickens, but they didn't necessarily want to get rid of the coyotes. The coyotes were impacting other areas of life inside the farm and creating those checks and balances. The moral of the story was the pests were necessary. They need to be incorporated into the fabric of what was going on and became the checks and balances. The problem was finding the balance. I took a lot from that as a confirmation of my attitude toward the skill continuum. There's going to be a situation where you run into a skill gap, and it'll be necessary to build the bridge to have access to skills on the other side. It was important to understand what I needed to do to not only solve that problem, but to introduce balance, a chance to have more diversity of skill, to open up a whole new room in the house of opportunity. Because with a bridge, we're able to access other things, and that provided more depth of skill for the player, which is ultimately what we're after. Our goal is improving all three of those areas: depth of skill, background knowledge, and awareness. What I call skill impacts is the impact on the entire aspect of this player's game and what predictability I could have inside of that.

One of the gentlemen I met early on in my development process who has been a constant for much of my career is Bill Gillmeister. Bill had a son who was coming to my hockey camp. His son was born in 1991. Bill is a trial lawyer in Buffalo and probably the most well-read person I know. He started sending me articles I initially thought had no correlation to anything relating to hockey. Yet when I read his takeaways and how they might apply to hockey, it was just fascinating. He'd send me a *Harvard Business Review* article on communication strategies in the workplace and the impact it was having on employees' productivity. Here's a process that might have some application from a hockey coaching perspective. Up until that point, I would look inside hockey or other sports to find answers. What Bill highlighted for me was there were a lot of other opportunities out there to learn what people were doing that could have a parallel even though it had nothing to do with sports.

Bill introduced me to a book called *Bringing Words to Life*. It was one of those books that just instantly changed my entire perspective. One of the things I was struggling with for the longest time was what I should teach these kids. There are so many skills to teach them and not a lot of time. If you wanted to teach skills one at a time, you wouldn't be able to produce a very good hockey player because it just takes so long to learn.

This is the same problem with teaching vocabulary. You cannot possibly learn each word by definition if you were trying to learn the English language. You'd struggle just given the sheer volume of words you need to know. The parallel for hockey was we also have a vast number of skills that need to be learned and mastered, but you can't isolate each one of them. There have to be some you're learning through the game and some you're learning through a different way of practicing that incorporates multiple different skills.

It's no different than how vocabulary relies on reading. If you're reading and can deduce the meaning of the words from context, you would then be able to infer that word's meaning even though you don't know its specific definition. That's very similar to hockey. There are things we can learn as we're playing the game, but it's contingent upon our depth of skill. The more words we know, the more fluently we can read, the easier it is for us to deduce vocabulary. However, if we don't have a high enough knowledge base of words, that's going to reduce how much we can challenge ourselves in our reading, which is going to reduce the new words we're actually able to understand. In hockey, you can learn some skills inside of where you're playing, but you have to be careful once you get into the competency bias, which affects that. What I mean by competency bias is that when a player's individual skill and/or processing speed is better than the competition, he has a distinct advantage to learn skill through his understanding or playing of the game.

Part of my development process is a three-pillar approach I call the Triple Helix. Rather than treating these three pillars as silos of individual elements we'd work on independently, they're all intertwined. Each of the silos actually twist around each other and are dependent on each other rather than things we look at in isolation. The three pillars are background knowledge, depth of skill, and awareness. I'm going to go through each one of these individually and then show how they connect as we go along.

For background knowledge, the two core pieces are we want to know what you know and how you know it. This is a critical component of background knowledge. We need to know how much of what you know impacts the way you view the game. Every player has a unique way of viewing the game—what I call a unique reading lens. This reading lens is what forms the backbone of their personal game structure, which houses their habits and movement patterns. The reading lens has different influences to it. It could be their favorite players they've watched endless hours on. It could be the way they're coached. It could be their initial exposure to the game and how that impacted their reading lens.

It's important for me as a skill instructor to understand how the player views the game. What are their biases? How do they read the game? What are their default reads they go to over and over? That impacts their mindset, their ability to see the game, and the types of plays they might make.

How are they able to acquire these skills? Are they someone who has learned through isolated skill training? Meaning, if they're working on skating, they work on skating. If they're working on stick handling, they work on stick handling, but it's independent of working on skating. If they're working on shooting, they work on shooting, but that's independent of what they're doing as it relates to skating and stick handling. It's also independent of all the decision-making they have to do as part of the tactical application. Isolated skill training is the equivalent of trying to expand your vocabulary by reading definitions of single words in the dictionary. It's a limited approach to development and can dramatically slow down a player's learning. There are players who are familiar with that because they grew up like that. I need to know how they learn. We can't learn skills one at a time, so if that's their learning perspective, then I'll have to put work into improving that player's knowledge.

You also have players who possess derived knowledge. These players read the game well and have a good functional knowledge of how they play through their lens, so they know the game based on their personal bias toward it. They can lack a lot of diversity and skill detail. These are players who know where they need to be based on how they read the game, but they have a limited perspective. These aren't people you could move from left wing to right wing, because they might struggle when they move to a different position. They're very good when they're F1, but if they have to be F2 or F3, the degree to which they're away from the puck is the degree they struggle with their understanding of the game. Those are important aspects for me to see.

For the vast majority of players, the games are not a playground to develop skill. One of the big challenges is that the game is based on results. There are certain results you're trying to achieve when you're playing. You're trying to win the game, so that creates restrictions. Most players, when they're trying to win, reduce the number of skills they are willing to use to only their best, most refined ones. This is not a time they're looking to experiment. If they have a one-on-one move and get in a one-on-one situation, they're going to the move they use the most and which has the highest degree of success rate. They're not going to try something new because that's foolish as it relates to trying to win. Development is the manipulation of risk and trying to win a game is the management of risk. You're trying to eliminate as much risk from your game as possible. These are opposite approaches and it's difficult for them to coexist. For most players, this is a big challenge. That's why playing a ton of games to the exclusion of enriched player development is problematic and can create a ceiling based on your perspective.

All this depends on which side you fall on the competency bias. A lot of players do really well by learning through games. But that's because they're on the proper side of the competency bias. We want to develop a rich skill knowledge, and the way you develop that is by creating multiple encounters with the skill you're trying to influence or have a high-quality exposure to a skill inventory. It's a problem when players only use skills in their own lens. Isolated skill development has a ton of transfer problems because players only have a single exposure to that skill and they're not aware of how it may apply in a game.

The easiest example of this is power skating. You see someone do power skating without a puck and without any situational pattern progressions. If you want to learn crossovers, you can go through it all: the balance, the edges, the use of your upper body, where your stick is supposed to be, all the posture elements, the actual skating technique. The problem is when you go play and someone passes you a puck. Well, you never learned to cross your feet with the puck. That changes your posture, which is going to limit fluidity. You worked on crossovers, but you didn't work on doing it with a puck. Now you get a puck and you're probably going to skate in a straight line. You're unlikely to apply the crossover. The next time we go, we're going to add the puck. We learn to skate and use all the same principles, but this time with the puck. The problem is crossover skating, or skating in general, has to have some kind of tactical application once we get into a game. If we didn't progress to teaching it in situational context, like in recurring play patterns, manipulating a defender, or using a crossover to move the defender or encourage the defender to cross his feet to create a competitive advantage, you're going to have a hard time with transferring. There will be no application recognition. So unless the player is consciously thinking of crossing his feet while playing, there will be no natural or fluid transfer. If you didn't move crossover development into other aspects of the skill, like putting it at the front of speed loading a turn or having a change of direction where you come out of it to maintain your speed advantage, you're not creating multiple encounters with the skill and you're going to reduce the richness of the skill knowledge. You're going to reduce its ability to be utilized effectively in the skill inventory.

It's like a carpenter who shows up to the job and has literally every tool he might need in his truck, so it doesn't matter what he encounters inside the job. He has the right tool to be able to get him to the next step in the building process, as opposed to a carpenter who shows up with only a hammer and a saw. Skill inventory is having every tool in the toolbox available to you, so you can apply the right one at the right time. Skill application is applying the right skill at the right time with the right speed. We guard against a player having all the tools and no toolbox by developing individual skill inside recurring play patterns and competitive advantage situations. This provides the player the opportunity to benefit from situational recognition and apply the right skill for the right play.

Learning from playing is a big touchpoint in hockey. There's a thought that the more we play games, the better we get. We're somehow missing the whole mythical idea of entire communities playing on a backyard pond and every kid having elite hockey sense because of it. Now we've adopted this hockey-sense myth and incorporated into it all these small games and games in general. The missing context is the value in the hockey-sense gains on the pond are true if you're on the right side of the competency bias, which is actually irrespective of the pond. If a player's competency level is at the speed of the game he's playing in, he's going to have issues trying different things because he's teetering on the level of the game. Then you have players whose skill set and ability to process are below the level of the game. They're just trying to survive, and they're of course not going to be trying new things because they're having a hard time processing the game as it is. Your competency and where you fit as it relates to the competition have a major impact in your ability to learn through playing.

One of the challenges players will come up against is the achievement gap. We have 15 kids on one team, and each one is reading the game at a different perception speed. We have four or five kids who see the game so clearly that it's easy for them to play well, make good decisions, and try new things. They have a rich skill set for the competition they're playing. These players have great ability to try different things, because they have the confidence and perception of speed in their favor. The more skill you have in relation to the competition, the more the game feels a lot slower for you because you can now play with your head up and move into a ton of open space. Then we have four or five kids who are desperately trying to hang on because the game feels like it's going a million miles an hour as soon as they get the puck. They feel like the whole world's crashing in and they're just moving the puck quickly. Those kids are going to struggle in trying to learn from playing. We have a large percentage of kids who are relying on games to teach them and are in desperate need of enhancing their skill repertoire. Because they don't have an ability to enhance their skill repertoire to meet or exceed the competition they're playing, they're going into the game with a skill deficit for the competition they're playing at, and that's going to impact their perception of speed.

There are two conditions that need to be met in order for kids to effectively learn from playing. The first is they would be given a fair chance if they were playing at a level in which they can skill and/or process the game significantly better than the competition. They would have the confidence to try different things because the game feels slow. The second condition is they must have the ability to infer skill application. In other words, using the right skill for the right situation. For example, let's say you have a player who's on the rush, gets the puck, and is flying through the neutral zone. He looks over his shoulder and realizes he's going one against two; his other teammates are not in the play. The ability to infer skill application would be instead of going one-on-two, he'd try to isolate one of the defenders and go one-on-one to try to beat that defender and take the puck to the net. That is a poor skill application. That's not the right skill for that situation. The right skill for that situation would be to realize he is at a competitive disadvantage, and in order to create offense he wants to be on the opposite side of that. He wants to be playing two versus one. This player would read that situation and say, "Okay, on the rush here I'm going one versus two, I'm going to attack this one defender, force him to turn his feet parallel to mine running toward the end boards, and then I'm going to turn up. By turning up, I'm going to eliminate the weak side defender, and I'm also probably going to lose this initial defender. Now I go from one versus two to going into open space and giving my linemates time to come into the play and create a new two-on-one opportunity, which is a much more favorable situation to create offense." These two conditions have to be met in order for the player to effectively learn through playing.

If you have players who are not able to play above the level of their competition or cannot infer skill application, you are now perpetuating the achievement gap. The best players will be the best players, the middle players will do things every so often that are okay, and the bottom players will continue to be the bottom players because we've done nothing to improve the achievement gap. The way you influence the achievement gap is by reducing the competency spectrum—you have to teach something new to the whole group. That's why you have to teach to the top. The more uncomfortable the top player is in his acquisition of the skill, the more he's on par mentally with everyone else in the group, even though his skill set and capacity to learn are way higher. All the players are on a level mental playing field, which gives them an ability to reduce the competency bias. Everyone has a fair opportunity.

We just don't do that enough. If you just drop the puck and let them play three-on-three, you're perpetuating the achievement gap. The top players are going to try new things because they have the time and space and the speed perception to do it. The kids who have a lower level of skill for the competition are going to get rid of the puck as soon as they get confronted with any level of stress. They're not going to perform with a higher level of speed or skill.

What we want to do is learn through application. This is the whole idea of the skill gap being the ecosystem of skill development and following the law of the farm. We want to target specific learning that's designed to improve the depth of skill. We're looking for intentional transfers. What that means is I've identified a skill gap in your game, I've gone through the process of trying to eliminate that skill gap, and I'm trying to improve or influence that skill. I'm also going to build all the ancillary skills that go around it and then I'm going to put it in a variety of different situations to acquire this rich skill knowledge. You've had multiple encounters with that skill, and now we have a diverse aspect of the skill inventory. Now I'm going to set you up to have an immediate application. Inside my development process, I'm going to hide the application of this skill and force you to recall it. If you can recall it, then we have an opportunity to have an immediate application, which is now improving your depth of knowledge. Once you know how you can apply it, you can anticipate its use and use it appropriately. You're now in a position where you can explore that skill and try to leverage the skills we've taught in other skill sets in other situations. That's more of a targeted learning environment and learning through application. That's the basis of our training-to-game transfer philosophy.

That's not to say players can't learn from playing. It just means I need to start at the beginning, adding skills that introduce new skills I want them to learn. I take them through the development process. I force them to recall it and challenge them to apply the skills in the game situation. It's not a free-for-all three on three; that's just the venue to apply skill. All of a sudden, I'm asking you to incorporate the skills we've learned as part this game. That's targeted skill development, learning through application or what I call training-to-game transfer.

The other aspect I want to explore with background knowledge is players' impressions of what "good" means. Often we don't really know what "good" is until we see someone who's actually good, and that goes for everything. It's important to consider if you want to have a good understanding of your background knowledge, which is often rooted in what your understanding of what good is. Good is relative. It's sometimes relative to the geographical area you're in. The best player in your mind is the best player in your league, and the best player in your league happens to play in your town because it's a house league. If you're only exposed to players in your own town—you don't go anywhere else, you don't see anything else—your impression of good is going to be whomever is good in your circle. The wider your circle, the more you're likely to be able to see what good truly is. That's not to say the best player in the world might not be in your hometown. But the best player in the world might not be in your hometown. So understanding what good is can really improve your background knowledge.

The first step is your exposure and your experience with players who are good. For example, let's say you're an 11-year-old hockey player. It would be important for you to know what the best 12-year-old looks like. What does he do? What's his skill set? How does he create advantages? What's that look like? Because if you understood what the best 12-year-old looks like, it would create a map for your development and where you should be the following year. It immediately gives you context and an objective.

I wanted to find out how good Nathan Horton was, because I did not know what good was relative to him. I went to Toronto and tried to find out who was the best player in the 1985 birth year in Toronto. At the time, the best player in the '85 age group was a kid named Anthony Stewart. I went to go watch him play; I wanted to see what he did that Nathan didn't. What was the difference between them? Once I understood what that was and started to get a profile, I wanted to know what the best '84 birth year player looked like. I took the time to understand what that next level looked like. It gave me some context about where Nathan's level was relative to the people who were good. In our area, he was the best, but he might not be in the top 100 players in Toronto. I just don't know. I'm not going to know that unless I do the research and understand it. Whether you're a skill instructor, coach, or player, the more information you have about exposure and what good actually is, the easier it's going to be.

The best part about doing that research, of course, is it gives you insight into what the next level looks like. One of the objectives every player and coach should have is to be at the next level of performance before you get there. You don't want to be an 11-year-old hockey player who's turning 12 and still playing like an 11-year-old hockey player. You don't want to be learning to be a good 12-year-old hockey player at the same time you are arriving. It's no different than if you were a draft pick in the Ontario Hockey League, and you show up to camp and you still have the habits of a midget player. It's going to be a harder transition for you to be able to play at the OHL level. It's way better for you to understand the difference between a midget hockey player and an OHL player and start pushing yourself to perform at that level before you get there. The problem with lacking context and not really realizing what that next level looks like is it will reduce your confidence and it will impact your risk willingness. You're only going to be constricting your skills, and thus constricting your ability to push to the next level.

The other thing to consider is your personal context. What do you know about yourself in relationship to what good is? We'll hear a lot of, "Well, that player is good for his age, he's good for his size." It create creates this glass ceiling of sorts and takes the shine off however good he might be. You're qualifying how good he actually is. You're not saying he's good, period. Your impression of your personal relativity to good will impact the glass ceiling you've put on yourself and your ability.

When I was training Toronto Maple Leafs center John Tavares very early in my relationship with him and he would do something I really liked, I would emphatically and enthusiastically describe how good the skill expression was. I would use words like awesome, or unbelievable, or beautiful. Sometimes the skill he expressed wasn't even very good. It was that he was starting to move on the right track, which I was excited about. The thing with John was I would say, "Oh, that was awesome," and he would say, "Yeah, I felt better." I was like, *Man, this guy is a bit of a killjoy.* Every time I would say, "You did a great job," he would say, "Yes, I felt a little better, let's do it again." I was trying to figure it out. One day I asked him about it. I said, "I thought that rep was awesome, but you said it was a little bit better. What did you not like about it?" He said, "Oh, I thought it was really good, but I don't want to put a ceiling on it. If I start saying that was awesome, it might impact what I think about it and if I think it's already great then I'm not going to push it and won't know how good it could be. I'm trying to maximize it."

In John's mind, if he just thought the skill was getting a little better then there was always room for improvement—which there always is. He's put himself in a position where he's not putting a ceiling on his skill expression. I thought that was brilliant. I've been very careful with my wording about things ever since, because I don't want to put a glass ceiling on a player. That's counterintuitive to development, and sometimes I don't know what good is. I know it's getting better, but I don't know how well the player can actually express it. That was an important level of understanding for me, because it highlighted the whole idea that I really don't have any business putting any ceilings on anybody because I lack the understanding about what good really is.

We do that a lot in our game. You know, "That player's good or that's the best player I've ever seen." We say, "That player's reached his potential," when we don't have the context to understand what that really means. We put this glass ceiling on the player. If the player believes that's true, then we have inadvertently stunted his growth because we don't have the background knowledge to be assigning those statements to the player and the player doesn't have the background knowledge to assign those statements to himself. So he's putting up a self-imposed glass ceiling, which reduces the motivation to push to the next level—and he may not even know what the next level is. He lacks the context to understand where this could go. If he's never seen what good is or someone expressing it at its highest level, then he doesn't have any context of what good is..

Once you see someone who's better than you, or you're exposed to what good actually is and you realize you were really good for your age group or for your town, but you're nowhere near *good*, what's your reaction to that? Does it inspire you to rise, or does it discourage you and you shrink? What's your reaction? Once you realize there are more levels ahead, what impact does it have on you? That's a critical aspect of background knowledge—revealing other contexts and trying to see what the reaction is going to be.

Often I will try to shape something for a player by leading him to believe the skill he's trying to express is very easy, even though I know it's actually incredibly difficult. All my wording and body language suggests this is a very easy skill expression, and yet it's not. When the player can't do it because it's incredibly difficult, I want to see what his reaction is going to be. Does this inspire him to action? Does this sharpen his focus? Does he get discouraged and want to avoid going down this path? He can see there's going to be a high level of failure, and he's not interested in that. It's a good barometer to see where players are in terms of their background knowledge and what their impression of good was prior to this.

When the player starts to move forward and realizes there are more levels he can get to, what is his impression of that? He came into it saying, "I'm a good shooter, I'm a goal scorer," then he gets into a situation where the context is being around kids who can actually score at a higher level. Shooting at lower levels has layers to it. There are players who can really shoot the puck off the pass with greater velocity and accuracy. All these things really matter. So, what's your impression of skill expression? What's your reaction when you realize there is a whole other level? How does that change your body language? How does that change your motivation? It's an interesting and important aspect of background knowledge to understand that good is relative.

There are a lot of players who would rather be the best player on the worst team in the league than an average player on the best team. Some players should absolutely avoid being the best player on a team. It's just not healthy for them from a skill development perspective because they become satisfied they're the go-to guy and they're not really pushing. Sometimes, it's better for them to be the second-line center, where they have to really push and find a way to leapfrog the top center. They know there are levels they need to get to, and they utilize the opportunity to be in the presence of someone who's better to continue to measure themselves, their effort, and their habits against that player every single day. That becomes the challenge. Eventually, they may surpass that player. Whereas, another player may put himself in a situation where he's the best player and he gets everything handed to him a little bit. It's a lot easier from a team perspective. Everyone thinks he's great and it creates a complacency that precludes him from moving to the next level.

Other players may get on a team where they're the second-line center and that has a reverse effect to their development. They're not able to handle constantly being second. It impacts their confidence such that it continues to reduce their level of risk and their performance. There's not a great environment for them to be able to push.

There are other players who, when they get into a situation where they're finally the best, thrive. They're constantly pushing and looking to leverage being the best player on the team. They take that as a real badge of honor and it inspires them to continue to push and elevate the people around them. It's different for different players and it's different at different times in a player's development. We have to try to get them to always be inspired to rise. That's a difficult thing to do, especially when you finally understand that good is relative. Players need to figure that out and it's always good to get exposure to someone who's better, which gives them the context to understand where the levels are in their own development.

TESTIMONIAL

JOHN TAVARES
on Darryl Belfry

John Tavares seeks Darryl Belfry's help because he trusts Belfry to improve his game. It's a relationship they've been building since just after Tavares entered the NHL.

But Tavares also brings his own ideas and feelings to every session with Belfry. It's important to Tavares and Belfry that both their voices are heard and they're on the same page. As Belfry likes to say, they're co-teachers.

"I think we're always talking," Tavares said. *"I'm giving him a feeling of what I'm feeling on the ice and what I'm sensing. I also have an idea myself of how I'm going to improve my game, what I like to work on. I think he has a sense of what he sees and how he sees the game and then you kind of collaborate."*

It's a process, too. Sometimes what they work on transfers immediately from practice to game. Other times, they need to work on it some more.

"Some skill sets, some things you're working on don't always transfer right away or the way you expect it and you have to adapt and adjust," Tavares said. *"He's very good at it. I always keep an open mind because I don't want to set a limit on what I can do. I always want to push myself to get better. To say it's not rewarding to go out there and play well and make good plays, I'd be lying. But I*

think I enjoy it when you're in the moment, and I think you see it when you make a nice play on a goal or score a goal yourself or you have a good game. To be at the level we're at, to be playing in the best league in the world at a sport or being a professional athlete, it's about being able to do it again and to be doing it consistently and not being satisfied where you're at. That's kind of my mindset. I think it's especially been good with Darryl because I think he enjoys being around people and players who are hungry to play the game and continue to explore where they're at and how they can get better. I try to really embrace that."

One idea Belfry had early on in Tavares' development was to have him perform linear crossovers on the ice. It was a way for Tavares to create more time and space and work less.

"I think for me something I still focus on a lot, whether it's with my skating or my patterning, as he likes to call it, is how I can be much harder to defend, much harder to read and also not having to work so hard getting to where I want to get to so you have the energy to be deceptive and be hard to defend," Tavares said. "That was an area he first looked at, a way he felt he could make me a little bit more dynamic going up and down the rink, a little bit more explosive and being able to generate a little bit more speed, a little bit more power and to bring out whether my puck-handling or my playmaking ability through that kind of skating patterning. That was kind of his first concept right off the bat."

There have been many concepts ever since. As Tavares as evolved and flourished in the NHL, he and Belfry have continued to find innovative ways for him to put his ability to use. They aren't putting a ceiling on what he can do.

Tavares has found Belfry has a unique understanding and mind for the game.

"I think something he really has a good feel for when he works with players and I think specifically with my experience is having a good understanding of who you are as a player and what you're trying to accomplish and how you want to be effective," Tavares said. "I think also getting his thoughts on how I see myself and applying my game and how I want to be effective and be productive and kind of correlating that right away and just his vision on certain things, certain ideas were great for me.

"I think something with Darryl that's always impressed me is obviously he maybe doesn't have a resume like some of the very high-end players he's worked with, but I think he thinks the game at an extremely high level. He may not be able to apply it, but his ability to connect the game and see it differently and apply these skill sets to many different types of players, many different types of people, and to help make the game better, to help make players better individually, even coaches, I think it's really, really impressive on what he's been able to do. It's been a lot of fun to work with him and I'm really thankful he's had a great influence on me in my career."

9

TRIPLE HELIX: DEPTH OF SKILL

THE NEXT ASPECT OF OUR TRIPLE HELIX IS DEPTH OF SKILL. Understanding depth of skill is a critical component to our process. The first thing I want to understand is what the skills are. Defining the fundamentals is one of the most difficult aspects we have in player development. There are basically four silos: skating, shooting, stick handling, and checking. Those are widely considered fundamental silos, but each one has a massive number of skills and an incredible amount of individual skills. Those silos are difficult to assign a level of understanding or a definition to because the topics are way too broad.

I always struggle to say, "Hey, you need to work on the fundamentals of skating." What does that mean? First, there are different types of skating. There's forward skating, backward skating, transition skating, trying to skate in a straight line, trying to skate a curve-a-linear, change of direction. There are hundreds of different types of skills and ultimately skills of skating. What actually are the fundamentals? Are the fundamentals essentially posture, balance, and edge control? Because that's your base starting point.

I struggled because I felt like the fundamentals of a particular skill set changed a little bit and what you needed to leverage for each of those "fundamentals" was different depending on what aspect of the fundamentals blanket you were focusing on. I was trying to define what skills were and realized this was a big animal to really understand. So I needed a better system to categorize skill.

With fundamentals, there are definitely interdependent skills or what you would call an undercurrent that are prerequisites to execution. If you don't have good posture when you're skating and you don't put yourself in the right spot in terms of how you're carrying your body, that's going to influence your ability to acquire those skills. That becomes an interdependent skill; posture becomes a fundamental because it's definitely going to impact everything else if you don't have it. If you don't have good edge control, at some point it's going to be limiting or precluding, so edges are definitely a fundamental.

But when I was going through my process to understand skill, I realized there was one area nobody was working on at the time. Weight shift was a true fundamental and appeared to cross a multitude of different skill applications. I would watch a ton of people who were trying to develop kids and noticed no one was even talking about weight shift. Yet when I was evaluating skating at the time at an elite level, weight shift was the core element that was consistent in every execution of elite skill. I thought, *This is obviously a fundamental, yet we don't really teach it; no one's exposing it.* For me, that was a competitive advantage. I wanted to understand weight shift and how it contributed to the execution of skill, and how the lack of weight shift ability contributed to a player's inability to acquire skill, at the deepest level I could. Understanding that weight shift in its skill expression was just a sketch of how it was interdependent on other skills dependent on that level of execution was a really important "fundamental" breakthrough for me.

There's one thing that permeates every elite skill. We are constantly bombarded with, "Keep it simple and work on the fundamentals." Well, obviously there are some holes in that. I really wanted to understand it better. One thing that was really crucial for me was going back to this vocabulary analogy and reading that book, which inspired me to read several other books about teaching vocabulary and the challenges involved. It was fascinating to me, trying to close the achievement gap as it relates to reading and its impact in the restricting aspects of a person's reading level and their achievement in school. I started to really pay attention to it and mess around with that book. What I was interested in with that book was how it categorized the different frequencies and utilization of words and how that impacted a person's reading ability. My goal was to replace vocabulary terms with hockey terms.

For example, I would replace the word *word* with skill.

Bringing Words (Skills) to Life

Legend of Word Replacement in Converting Vocabulary Terms
to Hockey Development Terms

Vocabulary Word/Term	Hockey Development Word/Term
Word	Skill
Vocabulary	Individual Skill Set
Reading Comprehension	Tactical Skill
Context	Game Situation
Instruction	Isolated Skill Development
Oral Contexts	Team Practices
Wide Reading	Competitive Environment
Word Meaning	Play Patterns
Mature Language Users	High Performing Player
High Utility Words	Competitive Advantage Skills
Spelling	Key Execution Points of a Skill

I went back through the book and started to take passages out and rewrote them exactly the way they were in the context of the book, but then replaced each of those terms with new words so it was hockey specific. When I read it back, the parallel was basically identical. It was exactly what I had envisioned going into it. When I was reading it, I could see this was an approach that made logical sense.

The book had indicated that in a decade previous there was little evidence on the acquisition of vocabulary in schools. I thought, *Well, hockey is kind of at that stage now where we're a decade behind with respect to emphasis on skill development on hockey teams.* For the longest time, people would say, "I don't have time to teach skill. The players either have it or they don't." That's what created a marketplace for people to want to learn more about skill.

The vocabulary analogy was also interesting in terms of my understanding of categorizing skills. I was able to categorize them based on frequency. How often does this occur? What can these skills be used for in terms of competitive advantage? What is required for learning? What's the core? What's the basis? What are the individual pieces that make up this particular skill? How many components are there in its execution? Then I would just build out a living skill inventory for the player, a live document as this player was accumulating skills.

What was the scaffolding effect of the translatable skill? What percentage of the skill set the player had access to was he actually using in the game? It was fascinating to me as I went through this process how frequently a particular situation would occur and yet a player who had that skill in his set wouldn't utilize it because he wasn't comfortable with it. If I took him out in a skill session and asked him to do it in isolation, the player could do it brilliantly. But when it got to a game, there was a disconnect. The player didn't understand its context, so he couldn't anticipate that skill could be utilized in a competitive advantage. Or he was utilizing skills incorrectly. He would utilize it, but not to create a competitive advantage. This all became important for me to understand as it relates to building out a development plan for the player.

The next step was trying to establish what skill categories could be. I used the vocabulary approach of Category 1, Category 2, and Category 3. Category 1 would be what we would call the fundamentals, but this is a little bit more defined. It would be the most basic skills players need to be able to function. So a player's skating in Category 1 would be just his or her balance, posture, edge control, weight shift. If a player didn't have those core elements, he or she would have difficulty acquiring skill.

Category 2 skills were more of the high-utility skill families. This is how you utilize skill to create competitive advantage. What's your knowledge of competitive advantage? How do you utilize your skill set to do that? How do you employ that and what are the skills you use to do it? If a Category 1 skating skill is a player's posture, balance, edge control, and stride mechanics, Category 2 is then utilizing that skating skill using tactical acceleration to beat someone one-on-one. The player uses his or her speed to take advantage of another player offensively.

Category 3 skills then became more elite-level skills. These are low-frequency skills amongst the average. They're more reserved for the elite players. They're like new skills that need to be added to the family of skills for a particular player. But these represent more high-level skill expressions and are often combination skills or blended skills, which we'll talk more about later.

Using this vocabulary analogy was critical for me because it allowed me to wrap my head around what depth of skill actually was and to be able to properly categorize skills. It gave me insight into how to build the continuum and understand what is next. This is why background knowledge is so important inside of depth of skill. If you don't know what good is or you're not exposed to how a great player at that age expresses skill, then you're going to have a more restricted understanding of depth of skill. That's going to impact your ability to push to the next level. If you're a teacher of skill and you don't have the context around what goes into elite play and what those categories are, it's going to be difficult for you to strip those skills back down. It's a whole teaching method. You know what you're trying to do. You know what it's supposed to look like in the end. You break it down into all its individual pieces and start putting it back together. Until you get to the final piece, which is the ultimate skill expression, you're not going to know how to decode that skill. You're going to inadvertently create a skill gap. My greatest fear as a skill instructor is not knowing what to do next.

This whole process of categorizing and decoding skill to strip it into its individual pieces helps you see the details. The detail you need to see changes given the level of player you're working with. Working with the top players in the world, the level of detail is so fine compared to working with a 10-year-old. While they're highly detailed for that level, it's relative to the level you're coaching and so the detail needed is much lower. That also gave me insight into the background knowledge I need to acquire to understand what the depth of skill actually was, so that I knew all the pieces and could properly diagnose what was missing. The ability for me to decode in order to teach was critical.

One of the things I stumbled upon while I was working inside this depth of skill stuff was how important blending skills together is. For example, there are players who can catch and shoot and make that look like one single skill expression, but really when you look at it, the actual catch and the actual shot are two independent components. A large percentage of players can do each of those two things, but when you combine them with enough speed where they're blended together to appear as one, not as many players can do that. The blended skills appear to be one skill, and there are lots of skills like that in skill instruction. We teach them as though they're one skill when really they're two or three. So decoding is the ability to take a skill that appears to be one skill, find its individual components, and determine whether this skill expression is elite for this player. If I break it down into its pieces, a very good AAA player at 10 years old could do each of these individual pieces well. The challenge for them is when we start combining two, three, four elements together to be expressed as one skill. That's what represents the level change. Those things became really important as my understanding of depth of skill started to expand dramatically.

10

TRIPLE HELIX: AWARENESS

The third aspect of our Triple Helix is awareness. How we utilize awareness is a major aspect of our development process. Awareness is essentially our ability to problem solve for the truth. We're able to paint a picture of what's really going on with the player by removing a lot of the external noise. We get that from the video because the video doesn't lie. That's why video is so important for us. It allows us to pick up on various patterns of thought, patterns of play, skill sequence patterns, and instance rates and to calculate success rates. These elements all create a personal game structure profile, which is what we're trying to influence.

Sometimes we're trying to bubble it up to the surface of consciousness. So much of hockey is patterns. It's a game of recurring patterns and responses to those recurring patterns. Everyone has a different response. Their skill sets are different, and that causes them to respond differently to situations. What we're trying to do is figure out which habits are helping them and which ones aren't. So much of the game is automated. There are a lot of patterns players use in every game that they don't even realize. They've adopted these patterns into their personal game structure and continue to utilize them over and over again even though they lead to a low success rate. Or the pattern could lead them down a road to success, but they're not always aware of what those habits are specifically because they've been formed, adjusted, and adapted over the years.

What are the tools we use to articulate this to the players? We use what I call the success equation. The success equation is a mental map of the order skills are expressed. Inside that order of execution, we can pinpoint where the player's habits are leading them toward success and where they're not. We also look at the two governing principles of our success equation. One is frequency. How often does it occur in a given game? The other is success rate. How much does it lead to a positive or negative result?

When we're building the success equation, it's unique for each player, but it gives us an opportunity to dig into these mental patterns and establish a priority list that we want to influence. If it's a high-frequency event and the player has a low success rate, then that becomes the highest priority for development because it happens so often and it gives the player the most opportunity to influence their game positively.

That's how we are able to pinpoint what we should work on. That's the hardest part of player development for me: How do you know what to work on and what are you relying on the athlete to tell you? Because athletes are only going to know so much of their game. That's a good thing, because they play with so many automated habits, they can't possibly know all those thought patterns or movement patterns. It's up to you to figure that out. That's why video is so critical, because it gives you insight into those patterns.

The advantage of this success equation and pulling the awareness to the forefront is it allows us to figure out which habits are conscious and which are unconscious. I can say to a player, "Do you realize you get the puck on your backhand coming up the wall from the goal line toward the blue line seven times a game? There hasn't been a game in 20 games you haven't had seven of these opportunities." Players will say, "No, I didn't know that." "And do you realize when you go up there the next play that occurs has an under-50 percent success rate? In other words, there is a 50 percent chance the possession sequence is going to end when you are in this situation." "No, I don't." Okay, well that's a high-frequency event we can work with. The fact you're unaware of it is actually a good thing because now we're going to bubble this up to the surface. We're going to go through the habit and rebuild some of the thought patterns going into it, the awareness of what options you have to manipulate the situation and bend it to your strengths. It could be the ice vision of properly looking at the right pressures or looking in the right area of the ice to be able to better see what your support might be. It might be that the way you move your body is precluding you from seeing a particular area of the ice, and that could represent our greatest area of opportunity. It could be a variety of different things. So we want to get a better sense of what's going on.

Basically, we want to understand what the good habits are, which ones are producing the most results—their movement patterns, skill sequences, and thought patterns. Those are all elements we're trying to evaluate to lead to positive results. We may not directly influence those because they're already leading to great results. What we might do is influence other patterns that lead you into those sequences at a higher success rate. I'm not going to talk about rebuilding or adding to a good habit. I'm going to find ways to get the player in that situation more frequently or get him or her to learn how to bend the game in their favor, to manufacture more of those sequences.

That's the pathway from good to great. Good players will take what's given to them. I'm sure we've all heard that phrase before.

Great players know exactly what they need to do to be successful. They bend the game in their favor. They don't take what you give them. They dictate to you what's going to happen. They create the conditions in which they can be successful. That's the difference. The more we can create awareness as to what these good habits are, the more success the player can manufacture.

How can you bend the game in your favor? It could be your attitude on possession after a shot recovery. The way you position yourself on shot recovery is the anticipation of the movement patterns. Where you go that will lead to more instances. It could be the way you interact with the D or your awareness of your availability and spacing in the sequence prior to that situation happening that allows you to influence where the puck goes. It could be a decision you frequently make on the other side of the ice that would allow you to then bend the game in in your favor. Again, it's multiple things, but with good habits, we're not looking to directly influence the habit in order to make that habit go from good to great. We need to up the instance rate. That's what we're after. We want to influence what happens and what those sequences are before it happens, so we can make sure we can bend the game further in your favor.

Then there are the habits we do want to influence. These are situations where we want certain things to become better. Maybe there are habits that are precluding the player from getting the puck. Maybe he has habits with greater potential because of the frequency to go into some interesting pathways. But in order to get there, we're going to have to influence the way he moves. The skill sequences he employs may have to be challenged so he can produce greater success. What we want to do from a development perspective once we've pinpointed these areas is make the habit top of mind, because it's been recessed into the subconscious. We want to positively influence the skills, movement patterns, and thought process that go into it. After we've influenced it positively, we want to put it back into automation. There's a whole way we go about that we'll get into more once we go through the teaching process, but that's the entire goal.

Sometimes a player has really good habits and a high frequency rate, but the habits are not producing results at the rate he's accustomed to. It's starting to fall off from a performance or a results perspective. When we understand the habit sequence and all the manipulation of where the player can assume control over the situation, the pathway to create more consistency or a higher rate of success reveals itself. It's crystal-clear if a player is in a slump in a certain way and he's still creating chances the way he normally creates chances, but his success rate is lower.

Let's say the player is on a power play shooting one-timers and his success rate is somewhere around 16 percent. It's a really high success rate for shooting. Now, if you shot 12 percent, all situations, in the NHL, and you have a high frequency rate where you're shooting 300 pucks a year, you would be well on your way to being one of the elite players in the NHL. So now you say, "Well, this guy is four percent above the average of shooting, but this is a favorable condition." He's getting the puck off the pass, which is already more favorable. It's on the power play, so there's more ability to create a repeated opportunity for the player to shoot. What's happened is they're normally a 16 percent shooter and now they're down to shooting 11 percent in this situation. We have to find a way to get five percent better in this situation, and we need to know why the player is not executing in this particular situation. It could be as simple as their footwork. It could be a situation where they're moving in an uncomfortable position when the puck is coming so their timing is slightly off. They're still shooting at the exact same instance rate, but the success rate is lower. We already know which habits produce the 16 percent. Now we're trying to evaluate what piece is missing. Well, it's going to be inside that movement sequence. It's going to be inside the preparation of the shot or the actual technical aspects of the shot. So the correction corrects itself; it's simple. It's a very easy thing to then diagnose. That's the advantage of coming at this from a success-rate perspective.

One of the things we're trying to do is influence the law of averages. We know you get the puck at a certain rate and we know the conditions that typically happen for you to get those pucks. What we're trying to do is create more lottery tickets. The percentages are always out of 100. We're trying to race to get to 100 instances and then influence the success rate inside that 100 and squeeze more value out of each instance. We want them more frequent with a higher success rate. That's how we improve the player. From a law of averages, we want to eventually turn the math to lend itself well to the player's ability so he knows he's creating a greater level of frequency, which gives him more lottery tickets to get a higher output by the end. We want to stack the deck in the player's favor. We do that by elevating frequency.

One of the things we know for sure is the seconds-per-possession rate for the players. In other words, how many seconds is the player on the ice on average before he gets a possession? We want to influence that. The lower that number is, the more frequently they're getting the puck. The higher the number is, the more disconnected they're getting from the puck, which then influences their instance rate. The problem with elite players is when their instance rate of getting the puck is too far apart, they lose offensive rhythm. It affects how they think and their preparedness for the puck and takes them out of feel.

We're always trying to influence and monitor how frequently a player is getting the puck, and we want to know how many possessions he's getting in a given sequence. As soon as our team has the puck, that is the start of an offensive sequence. When you're on the ice, how many times do you get the puck inside that given sequence before the puck turns and the other team has it? What we're trying to do is compound possessions, because the conditions that surround a possession change with the number of instances that occur in the same sequence.

If I get the puck and we get a possession sequence, that first touch is likely not going to be as favorable as what would occur if I got the second touch. The first touch is typically a loose puck or a forced turnover, something like that. We want the puck off the pass, but once we have that possession sequence and you have your first touch and you make a positive play, the odds of you getting the puck back improve because you've made a positive play. The person you've given the puck to has acquired the puck off the pass. If you're an elite player, that means you've probably led the player into open space. He now has a better opportunity to make a good next play because the conditions of his puck have improved. He has a better opportunity to make a better decision because you didn't put him into small space and you gave him more time. Now, if you get the puck back again, that puck in terms of time, space, puck location gets much better again on the third possession. We're trying to compound possessions because we know the conditions that surround the possession will improve *and* the opportunity to attack offensively and be able to generate a higher rate of result is great.

If we only tracked seconds per possession and all we wanted to know was how frequently the player got the puck, we'd lack context. What know we need favorable pucks. Those are the ones we're going to have the best chance to be successful with. We need to know the possessions per sequence and how many times the player gets the puck in the sequence, because we know we want to compound the possessions. If the player gets the puck three times in the sequence, that third possession is going to be his best opportunity to attack. If he doesn't get that one, then we need to figure out ways to improve the lottery tickets. We want to stack the deck in his favor by improving the quality of the puck the player can attack on. That comes from our research and understanding of how the player moves and how he reads the game. This is going to influence how we try to get him the puck more frequently. We're trying to bend the game ultimately in his favor and pull in his best assets. That's how we improve his results.

The biggest advantage of a player having a solid mental map and an understanding of his success equation is then he has the ability to play with expectation. I've told him how frequently he gets the puck. A game is 60 minutes of actual playing time, his contribution is somewhere between 18 and 20 minutes, and I'm telling him, "You get the puck on your backhand climbing up the wall seven times." The frequency of that occurring over the 20 minutes will be difficult for the player to recognize on their own—that's a hidden area of opportunity that has a low-success rate. Initially, seven possessions that occur at the same consistency may not seem like that many. If a player's going to touch the puck 40 times a game, it isn't. But when you look at it over 80 games, that's 560 opportunities per year, and that gives you the perspective of how important those seven possessions are. If you're not getting positive results out of that, then that represents a massive opportunity in the course of your entire season. By bubbling up this opportunity, we allow the player to play with expectation. He knows this is a high-frequency event that gives us an opportunity to get the puck to recreate these situations and execute.

Here's why playing with expectation is so important. Let's say I get that first opportunity in a game on my second shift. I get the puck, climb up the boards, and I have a poor level of execution. Well, I know there are going to be six more opportunities. So it creates excitement for the next opportunity. I can evaluate that situation in my mind and figure out what I did wrong. I didn't shoulder check, so I didn't see that check coming, I didn't realize how close he was, I didn't build the space beforehand to give myself the trap door escape option, and that's why the possession ended. Next time I get in that situation, I'll build myself the space beforehand and have a little more time once I get the puck. Now it doesn't matter how close that guy is, because I have my trap door where I can extend the possession. Invariably, on the fifth or sixth shift, I get the opportunity again. I see the other player coming up the boards and I move two or three more feet inside; that gives me my trap door when I get that puck. What are the odds the conditions are going to be exactly the same as the first opportunity? None. Every play is different. So now the pressure is different. Initially, the pressure was other player being on me, and that's why I created this condition to give myself options. Of course, on the next possession, no one's on me, so I feel that time and space. I'm playing with expectation. I've improved the conditions to be more successful and execute my pattern of play at the highest level, which gives me more opportunity to create better results. That's the idea behind it.

The better the athlete, the more refined his personal game structure is, the more consistent and predictable his habits are going to be. The most elite players in the league have the most consistent habits. They do the same things more frequently with a higher success rate than everyone else. But the more uncomfortable a player is with the speed of the league, the less he's going to do the same habits over and over again. The erratic nature of his habits is going to lead to a lower overall success rate.

No matter who you are, you're going to have something you do frequently. Do you know what it is? Can we influence its success rate? The best part of the ability to play with expectation is it allows the player to expect these recurring events. I know average seven of these opportunities a game. I can now be looking for them or recognize when they happen. I now have a better ability to mentally prepare for these things and I have the advantage of expectation.

I have a level of excitement about these possessions, and I get less stress from missed opportunities.

If I combine playing with expectation, the success rate, and the frequency of the opportunity, I can say, "Listen, the goal here is to be 8 out of 10 positive, so you really have two to give." That's a fascinating concept, because I've found the allowance of failure is actually what allows a player to reduce the instance of failure. Building in an allowance of failure gives the player more mental permission to move on from that instance, rather than carrying it with him to influence his next shift and ultimately the next instance.

A lot of players are so caught up in the pursuit of perfection they do not allow any failure, and then they struggle with bouncing back from instances of failure. I've found over the years that building in an allowance of failure gives the player a more positive frame of mind when he has a feeling of expectation on the subsequent instances. This has been a big breakthrough in my teaching approach. In some games the success rate is going to be less, maybe 7 out of 10, 6 out of 10. But you know you're going to get a high frequency. Let's say on that first possession, the player gets the puck and doesn't execute properly. That's fine. We have two to give. The next possession, he tries to improve the conditions and he does a better job, but he gets a negative result again. This is not going to crush the player because he has a high level of understanding of the success rate here. He knows he's typically 8 out of 10, so he's going to go on a good run. It gives him more confidence and less stress in missed opportunities because he knows it's going to come back around. He's going to get another opportunity, and that miss actually improves the conditions of his anticipated success rate because now that's one miss out of the way. He has another miss out of the 10 opportunities he usually has, but he has 8 good ones to look forward to. Mentally, the player is in a much better state to handle the negative results because he understands success rate and how frequently he gets the puck.

The other thing we're trying to do as part of the mental preparation process is improve players' automation. If you know you're going to get the puck in this situation a high number of times, it allows you to anticipate the event. Because you can anticipate the event, you can see the start of the sequence that typically creates the event. That will create a higher degree of automation of your responses. Your responses are based on the frequency of event. When you can see the play pattern starting to occur, you can see where it's going. You can automate your response, so you get there with better timing and awareness of your surroundings. The play starts to slow down for you, so you're able to collect more information and manipulate circumstances.

It's interesting to see how collecting this information changes the player's response. If, as he was climbing up the wall on the backhand in the offensive zone, he knew that a defenseman was defending him, would that change his approach versus if it were a forward? Let's say it's a forward defending him. Well, that's a clear opportunity for him to be more aggressive because forwards are less adept at defending in one-on-one situations in a corner than defensemen. Defensemen have a higher success rate defending in a corner because they do it more often and it's part of their expressed job. It's a higher priority job for them, but forwards aren't in that situation as often. They're not as fluent in the skill depth of being able to execute, so a lot of times they don't even want to be there. This is not a situation they're looking forward to. So this is a huge opportunity for this player to attack aggressively.

It's no different than if there's a skill difference between two players. Perhaps there's some way I can manipulate my asset base against that player to produce a higher result. If I'm bigger than you, I want to use that asset to impose my physical will against you. But if

I go against another guy who's bigger than I am, I can't use that asset and have to find a different one. But I would have a better automated response to whatever the situation because I was able to collect the information. I knew who was defending me. I knew the space and pressure. I might also know what the anticipated defensive responses are. If I beat this forward out of the corner, maybe I know which guy in their system is going to rotate next to defend me. All this allows me to play faster. If no one comes, I attack the net myself. If the net-front defenseman all of a sudden comes, then I know who's open. If a guy comes out of position at me, I just pass to the person who he left open to execute. This is what goes on in the minds of the best players. They have automation of movement based on frequency of events, and their habit base is so strong that they do these things over and over and over again. They don't need to think about it. It just happens.

In this element of our Triple Helix, my job is creating that level of awareness and being able to problem solve with the athlete so he knows which things he's doing at a high frequency rate that are leading to his greater success. If it's not something that leads him to a high success rate, then we need to bubble it up to the surface, influence it, and reshape the patterns to produce better results and then put it back in his subconscious so he can play.

These are ways you can manipulate the situation or bend the game in your favor so you can get more lottery tickets. Then there are situations that happen at a high frequency rate but you don't get the puck as often, so your success rate is low. These are things we need to influence, so let's focus on those. We know how many times you get the puck. Let's take a look at all those times and see which ones you execute well. Let's see the ones you don't execute as well. Let's compare what you're doing from a movement perspective. Are you more prepared? Do you look like you're surprised by the puck?

That gives us a clear path to influence it. It's why awareness is such a key part of our Triple Helix as we go through the three pillars of our development process.

TESTIMONIAL

MATT ELLIS
on Darryl Belfry

The work and the effort were never the issues for Matt Ellis.

There probably aren't many before or after him who worked like Ellis did to become a professional hockey player. His off-ice workout routines were the stuff of legends.

And even before he and Darryl Belfry discovered each other, Ellis had established himself as an AHL player and was doing just fine. But then they did meet, and that changed everything.

Ellis was built and operated like a truck. He was all strength and power. There were positives to that and it had carried Ellis pretty far, but there were also limitations, especially in his skating. It was those limitations Belfry sought to dig into, understand, and correct.

"Darryl was intrigued by the ice," Ellis recalled. "It was to a point where he'd be coming to me after and point out skate marks in the ice, whether it be off a start where I was inches deep or even on a turn because I was heel driven where I was really down into the ice. The older school, classic mentality [I] was always taught that sound means speed and fast and power. I'd almost take it as a

compliment. Once we got into it, I'm like, man, that's not right, that's actually slowing me down."

Belfry and Ellis' strength coach, Pete Dobbin, got together and began brainstorming. Belfry identified Ellis' inability to move laterally, stay light on his feet, and keep his posture forward instead of on his heels. Dobbin tested Ellis' lateral movements and whether his hips were activating that movement.

"Sure enough, they created a connection," Ellis said. "I'm seven years deep into pro hockey at this point. Well, 'Matt Ellis doesn't activate hardly any of the muscles in his posterior chain.' Right then and there obviously we got to a really good place. I basically had that wheel now that was working together and working in the same direction which really essentially rebuilt the way that I moved and rebuilt the way I approached training, which allowed Darryl to be more effective."

Ellis was a different player the rest of his career due to that.

"It changed my game because I was able to move better and I was able to start creating different opportunities for myself," Ellis said. "My calling card as a player was, if you ask anybody who had ever seen me play or my reputation, I was always the hardest worker you'll ever see, which was accurate, but on top of that, it was always, 'He doesn't skate well enough to play in the NHL.' Well, I found a way to play almost 400 games in the NHL. It was through a different type of training and mentality we started *painting a new picture of this, and he started pulling certain things out of my game.*

"We spent an offseason on helping me laterally and doing more than one thing at once. We started in '08–09 rebuilding my shot. I used to catch a pass, but when you catch the pass, you stop moving your feet. You were an athlete that was only doing one thing at a time. We got to a point through the approach and the training where I was able to start layering skills on top of things. When I started to do that, I started to grow and started to gain confidence to move different ways to apply things. Things that I maybe couldn't do before were starting to become easier. I was finding a different time and space on the ice. I was finding different angles of attack. And it all kind of connected, my body changed."

There was no better feeling than Ellis arriving to Sabres training camp the following season and blowing everyone's mind by what he was doing on the ice.

"All of a sudden, my teammates are like, 'Wow, Elli, where'd you learn how to do that?" said Ellis, who is now involved in developing players as the director of coaching for the Buffalo Jr. Sabres. "And I'd be shooting the puck in a unique way where I'm able to pull the puck in right off a catch, but where everything was hidden within my feet. It was explosive. It was deceptive. I'd be catching our goalie Ryan Miller with his glove down and I'd be going up over a shoulder. Here I am, a marginal three-to-four goal scorer per season, and guys are like, 'Elli, where did you learn how to build that?' I'm starting to get that snowball effect of moving a whole lot better and doing things that

I never did before, and with that comes a kind of belief and confidence.

"*The second thing that happened in that given training was management wanted to see me. They're like, 'What did you do for your skating this summer?' In the back of my mind, I'm like, I didn't do anything. I worked tirelessly on rebuilding my shot and opening up range of motion throughout my body. But obviously I wasn't going to tell them that. They're like, 'You are moving in a way that we've never seen you move before.' They gave me pats on the back, 'Awesome job.' That was a byproduct of a summer of just identifying certain strengths, certain weaknesses and building a roundabout program that was going to assess those things.*

"*When Darryl rebuilt the shot, it started to capitalize on the most explosive movement in the human body, which is a hip hinge. It was all hip hinge, which hammers the posterior chain muscle-wise and all of a sudden the range of motion in my hips and explosiveness and pop to my game. All my teammates are like, 'Wow, that's shot's incredible,' and I know for a fact a bunch of them called Darryl right after.*"

11

SKILL CONTINUUM

EARLY ON IN MY CAREER, I REALLY DIDN'T KNOW WHAT TO TEACH. I would just teach whatever I thought was relevant at that time. But I had really no structure to deduce what was next in the progression— or where to start, for that matter. I would go on research tangents where I would go on a full exploration of the topic to learn as much as I could about it and as much as I could about different ways I could teach it. Pursuing that tangent was really important to me at that time. I'd go on a run where I would just teach that, and it became a theme of mine. As my knowledge and depth of skill improved and the collective talent of the players I was working with got better, I knew I needed to develop a structure that would lead me directly to what I needed to teach. There had to be a system in place to assess and evaluate a player's needs and where they were in the development process.

I wanted a crystal-clear guideline that would take a lot of the arbitrary decisions out of my hands, so I could make a maximum impact in a short amount of time by teaching the most relevant thing at the right time. We run into trouble sometimes with the way we approach skill development, because we can get very random in what we're deciding to teach or very generic in what we present. Both of those extend the development time a player will need, which can leave the player in a precarious position when he has a very short career coupled with very short offseasons. We don't have a moment to waste on aspects of skill development that are irrelevant to players' next level of development.

NHL players especially don't have a tremendous amount of disposable time to just be messing around. We have to have a structure in place that tells us exactly what they should be learning and why. We want to cut right to the chase on things that are going to make the maximum impact in the time they have so they're as prepared as possible to play the next year. In viewing it from this lens, what emerged for me were two aspects that dictate how I decide what to teach.

The first one is the player research. I haven't worked with any NHL players in recent years I hadn't previously studied first. I need to know what's relevant for them at that particular time. I need to understand their personal game structure. The start of my system came from developing a way to research each individual with a custom video analysis system that we built and refined. Video analysis for us has grown exponentially each year. Over the years, I've really fine-tuned exactly what information we need to know and gradually tightened up that process. Now I feel like we get a lot of important data points that reveal exactly what we want to know. The critical element is to have the data markers correlate to frequency and success rate. I also need to know what the expected success rate number should be for each player. However, perhaps most important is not just collecting the information but understanding what one number means to another group of numbers—the chain reaction or compounding effect of success rates. That takes us immediately to a set of skills that lead directly to success and situations that are happening frequently where the player is not having success. That targets a specific area we now know we need to explore. Starting the exploration process shifts right into the skill continuum I've built that allows me to dig into exactly what these aspects are so I can get highly specific in the teaching process. There's not a lot of arbitrary decision-making. It's very specific.

There are three areas of the skill continuum I'm concerned with. The first one is skill types. I want to know what the skill types are. That's similar to what I discussed with depth of skill. That whole area is critical. The second area of the continuum is skill gaps. The third one is skill speeds. All three are considerations inside of the continuum.

There are several skill types. One is ancillary skills, which are basically a skill inventory you have that could potentially support anything I want to work on. It's any skill that has been identified as an area of yours to be focused based on our research. It's been highlighted as a low-level success rate for you. The first thing I want to know is your competency at the skills that surround or support that skill. If you are creating a lot of two-on-ones and you're not generating any shots off that, then I can trace back the way you handle the puck, the way you skate, the angles you take, the ways in which you're creating those two-on-ones in the first place, the reads you're making, the shot selection—all those factors. Then, I can look at all the ancillary skills that support what you're doing inside that two-on-one.

To me, this is where the value of Malcolm Gladwell's 10,000-hour rule is. When Gladwell said you would need 10,000 hours to have any type of mastery you want in a skill, there is truth to that in the Triple Helix depth of skill. It's not necessarily in specific skills in our sport, where it's so fluid and there's so much skill blending that goes on. When we were talking about our vocabulary analogy, there's just so much information and skills you have to have that it would be really tough to spend 10, 000 hours on a given skill set. What you're trying to do, though, is build depth of skill. So the 10,000-hour rule is relevant to the depth of skill. I see it when I'm working with our NHL players. A big part of what separates them is they have extensive ancillary skill sets, so it makes it easy to then target a single skill and work on it because you can always leverage the ancillary skills to support the skill acquisition you're trying to focus on. Therefore, it's way faster for them to learn skills because they have all the supporting structures. To the degree in which you are inexperienced or don't have a high skill level, you also don't have the depth of skill to support the individual skill you're trying to impact. This is why so many coaches value athleticism. Athleticism is a reflection of a deep resource of ancillary skills, which makes learning new skills easier.

Again in this two-on-one example, let's say you know the patterns of play you can anticipate to put yourself in great positions. You get the puck and now you're able to establish these two-on-ones at a high frequency. The good news is you have the intelligence level to recognize the patterns that allow you to create the play in the first place. The problem with execution is you don't have the ancillary skills as it relates to the way you handle the puck and your skating. Those two pieces have severe deficits. To really get to the heart of the matter, we would figure out which ancillary skill you're lacking, which might be deception. You know the reason you can't execute on the two-on-ones on your strong side is because you don't have that necessary deception. Deception is reliant upon the interaction between skating and the way you handle the puck to create the deception. You could lack just all that ancillary skill, so I would have to go into a much bigger and broader development process to impact that single skill set. A player who has a high depth of skill can escape with his head up; handle the puck effectively close to his body, away from his body, in front of his body, beside his body; and can utilize his skating inside of his stick handling. It's just a matter of spacing and timing and making the correct interaction between his feet, his hands, and his eyes. That's really what we need to do. The more depth of skill a player has, the easier elite skill acquisition is.

Another skill type is translatable skill, which is based on how relevant the particular skill set you have is to the level you are trying to play. Is the skill you're using a placeholder skill or a platform skill? There's a big difference between the two. A placeholder skill is something that can be relevant at a lower level of play. For example, it might be something you could use when you're in peewee or bantam hockey. But then, as you approach minor midget and start looking at going to the OHL or college, this skill set is not going to be as relevant, so it needs to be updated or replaced with a more translatable skill that would be relevant at that level.

An example of a placeholder skill might be that you can skate and rely on scoring by utilizing a slap shot off the rush. You get the puck to the neutral zone, fly in a straight line, and shoot the puck with tremendous pace to blow it past the goalie. That's a placeholder skill because at the peewee level, you're bigger and/or stronger than everyone else. You can get into those areas and shoot the puck, which is great, and that's what allows you to do it. The goaltending is not as sophisticated, the defending is not as sophisticated, so you have time and space to shoot the puck.

The problem is, as you move up, the time and space decrease and the goaltending and defensive process get much more sophisticated. Now you get to minor midget and you want to execute this wonderful slap shot. You're carrying in, skating in a straight line, and the goaltender gets square to the puck line, giving you nothing to shoot at. The goaltender is not intimidated by the pace of the puck, and in order to score, you have to hit such a fine spot on the net that might not even be available. So the goaltender can effectively eliminate the entire net based on his positioning, and he can do that because you skate in a straight line and the shooting release angle never moves. Once he establishes his puck line, he's golden, and your projection for scoring this way goes down significantly. Not to mention the defenders play a much tighter gap, and the space to shoot is greatly reduced to the point where you may not have the time to shoot in the first place.

Now that skill has to be updated. You need a multitude of different things for that skill to have value. You would have to come at it from a variety of different angles. You might have to shoot it off the pass rather than skating it in because we need the puck line to be changing. Instead of it being a skating-in slap shot, you'd need to utilize more of a one-timer, which is reliant upon your ability to have great timing, give the puck to someone else, get into a soft spot, and make yourself as available as you can to get the puck back. Your teammate finds you with a pass, and then you have to have great range of being able to shoot the one-timer in a non-perfect pass position that relies on your footwork, hand speed, and ability to process where the puck is coming at an earlier rate and earlier time. To execute that shot, you may use this slap shot. Or you might use it as a deception component to set up your next shot. You might make it look like you're going to shoot this slap shot as you sprint down the wing in a straight line, then you fake the shot and change the angle in the next movement, which is what the real shot threat actually is. You bait the goalie and the defender to get to the puck line, and then at the last second you change the puck line to shoot, which opens up the net you need.

We've taken a placeholder skill that has no realistic projection of going to the next level and gone through a translatable skill process to make it relevant in some way. That's really important. There are a lot of skills like that, skills that have a shelf life. At one level, these skills are highly successful, and you're able to generate a ton of offense off them, but then you move to the next level and you go from scoring 25 goals off them in a year, to scoring two, to scoring none. That doesn't even take into account the frequency of the event. You may not even get those opportunities like when you were in peewee hockey. You might get the puck, skate in a straight line, go past everybody, get to the top the circle, and shoot it five to seven times a game in peewee. Then you move up to minor midget and there might only be one time the opportunity even remotely presents itself, and even then it could be contested with defensive pressure. You go from a high-frequency situation with a high success rate to a very low-frequency situation with an almost impossible success rate. It needs to be updated. If it's not, and you continue to go with it, you're not translating your skill set. You go from being a 50-goal scorer to a five-goal scorer overnight. We have all seen this happen in our local area to more than one player.

Translatable skills are an important skill type to understand. That's why, later in my development as an instructor, I've stayed away from skill sets I believe are placeholders. I won't even teach them even to kids in atom hockey. I know that if they had that skill, it would lead to a high level of success, but I won't teach it because I know it's a placeholder skill. I don't want the player to become infatuated with a skill set that is going to become irrelevant at a given time. I would prefer to go more toward platform skills. Those are skill sets you could use from atom hockey and it would be relevant in peewee, bantam, midget, junior or college, and then pro and ultimately in the NHL. It would not expire. It's something that is relevant in all leagues. Those are the types of skills I prefer you learn early to have the maximum amount of time to build as much depth of skill around them as possible.

But how do I know which is a placeholder skill and which is a platform skill? Well, that's from the experience I've had understanding skill types and the research that has gone into it. That's what's allowed me to allocate a skill type or skill set to be able to see things. That's the true value of my younger years in being able to see the high number of kids we had in our program who we started with when they were eight, nine, 10 years old and then followed every year all the way to the NHL. Each one of them took different paths. Some kids made it all the way, and some kids appeared to be shoo-ins to make it all the way and then didn't. That's what gave me insight as to why some kids had a high number of placeholder skills that created an illusion of being great. When they didn't go through the translatable skill process to convert that skill set to be relevant at the next level and ran into adversity, they kept going back to thinking, *Well, this worked, it's always worked, it's part of my identity, this is who I am.* But it's irrelevant, and they end up getting nullified.

I started to really identify those things and become aware of them. I started to watch players at different levels. Although that's a kid who scores a ton of goals, let me watch him and see, knowing what I know about the demands and speed at the next level, if he could score there the way he scores now. No? Okay, well, let me watch this kid again next year when he moves to the next level and see if he adapts. If he doesn't, I would suspect he's going to regress and I'd want to see how he reacts to that. It's a fascinating process sometimes on a coaching level for players at a younger age, because this is where role changes occur. You have a highly skilled player at a given level, let's say peewee. This kid shoots the lights out, scores all the time, a really high-profile player. Now he moves up. Two levels later, he gets to midget, and he's not the same player he was. He's not scoring as much. What happens is he loses confidence. The people around him lose confidence in him. They say, you know what, you're clearly not a scorer anymore. You're a checker. You're going to be this effort guy, penalty kill, go get the puck, but don't do anything skilled, because clearly you're not that guy. It's less fun for the kid. You can see these kids who are really successful at a younger age and then they don't go through the translatable skill process because the people around them just don't understand how to tell a placeholder skill from a platform skill. They allow the kid to go to the well too many times and now he loses confidence, they lose confidence in him, and he can feel that. It becomes less fun, and a lot of kids will quit the game because of it. It's a shame, because the better understanding we have of translatable skill, the more elite players we can keep in the game. The truth of the matter is that player had the potential to remain an elite player had he gone through the process of converting placeholder skill sets into platform skill sets at the right time. He could have maintained his effectiveness and continued on.

The reverse is true when we have players whose game just does not work at a younger age group. They're not offensively minded players. It appears their skill set is not very relevant. They don't get into open space because they don't skate as well as others. Maybe they have some sort of restriction. They may not have the foot speed at that level because they haven't had an opportunity to build it yet. All of a sudden, they go from not being as effective to being ultra-effective, and they pass all the kids who were the early starters because they are working off platform skills and skills that are much more relevant. They translate and so they go from kids who no one would have invited to play on the summer elite teams to being the best kids at their age group within a three- or four-year period, and no one knows why. The reason is their game is better built. You hear that phrase a lot: "This guy's game is built for the pro game, he's more of a pro player than a junior player." It happens all the time. The assessment of translatable skill is critical inside the continuum to decide what we should be teaching and, more importantly, what we should be monitoring. In the translatable skill process, much of the early monitoring is to see what adjustments the player makes when his placeholder skill is losing its effectiveness. That self-discovery process can be fascinating, and instead of swooping in and telling the player what he needs to change, just stoke the fire of creativity and problem-solving by getting into "what else" discussions with the player. "What else could you do....?" Over the years, I've found facilitating translatable skill through advocating for the player to problem solve can be a fascinating insight into the mind of the athlete, and that will be invaluable every day moving forward.

Skill impacts is a critical component, because one skill can impact a variety of different skills and some skills are just one-offs. They're important skills, but they don't leverage well into other skills. We want to focus on a lot of these skill impacts early in a player's development, and how we pick this skill is really the trick. You have to have some fluency as a coach or an instructor in understanding how skill impacts really work. In terms of teaching, we want to have a small focus and create a big impact rather than have a big focus with a small impact. That's really important. A lot of times as skill instructors we run into this problem of working on things that have a big focus on a particular skill set, but their overall impact in the player's game is very small. We want to have a really tight focus on something very small. We want one skill to influence other skills; if we were to make a major impact in that particular area, it would have a major impact in multiple areas of that particular player's game. We want to have a domino or compounding effect on the player's skill set.

Usually you start by developing one skill and it immediately has an impact on a multiple areas. Not all skills are equal. Some skills have a multiplier effect. For example, if I want to improve your skating, one of the things I have to make sure I impact is weight shift. I have to get you to move through your hips. If I can get you to move through your hips, that's going to impact every aspect of skating. It can impact the way I'm going to teach you to accelerate, to change direction, to handle the puck, to shoot, to get body position on people, to handle contact. All those skills are influenced by the quality of your weight shift. If you have a poor weight shift, you're going to have problems in the development of that skill. But if you have a great weight shift, it has a multiplier effect where it impacts everything. Skill impact is essential in creating a chain reaction into multiple aspects of the game and having a small focus with the biggest impact.

Undercurrent is a teaching technique I've used for years. I'll have a particular skill I believe is a high-frequency skill set that is important to the execution of a high-frequency event. I would have that skill in every drill. We would be on the ice for an hour and a half, and no matter what, every drill would have this particular skill in it. One of the easiest examples is an open pivot. I don't want players in a lot of cases to use a crossover pivot. I'm not saying it's wrong, I'm just saying that the open pivot is much more effective in more situations. We need that skill in the player's skill set, particularly defensemen. On retrievals, that crossover pivot can really cause some problems, so we want to have this open pivot. Some people call it a mohawk pivot. I call it an open pivot. It's basically opening your hips inside of a change of direction and changing from backward to forward. When we're working, I'm going to isolate this pivot. I'm going to make sure I teach all the ancillary skills that go around it and then I'm going to drop it in every skill we're doing. It might be the first skill you do before you go into the rest of the sequence, it might be the last skill you do at the end of a sequence, or I might hide it in the middle, but for the entire hour you're going to be using this pivot on every single drill. That's an undercurrent skill. It's something that is critical to your development. It's important in a lot of areas of your game and it's a high-frequency situation.

The undercurrent technique also allows me to hide the volume of reps you get in a given hour. A lot of times we view reps inside of one drill; how many reps did he get in that drill? We need to have more reps, so we structure the drill to get more reps. When the drill is over, we move on to the next thing, which does not contain any of the skills we were working on in the previous drill. Whatever reps we had were only contained to that eight or 10 minutes we worked on that drill. What I want to do is have players carry this undercurrent skill through each drill so they can feel it all the way through all the situations.

There are several skills you can use as undercurrent skills that can dramatically help the player but can also be viewed as undercurrent in their game. It's a key execution piece as it relates to who they are as a person, as a player. That's an identity element and is a critical component to have as an undercurrent transporter skill. Transporter skills are really interesting skill sets because these are skills you can use to carry other skills into variants. We want to have some skills that allow a high number of variance of opportunity coming out of that skill.

Take turns, for example. There are all kinds of different turns. But there are some turns you can teach that give the player a high degree of flexibility as to how they exit them. This type of transporter skill carries other skills that can be used on the exit of that particular skill to provide a lot of options that can enhance the athlete's skill set more effectively than if you didn't use a transporter skill. In other words, the turn would come to an end and the player would then have to select another skill to add on, whereas by using a transporter skill he could fall right into any number of other skills.

To be more specific, a hook turn provides you the most effective way to keep your feet moving inside the execution of that turn and the exit. By using that hook turn, what happens is I keep my feet moving and it can vary from there. I can use crossovers. I can use straight strides. I can go into another change of direction if I want. I could do any number of things if I'm using a hook turn on the exit.

If you use the regular two-foot turn, where that inside skate is on the outside edge and the outside skate is on the inside edge, weight is evenly distributed. The problem with this is that as soon as your weight is evenly distributed, you're going to have to wait for the full execution of that skill before you can move to the next one. We call it having to move to move. You have to ride out this turn and then you have to move to move. It creates a low level of variance for the player. There's no transport ability, so they can't carry other skills, and that becomes limiting. We need to include that as part of our decision-making as to which skills to work.

Another skill type is a signature skill. These are asset-driven expressions of skill. These reflect what players are best at, and we want to put them in those situations as often as possible. But we're trying to leverage their assets to build skills that are unique to them. It's more natural for them to acquire the skill because it's right in their wheelhouse. We can begin to build other skills inside of their skill set based on their assets, and we can leverage these assets to build other skills because of the players' exploration of the skill set. Because it's so easy for them, they can combine unique combinations of skills. Signature skills are like the holy grail of skill development in a lot of ways because you're trying to create uniqueness of skill expression while having good movement principles and the like.

Another decision-maker for us is skill gaps. Looking at skill as a continuum that moves on a competency line, if there are 10 skills that need to be acquired in this particular line and the player has a good execution quality of the first three but struggles with the fourth, that is a skill gap. They're going to go through skill one, skill two, skill three, and then their competency is going to fall off at skill four. They're going to have hesitation. They're going to have failure once they get to that fourth skill. That precludes them from getting to the fifth skill or the sixth skill or seventh skill. It could be a movement restriction. It could be their ancillary skill support. It could be a missing read. It could be something physical; maybe they don't have the physical strength to execute the fourth skill. Whatever the case, a skill gap needs to be filled in. It needs to be isolated. It needs to be built and then put back into the skill sequence. Once it's put back in the skill sequence, one, two, three, and four are now well-supported and you have access to discovering five. Sometimes four is the only skill set in the entire sequence. Once you get past the execution of the fifth, sixth, seventh, eighth, ninth, tenth, those are easy skills for them, and they fall right into it because they have the ancillary skill to support it.

But the missing skill is problematic, and sometimes you have to build a bridge to get over it. That's where we talk about bridge skills. You have to give them a bridge to get to the fifth skill, and then you can continue to work on the limitations of that fourth skill.

These skill gaps resemble the problems in the law of the farm. They're like a pest, but rather than trying to eliminate the pest or ignore it, we embrace the opportunity because it allows us to use a bridge skill, which then creates more depth of knowledge for the player and gives him more options once he has all the skills. Skill gaps are problematic initially, but they're really rich in opportunity for the athlete.

Another aspect of skill is skill speeds. Anatoly Tarasov had a really interesting section in his book about the three skill speeds of hockey. He called them speed of feet, speed of hands, and speed of mind. After really looking into this on my own, I wanted to understand the interaction of these skill speeds because it's obviously critical to the execution of players' development. What I have come to understand is that players play and project at their weakest skill speed. Let's say you rate a given players' skill speeds out of 10. How good is this guy's skating speed? Well, relative to his peers, this guy has really good skating, so we put it at a seven. He also has excellent hands. He can shoot the park. He's very good one-on-one. His hands are actually a little better than his skating, so he's an eight there. What is his processing speed like? How's his hockey sense, his ability to understand patterns? Well, that's his weakest skill speed. Sometimes he can be really fast going nowhere. His processing speed is a five. At some point, when he gets high enough in the pyramid of hockey, he can be projected at the level of his weakest skill speed, which would be, in this case, his hockey sense. His inability to recognize patterns or misunderstanding of timing is going to preclude him from having tactical access to his skating and his hands. Because his mind is lagging behind, he's not going to get the opportunity to utilize his actual best assets.

Let's look at another case. For Player 2, his mind is his best asset. This guy's a really smart player. He's an eight with his hockey sense. He's a seven with his hands. But his skating is poor: a five. He can think his way around the rink. He can score a lot of goals because he can slide in the right spots. He can manage and make plays with the puck. But at some point, his skating is going to present itself as a problem, and it will preclude him from playing at the level of his mind and his hands. He will ultimately level off. When the game is at his highest level, his skating will prevent him from pushing forward and utilizing his best assets.

The crime of it all is that a lot of these things can be influenced way earlier in his life. Because it wasn't influenced early on, he's trying to chase this from behind. Now he gets to a level where it becomes problematic and he wants to address it. It's not something that's easily learned on the fly. It's going to force him and the people around him, the coaching staff and the management staff, to question his ability. His role starts to change. He goes from being this really smart guy who makes a ton of plays and scores a lot of goals to reaching a level where those around him have some questions about him. His role on the team gets reduced or eliminated. He's out.

The way in which you approach these skills is so important. This is why developing players in isolation is so limiting. It's best to develop skill in simulation. You want to have these three skill speeds factor into development as often as possible. When you're working on skating, you're also trying to work on hand speed and processing speed.

If you're working on something hands-oriented, you're always also trying to engage the lower body. You're also trying to determine other things as it relates to his hockey sense. It could be spacing, timing, play selection. You have to create some level of decision-making in whatever it is you're doing even though you're focused on developing his hands. Even when the focus zeroes in on one of these three aspects, you still need to incorporate the development of the other two all the time, so that they're always developing at the same rate.

The idea of, *This player needs to work on his skating, so let's dig into skating in isolation,* that's not going to work. It's not going to have the same cumulative or speed of acquisition effect in terms of how it translates into his game as if you develop them at the same time. Even as you're working on skating, you work on skating inside of recurring play patterns. So he's familiar with how the footwork works inside of what he normally does and how his puck skills in those situations are influenced by the new types of skating capacities you're trying to add.

It's important to talk about processing speed as the first one of these three. What is processing speed? It's essentially play pattern recognition. Hockey is very pattern-oriented. The same patterns tend to occur very often. This is why there's the old adage that it's easier to play in the NHL than it is to play at other levels. The reason is because the patterns are clearer. The players are in the right spot more often, and because they're in the right spot more often it creates a level of comfort and predictability. For the better players, they have an easier time there because they have more consistency. The lower the level, the more erratic people's hockey sense is and the less detail they have as it relates to positioning. It's much harder to play with those guys because they think, *He's supposed to be there, but he's not. The defender's supposed to be here, but he's not. He's not supposed to be here and now he is.* A lot of skill players find it easier to play higher because there's more predictability not only with their teammates but with their opponents, too. The defenses are much more structured. People are in similar spots all the time. It gives them insight into how they can play and get time and space inside. *If I go this way, I'm adding space and time. If I go that way, I'm closing space and time.* Processing speed would be understanding the difference.

A player who has excellent processing speed would understand pressure angles and make good decisions based on the available options. He would be able to read in advance what the available options are and would know which is best. He could pick the best one in advance because he has seen it again and again. So much of processing speed has to do with being able to handle the puck with your head up, which refers back to the way processing speed is still reliant upon the other two skills. If you have fluency in your skating and in your hands, it can really improve your processing speed, because now you can play with more ice awareness and create more availability. It's not altogether true that you can have great hockey sense and be terrible skater, but if you're a better skater, it's going to improve your processing speed because you'll get into areas of the ice of people who don't skate as well can't go.

Another element of skill speeds is changing environment. Hockey is a very fluid sport. Let's say you're a defenseman and you're defending the rush. The guy who's attacking dumps the puck in, and now you're in a retrieval. You open pivot, head back, and do a shoulder check. You take a look over your right shoulder, which is closest to the middle of the ice, and while you're looking into the middle of the ice, you notice where your puck support is and where the pressure is. Now you look over your left shoulder to see what's going on the short boards and you've processed some information there. If you don't look back over your right shoulder when you pick up the puck toward the middle of the ice, the conditions are going to change. Someone might go for a line change. Someone might move in a different position or change his angle of travel. The conditions of the pressure and the support are changing. The ability to have high processing skill would allow you take in that information more frequently. You would look more often. A player with better hockey sense will look over his shoulder more frequently than a player with poorer hockey sense because he values taking in more information in the changing environment. He knows the changes in the environment impact his decision-making and helps him make better decisions, which is ultimately what you want.

Now let's discuss leading passing. This is something I've been exploring over the last several years. A leading pass is an ability to leverage your hockey sense on a player who doesn't have the same hockey sense. This is what happens when you play with a great player and you are not at their level. If he is truly a great player, he will start putting pucks in areas that force you to go into those areas. If you want the puck from him, he doesn't just see your line of travel and pass it to you so it's easy for you to pick up. He might pass it to you on an angle that forces you to change your line. Instead of passing it in front of you, he passes it slightly behind so that you're forced into a turn or you'd have to adjust. All those things are designed to impact where you're going. He leads you where he wants you to go because he understands what the sequence needs to be. He understands where the competitive advantages are. He understands you don't know where those are, so he puts pucks in areas that leverage his processing speed to put you where he wants you to go. Those are leading passes, and that's a skill reserved for the elite.

These are the things we talk about with those types of players—leading passes, leveraging. You don't like the linemate you have?

That's too bad, because you're playing with him anyway. You can't control who you're playing with. Don't think he sees the game the same as you? Okay, I feel bad for you. How are we going to influence that? Well, we're going to use leading passes. We're going to train him to go where we want to go. Because we work in recurring patterns, we can train him by putting the puck in these areas and he'll start to go there automatically. Then you don't have to lead the pass there; he's already going there. Now you've trained him where you want him to go. That's how a great player can leverage other people.

Two of the best players of the modern era that jump to my mind are Sidney Crosby and John Tavares. They've done a masterful job for years of playing with players who haven't had a reputation for high-impact offense and found a way to leverage their assets inside of their games and put their linemates in situations where they can be productive and contribute. You might have a harder time finding a guy who is more productive with players who have come to his line without a previously established offensive resume in the National Hockey League than Sidney Crosby. He does a wonderful job of that. The difference between Crosby and Tavares is Tavares does a really good job of leveraging his processing speed into what he wants and puts the puck in areas that help the player go where he wants him to go. Crosby does a great job of adapting his game to fit the assets of the linemate. There's a subtle difference there in how they do things, but it's still the same principle. Tavares tries to bend you a little more toward what he wants you to do. Crosby acknowledges your restrictions and adapts his game to work with you. For the longest time it was said that Crosby was one of the hardest guys to play with, and now he's probably one of the easiest. He just does a wonderful job of that, and that's a guy who's adapted and figured out how to leverage his processing speed to influence the people are around him.

Now, let's get into skating speed. You have skating speed inside the first three steps. This would be your separation speed. This could be from a stop. It could be from moving at half-speed and now you're looking to change speeds inside your first three steps of acceleration. That is a given skating speed. After you get to full speed, what happens? Do you have any other gears you can get to after it appears you're at full speed? That's another aspect of skating speed. You have change of speed, the ability to decelerate or accelerate. Those are critical components, and you can imagine the amount of timing that goes into that. It's massive.

Then you have your change-of-direction speed. This is all your stops and starts, turns, pivots, forward to backward, all your transition speed. Anything to do with a change of direction, there are speed elements that go into that.

Then you have your speed differential, which is really your higher level expression of skating speed. Speed differential is creating a differential between your speed at the time you attack a given defender. Speed behind the puck is important. If you can get off the rush, the forward who appears to be a threat has a given speed, the defender matches that speed, now the player passes the puck to a guy underneath who has a different speed than him, so he's coming out with a higher level of speed. Because space has been created off the pass to a new guy, the defender is now defending a guy with a much wider frontal gap. The defender starts to slow down to try to get his gap sorted out. Meanwhile, the attacker is speeding up. That's a speed differential. When I speed up, I've created a differential. This is a critical component of speed differential, because if I can force you to stop, then I've eliminated your speed. You're playing catch-up all the time. This is more of a tactical expression. It's an ability to create speed based on an understanding of how you want to attack.

Angle of attack is another important part of speed differential. If two of us are racing, it's a 50-50. Rather than racing directly to the puck, I just race two steps and cut in front of you. By cutting in front of you, I've influenced your speed. You've slowed down and changed your posture. Between the two of us, I now have the best line to the puck. You'd have to try to go around me to get to the puck, so I've established body position on the puck angle, which naturally makes me faster and in control. That's not the speed you want to be going at, but you're forced to slow down because I have body position and I can get there whenever I want. I'm in total control of the speed at which we are going to acquire this puck.

There are a ton of elements that go into speed. There's hand speed. Your hands can be evaluated by the quality of how you catch the puck. We call it a sticky catch—the ability to catch the puck at any angle and the speed in which the puck is glued to your stick. It doesn't bounce off and you have to re-collect it, which happens to many more players than would like to admit.

Then there's traffic hands. This is the level to which you can manage the puck in high-traffic situations. What you're doing with your hands is independent of what you're doing with your feet. The ability to separate your upper body from your lower body could be incorporated in your skating. For example, you can handle the puck while you're pivoting, while you're crossing your feet, or while you're shooting. Most players have to stop skating in order to execute hand skills.

Range is another factor. How far can you stick handle? How much distance do you have from your forehand to your backhand where you can comfortably handle the puck? What's the skill level of your backhand? Understanding and controlling all of those elements is very important.

Then there's shouldering speed, which is the fourth skill speed I would add to the model. It's the time between skill execution. If I were catching the puck and shooting it, those are two skills—the ability to catch and the ability to shoot. Now, truth be told, there are a lot more skills in there. There's the way you weight shift on the catch. There's the way you weight shift on your shot. There's a lot going on there. But for argument's sake let's keep just the two skills, catching and shooting. An average player is going to catch the puck and there's going to be a space of time that elapses before he or she is prepared to shoot. That time lapse is called the shouldering speed. The goal would be for the player to catch and shoot the puck all in one motion so that it looked like it was one fluid skill. That would be high-quality shouldering speed; they're blending those two skills together and it looks like one. The degree to which you do one skill at a time is the degree of sophistication of your skill set. The more sophisticated your skill set, the more things you can do in combination—two skills together, three skills together, four skills together, five skills together—and it looks like one fluid movement. Shouldering speed, to me, is a critical component of the three skill speeds, and why I say it's the fourth skill speed. Those four elements, in turn, are critical to how we set up the skill continuum.

The following is an example of how the skill continuum works. I'll illustrate establishing body position, which is a fairly popular topic among players of all age groups. Everyone wants to teach their players to create better body positions more effectively.

There are a lot of considerations here. The first one is assets. What are the player's assets and how can he leverage those assets against his opponent? There's the situational awareness of how he reads what's happening. There's spatial awareness—how much space he has or where he can go into puck acquisition. How the puck is acquired impacts your ability to establish body position. There are the types of strategies you use to earn the body position in the first place—how to build a trap door, which is pre-planned space that you can use to allow you to extend the possession; how to manipulate the check and then ultimately making a play.

The often forgotten piece of this continuum is the making the play after using body position. Too often when we are training players to improve their ability to protect a puck or establish body position we don't spend enough time on the making of a play. Ultimately, that comes back to what it is you're really trying to do. Do we want the player to protect the puck for the sake of protecting the puck, or do we want the player to protect the puck just long enough for the right play to reveal itself and then be executed? To me, it's about making a play. You're trying to protect the puck for the purpose of making a play. If that's the case, it does cause that little shift in focus and change how you approach teaching body position.

The first part of the continuum is assets. Every player has some assets he can use, and it's about figuring out how he can leverage those assets. Do you have speed? Do you have quickness? Do you have size? Do you have strength? Do you have length? Are you low to the ground? Do you have a wide base? Do you have quick hands? Do you have an ability to blend movements? Can you handle the puck while you're skating or accelerating? Is one of your assets just good spatial feel? Some players have an excellent feel for where people are and for timing. So those are all assets that can be leveraged.

The next component is situational awareness. In order to have good situational awareness, you have to have a pre-check. A pre-check is what we call a shoulder check before the play happens that allows you to collect information that's going to help you. The constantly changing play variables will be lost on you if you don't have a pre-check; now the situation closes in on you and you don't have awareness of your surroundings. If you did have awareness of your surroundings, you might make a play a lot sooner, or it could be a lot easier. What are the characteristics of your opponent, both as a team and as an individual? That's going to dictate how you use your assets. What's the score? Is this a situation where a prolonged puck protection would be beneficial, and we try to kill the clock in the offensive zone and extend the possession? Are we behind in the game where we don't really want to be in that position of long-extended possessions and just want to make quicker plays because we're looking to advance the puck toward the net to try to tie the game? What's the time on the clock? Are we in the last minute of play? Are we in the first minute of play? What's the time of your shift? What zone are we in? How much space do you have? And how did you acquire the puck? All those aspects of situational awareness are going to influence your puck protection or how you're going to establish body position.

Also, there's your approach to spatial awareness. How much space do you have? What are the pressure points? One of the interesting parts is checking angle. Is the guy coming straight at you? If he's coming straight at you, he can only pressure you really from one contact point. If you are in a situation where you maintain your speed and he picks the right line, then he's going to be able to put a ton of pressure on you. But if you can quickly change that line, he's going to have a hard time adjusting because he's only picked one angle. It's all or nothing. Or does this guy pick an angle where you know he has done a great job of creating multiple contact points? Or is this a situation where you know he's late and you can stay ahead of him by taking the space in front of him, establishing better body position early?

What is the pressure point, and how many pressure points are there? Is one guy coming, or two? We need to know. What's the spatial awareness as it relates to pressure? What are the structure outs? These are the outs you can count on as it relates to your team structure. We can rely on the familiarity of where people are supposed to be. Can we rely on that if you're in the offensive zone? Do we know where the defense is supposed to be? Do we have a high forward? What is your structure? If you're in the defensive zone, is your center in a good spot underneath the puck? Where's your weak side winger? Can you pass the puck to the weak side defenseman? Those are the types of things you want to consider in fractions of seconds.

What's the rotation response? In other words, if you beat your check, what's the next play that's likely going to happen? Who's coming next? How do you alleviate the pressure? Do you do it by manipulating the angle from which the pressure is coming? There's an opportunity to alleviate the pressure just by changing the checking line, and that puts you in a in a situation where you have an advantage. Is it a situation where you want to just turn his feet and then escape the other direction?

What are the opponent's characteristics in spatial awareness? Where is he positioned? What hand does he shoot? You're trying to collect this information inside of a pre-check in fractions of a second, so quick glance probably isn't going to gather enough information points to get it done. This is where playing with expectation is so helpful, because you won't be surprised by getting the puck. You'll have an expectation that you're going to get it. You're scanning the ice and you're taking in this information, a lot of it subconsciously, that leads to decision-making.

In terms of puck acquisition, there are three ways to acquire a puck: a loose puck race, receiving a pass, and forcing a turnover.

In a loose puck race, I've identified three main buckets. There's a 50-50 race. You're trying to just win the line and control the exit. There's a line the each of you is using to get to the puck. Your job is to push your check off the line, establish or win the line. The earlier you can win the line, the more control you have of the line, which gives you easier control of the exit and how you're going to escape. It gives you all the deception once you establish the line. You could have a 25 percent chance of winning the race as the other player is ahead of you. So, what strategies are we going to use? We need to use a wedge, where I'm going to get my stick under his stick and wedge him off the puck to create a seal. I get in front of or through his hands and it allows me to pin or rub him out on that seal. After he picks up the puck, I can improve my 25 percent chance of winning by establishing good position on his forehand side and forcing him to go to his backhand, which makes the seal and the wedge a lot easier. I can control my exit by establishing a sealed body position coming of the wall. When I exit, I'm the first one off the wall. Let's go through the opposite. I have a 75 percent chance of winning the race. This is a situation where I'm ahead and the check is behind me. Now I can easily establish the line. I can manipulate my escape by using deceptions and control the exits by controlling the feet of the checker

The most ideal way of acquiring a puck is to get it off the pass. One of the pre-check situations I want to have is to position myself so that when I catch this pass I'm between two checks. That creates a slight awkwardness as to who is actually responsible for checking me. Either neither of them come, both of them come, or I can anticipate where each one is going to come earlier. Playing between checks gives me a huge advantage to establish body position. If I don't play between checks, I am not aware of my spacing inside the structure of the defense and I could put myself where it's clearly obvious who's responsible for me because I'm lined up beside them. Now, when I get the puck, it's very easy for them to initiate the check because they have no decisions to make. The idea behind playing between checks is it forces a defensive group to communicate and identify who I am. They have to make decisions, which means I've improved my ability to control the situation because it's likely they're going to make some kind of mistake that improves my position. They could both be looking at each other, and by that time I'm gone. When you're an offensive player and you're trying to acquire a puck off the pass, you're trying to give the defensive team every opportunity to make a mistake. You do that by forcing them into making collective decisions.

In terms of a forced turnover, I can steal the puck off a strip, I can intercept a pass, or someone can pressure the opponent and force a giveaway to me.

Those are all the ways in which I can acquire the puck, and each way influences how quickly I can get body position, what my escape routes are going to be, and how well I can dictate the contact and influence of the defender.

In earning body position, my goal is to influence the checker's posture. When they come, I want to force them to lift their body posture. I do that by getting access to their hands. I take my hip and drive it through their hands, which is going to naturally cause them to lift, and that improves my leverage. It also puts them on my back, which is where I want them. I want the check on my back which allows me to be more in control, more manipulative. I want to dictate how the contact is coming. I don't want the checker to feel like he's in control of the play. I'm the one with the puck. I control the play. I'm going to use a weight shift nudge, which is similar to a reverse check or a back hit, but it's not necessarily a straight contact. It's to nudge in front or get this-hip to-hand. I'm not going to wait for the check to come get me and then protect the puck. I'm going to initiate that contact.

We use a Kane Push to get the body position in front and lean more back toward the boards. Once I have the check on my back, I lean back, encouraging the checker to push me into space. Recall that I call that the Kane Push because Patrick Kane is a master of it.

When it's difficult to get my hip to the hands because the defender is even with me, I use a chuck. I take the arm closest to the defender and I get it in front of him. I use my arm as a lever to then push my body ahead. It's almost like a stiff arm you would use in football, but instead of pushing them, I'm putting my arm in front of them and use it as a lever by pushing against them. Then my hip can clear their hip and get through their hands.

Now I'm in a great position where they're slightly ahead of me. They're in perfect position to defend the space in front of me and in a terrible position to defend the space behind me. I recognize that and spin into that open space, building a trap door. This why, as part of the pre-check, you need to understand where the space is. Once you realize you're about to accept some pressure, you understand where your out could be. So you build this trap door before it happens.

The analogy I always use is that the best time to dig a well is before you're thirsty. You don't want to be starting to dig your well when you're already thirsty. You want to anticipate it. So prior to puck acquisition, you get yourself off the wall. You don't put yourself against a wall. Old-school teaching of body contact would be to get against the boards and absorb the contact. There's a lot of value in that to help you if you are just going to accept the contact, for sure. But I don't want the player to accept the contact at all. I want him to be like a ghost, who looks like he's there and then he's gone. In order to do that, you have to play off the wall and use the contact to spin into space. You draw the check in and spin, and you do that confidently by manipulating the checking line. If you understand how to manipulate the line, you can put the defender in a spot where you become really small. As a checker, you can become really small or really big depending on your level of understanding of the checking line and the defender's understanding of the checking line. If you understand it better, you can do a tremendous amount of work to become a ghost. You're just not there, because you understand the line.

Once you have the puck, you go in possession. In possession, you're looking for a seal escape. You want to put the defender on one side of your body, so he's perfectly defending one side and in a terrible position to defend the other. Once you realize where he is, that tells you what your escape route is. It's based on his body position, and you can either react to it or you can influence the line, which allows you to control the escape. Now, inside the escape, you're trying to determine whether you can threaten coming off the wall right away or if need to extend the possession inside the escape. You already know where your outs are. Is this a situation where once you beat this guy you have space to attack? Or do you have to extend the possession because when you look, you don't really have an out?

While I'm inside all of this, I want to manipulate the check by turning the defender's feet. The more I can turn his feet counter to the direction I want to go, the more space I can create, the longer I'm going to be able extend the possession, and the more likely it is they'll have to bring someone else to check me, which is ultimately what I want. I want to force a check change, because it's way easier to make a play inside the space between the times you're being checked. I want to make a play by maintaining my vision. This is why, on the opposite weight shift, which is the body position we're actually trying to get in, especially when we're using the nudge, once we have that great puck protection position I need to be able to use my head to see my outs. Once I see my outs, it allows me to improve my possession. I have more time and space, so now I have an opportunity to extend that possession or make a better decision. The less time and space I have, the smaller the window to make a play and the more errors are going to occur because I'm working off the opponent's time, not my time. I want to work off my time and understand when I can attack.

I have the means to attack because I have good support positions. This is a good opportunity to attack. I need to be able to make that play. This a situation that happens to too many players as they get caught in chains of battles. It becomes self-fulfilling competitiveness because they don't make a play and they go into the next battle. Let's say you're on the forecheck, you've stolen the puck from the defense, and now you're in puck protection. Because you're on the puck and use your body position to put the check on his back, you turn your back to the most amount of ice and limit your vision. Now, you're in a board battle. What do you do? Do you just pitch it back down the boards? Well, that's perpetuating a chain of battles. You're not solving a problem. You are basically passing your problem off to your teammate. You can't classify that as making a play. You classify that as transferring the problem. Your responsibility is to make a play, not transfer the problem.

We have too many players like this. We have to decide what we're really valuing in this puck protection situation. Do we just value the idea the player can protect the puck, or are we valuing the idea the player can protect the puck and make a play? I want him to do three things on a possession. The first thing is he needs to protect the puck and extend the possession, so he takes control of the time and space of the possession. Then I want him to manipulate the check. I want him to turn his checker's feet, so he can buy the time. Then I want him to force a check change, which immediately opens up opportunities for his teammates. Because he's manipulated the check and forced the check change, he now has the ability to make a play that improves the quality or conditions of the possession for his team.

If those three pieces are present, you have done a great job with your body position. If you haven't, then somewhere in this continuum you have a problem. You didn't leverage your assets. You had poor situational awareness. You had poor spatial awareness. You didn't understand how to acquire the puck. You didn't react well to acquiring the puck. You put yourself at a disadvantage before you even started. You didn't earn body position properly, so that is going to impact your ability to maintain possession. You didn't build the trap door. You didn't manipulate the check, and you weren't able to make a play. It could be you leveraged your assets, you had good situational awareness, great spatial awareness, you prepared to acquire the puck in a great position, and acquired the puck in a great way, but then you weren't able to earn good body position. So we don't need to work on the first four assets. We would start your development with earning body position. But we always go one back, so we would actually start with puck acquisition then go into earning body position. We link those things together and move on to the trap door. But in order to build a trap door, you're going to have to earn body position. In order to earn body position, you have to understand puck acquisition. So you see why it works on a continuum. Somewhere there's a skill gap, and that's what we're trying to influence or fill in. Once we fill that gap, it gives you access to the next asset.

For example, maybe you really have a hard time earning body position in any situation where the defender's even with you. You can't create a chuck because you don't have the strength and you don't have the edges to be able to use a lever and create a slingshot effect. You can't handle the puck with one hand on one side of your body. These are all situations that would require us to influence that particular position and leverage your assets. But you don't have the strength to do that, so we need to build a bridge. The way we would build a bridge is by using more weight shift nudges, which would mean we would change speeds and not put ourselves in situations where the player is even as often. We would be conscious of the fact that it could be difficult to create the chuck, and until we learn all the ancillary skills that go with the chuck we've got to go out in a different way. Then, once we learn the chuck, we have more capacity and a very sophisticated way to use the weight shift nudge. We understand the Kane Push once we get into that position. Now we can use the defender's leverage against them where they're pushing us into space. Once we learn all the things that are related to the chuck, we can put that in our tool kit. We're more diverse in our ability to establish body position.

That's really just one example of how to teach body position inside of a continuum. Everything that you're trying to teach takes a similar approach to this and operates on a similar chain. That's how you diagnose what to work on.

There are three categories of the skill continuum. The first one is your basic skills, the second is your higher frequency skills that are more related to competitive advantage, and the third is more elite expression skills

The first element of Category 1 skills is assessing posture and balance. The most ideal posture for movement is the movement angle of having your shin angle and your back angle be parallel. We want to establish your sit position, which is a term I learned from Andy O'Brien, a strength and conditioning coach for a multitude of NHL players, most famously Sidney Crosby. The sit position is effectively just how low you can get in your stance and be able to establish these two acceleration angles. One of the things with the balance element is once you're in this particular posture for body position is whether you can use contact as an accelerant. Your body posture will either help or hurt you in this regard. We want to make sure as part of the Category 1 skills that once the player has established body position and encounters contact, he's able to use the contact as an asset—an accelerant or an ability to create separation.

The second element is edge control. You have the outside edge of your inside skate and the inside edge of your outside skate. There's timing that goes into the weight shift. That is critical, because we don't want you at any point to be centered, meaning your weight is evenly distributed between both feet. We want to have weight on the inside foot as much as possible so that you have the capacity to move. Once your weight is centered, you have to move to move, and that creates some restrictions. The other thing we want to be able to do is turn and change direction inside the edge control. This would be how you would get into body position and, once you're in it, how you manage that body position and get out of it. Your escape comes from your turning, change of direction, and weight shift skills, which all come from that edge control.

Now we're going to talk about separating the upper body from the lower body. This is where you get into your opposite weight shift, which is really the puck protection component where your upper body is twisting counter to the direction of your lower. That's what allows you to protect the puck, put the puck beside your body and beside your outside skate. That's an opposite weight shift. Because you're twisting your upper body counter to where your feet are directed, we now have to turn your head toward the anticipated pressure, so you're building a wall with the side of your body, the shoulders, upper arm, side torso, hips, and legs. You're trying to build a straight line against the wall. Your shoulders would turn in the direction you are protecting the puck or where the puck is on the outside skate. You need your head to be turned in the opposite direction to look past the pressure and into what your support options might be. Then you can work on all the stick skills that go with separating your upper body from your lower body—your forehand puck skills, sometimes with one hand, especially if you're going to use a chuck. You have to have your one hand off the stick while your other hand is controlling the puck.

Now you get into Category 2 skills, which are your weight shift scaffolding. You want to be able to target your hips to or through the hands of the defender, and you want to be able to change speeds to get that position. If you have a quality weight shift, you can cross your feet to get in there; you can use a turn; you can use all kinds of different skills before you get into that weight shift. Then you have weight shift away, meaning you would go away from the pressure. So you would allow the defender to assume there is an anticipated contact line or a contact point, and you would change the contact point by going away. You present your wall, and the defender would come in anticipating he's going to have resistance on that wall and that would be the contact point. As that defender is coming in, you would shift your weight away and you would elongate or change the contact point to a further distance going inside. While you're doing that, you would then spin off the check so that the defender is fully extended and you've influenced his posture. It gives you better escape ability.

Then there are consecutive weight shifts. These are weight shifts you're using in tandem. So you go inside, then you go outside. You're constantly looking to change or manipulate the contact point. Using pattern skills, as well, can not only change the contact point but also lead to excellent deception in your escape route, which makes it difficult for the defender to stay with you. I'd also encourage you to get into more open space, which would then force other players to decide how they're going to defend you.

Another Category 2 skill is controlling the defenseman's skates. You can control a defenseman's skates a couple different ways. One, you can go through his hands and threaten that you're going to go all the way across his body, so he now believes you're going to just cut right in front of him, go all the way across, and end up on the inside of his body. That causes him to react by turning his feet to try to protect that space or to chase that body position he just lost. Or, you can push him inside. You would use that wall of your body to get even with him and just push him where you want him to go with your feet. At any rate, you're trying to control the defenseman's skates and push him counter to the direction you're trying to escape and make it very difficult for him to hold that back contact point.

Finally, let's discuss Category 3 skills. These are much more advanced techniques you can get into depending on the caliber of player you are. The first one is a hook turn, which is a subtle change of speed and direction change using your outside skate heel to hook but not be on your heels. That's the hardest part. You're not on your heels when you execute this skill. That's why we call it a hook turn instead of a heel turn or a single leg. We don't want the player to assume that he's on his heel. We're just using the heel. It's a subtle way of changing speeds and getting body position. It doesn't appear as though you're making any rash movements, and then all of a sudden you end up in a great body position. You use the hook turn to do that. It's a much more subtle and finesse way to establish body position.

Manipulating the line is another one. Again, you're trying to change speeds and change the contact points. You're trying to use the ghosting technique. You make it look like you're going to initiate contact, and then when the defender responds you go away from that contact. The defender can't get a handle on where the contact point is, and if he's too aggressive he's going to end up off balance.

There's also dictating the line. You choose to create a line to match the play potential. Rather than manipulating the line, whatever it may be, this time you choose the line based on what the next play might be. You might slow down to change the contact line so that you give space to turn. So, you encourage the defender to be on your top side, and when you turn you're now on the bottom, which opens up all the passing lanes on that side. You might see a play behind you. That's your best option, so you dictate the line to be advantageous to you for the next play you're trying to create. You could see an opportunity on the top side of that defender, so now you change speeds to go faster and get ahead of him because the play potential you see there is better. Because of the information you're collecting with your pre-check, you can see a great opportunity to make a play on the top side.

Another element of Category 3 skills is playmaking. There are several types of plays you could make. You could use an offensive stick check, which would be to eliminate the stick defense. As the defender is coming, he's leading with his stick. He's trying to get stick on puck. You would lift his stick so that he cannot defend that area, and you would be able to then improve your passing lane. He would only have his skates to defend the passing lane because you've eliminated his stick. The offensive stick check is becoming a very important skill set in today's game, and I'm sure it'll continue to evolve. I can already see several iterations of where we can go with this, but right now players use this offensive stick check as part of their playmaking package in a Category 3 skill.

Then you have all your passing skills. There's the hook pass, where you hook the puck around. Let's say you're cutting in front of the defender and the defender has his stick; you can use the hook pass to be able to make the play. Also, in the offensive stick check, you can use your stick to pop the defender's stick or you can use your inside knee to target his stick to knock it out of the way. We have a pull pass, where you get the defender to declare his stick. Once he declares his stick, you know where it is, and you can pull around and use the space between his skates and his blade as a passing lane. There's the saucer pass, in which you can just sauce it over top of their stick. Leading passes, which is what we talked about before, are where you get into trying to leverage your hockey senses. It's more like Patrick Kane, where he's making plays by leading his support where he wants him to go. He passes the puck to get his teammate to go to the next play.

There's the second layer. Second layer, in this context, means the backside of the ice. You might be in the right corner and you want to make a play over to the left side top of the circles. You're using the weak side of the ice. It's not an immediate pass. That's why dictating the line is a really important skill for those players who have the ability to make plays to the weak side. Controlling that line can really bring out the best in those assets. That's how they have access to the weak side because they can see something, create a line that maximizes the potential, manipulate the defensive pressure, and then escape into space that allows them to utilize the weak side of the rink.

Darryl Belfry stands alongside Patrick Kane (No. 88) and Auston Matthews, two of the top U.S.-born players in the game.

Darryl Belfry instructs Patrick Kane (No. 88), Michael Matheson, and his daughter, Ella, during an 88 Summit.

Darryl Belfry taught himself a lot of the necessary hockey skills to become an effective teacher.

Darryl Belfry instructs during the 88 Summit camp, which is an invite-only NHL camp.

Darry Belfry has worked with Patrick Kane since Kane was nine years old.

Darryl Belfry also works with the Chicago Steel in the USHL.

Darryl Belfry's daughter, Ella, with Nathan MacKinnon (left) and Sidney Crosby.

Darryl Belfry instructs players, including the Chicago Blackhawks'
Patrick Kane (No. 88) and Alex DeBrincat (No. 12), at his NHL camp.
(allarsonphoto.com)

*Darryl Belfry's daughter, Ella, with Patrick Kane (left) and Auston Matthews.
(allarsonphoto.com)*

*Ella Belfry chats with Patrick Kane during a skills camp.
(allarsonphoto.com)*

Darryl Belfry hosted some of the top U.S. and Canadian women's players at a camp in Florida. (allarsonphoto.com)

Darryl Belfry works with Pittsburgh Penguins captain Sidney Crosby.

Darryl Belfry instructs players, including Claude Giroux, at his NHL camp in 2017. (allarsonphoto.com)

Threatening escape is a skill that means finishing on the offensive side position. It's not enough to get the puck in a good spot, protect the puck and extend the possession against pressure, and make a play or manipulate that pressure to then make a play. You still have to finish on the offensive side. You want to have numerical advantages for as long as you can. Getting on the inside is critical as part of your protection habit to extend the possession, make a play improving possession, and then win the body position for the next play so you can cut behind the check. After you've cut in front of the defender, you would then cut behind him and make sure you have exclusive access to the best line to the net, which eliminates his check. You're putting him on your back.

Finally, there's trapping the defender's stick. You might put him in a situation where you turn his stick in a way that when he tries to move it, he's going to hit your legs because you're so tight to him. You've trapped it so he can't recover with his stick on the other side of the body, thus giving you more time and space. He has nothing to prevent you from being able to establish that offensive side positioning. That's a critical component to Category 3 skills for players who can threaten during or after their escape.

KYLE OKPOSO
on Darryl Belfry

Kyle Okposo just knew there was something more to his game than what he was seeing. What he needed was help exposing it.

So, he called Darryl Belfry. And, as Okposo says, "The rest is history."

Okposo sought out Belfry during the 2013 lockout season. Okposo had started out the season on a rough note and was frustrated about where he was as a player. He was getting 10 minutes a game and playing a middle-six role. He was confident there was more to his ability. But to his credit, he also recognized he needed someone to assist him in finding it.

"I just kind of really lost my game," Okposo said. "I contacted my agent. There were a few guys who had used him before and a couple guys I know used him, so I gave him a call. I remember talking to him and we talked about building a game. My game was always in there, but I didn't exact know how to bring out my game the best way that I could. He helped me do that just by doing some simple things. Like he had watched me play a lot before, you know he had been working Johnny [Tavares] for a years at this point. He had watched my game and knew what I did when I was playing well. All he did was give me a few things to think about. That helped me get back on

track and just helped me feel good about my game again and the rest of history."

Belfry began focusing on Okposo's down-low game. Okposo was good at battling on the boards and winning the pucks. His problem was figuring out what to do next after winning that puck. Sometimes he'd just go and win another puck.

"We just talked about getting off the wall and being a beast down low," Okposo said. *"That's kind of when everything else falls into place in my game is when my game in the offensive zone below the dots is really strong. That was one of the first things that we did, just making good plays down there and being confident down there and getting off the wall when I could. That's still something I go back to quite a bit if I'm struggling. That was basically the first thing that we did.*

"It's making good plays back there. If there's space there, you take it, you be aggressive. But you don't try to get stuck on the wall. I find sometimes I get stuck on the wall and just get in the mode of mucking it up and grinding. Yeah, that's fun, and I am pretty good at that. It's so much better just to look for that next play. Just have that next play, know what you're going to do. You see a guy in the middle, it's like, how do I problem-solve to get the puck to him with space and then keeping moving. It's a lot about making the next play off the wall and putting yourself in the right position to do that."

Okposo's focus as he's gotten later into his career has been improving his skating. With that comes a whole other level of possibilities for Belfry.

"I think everything is interconnected," Okposo said. *"It's amazing how Darryl teaches how shooting is all lower body. That's what he looks at first, just very different than most people. For me, the biggest thing is my core. If that's sitting on top of my skates and sitting on top of my hips, then I'm doing well. When I'm leaning, that's kind of where my game goes sideways a little bit and I start to fall and lose my balance and then I'm not able to do things I'm talking with Darryl about. Definitely just core stability and not being in a hurry to go somewhere with it sacrificing stability."*

Okposo and Belfry continue to find ways for his game to evolve as he continues playing in the NHL into his thirties. For Okposo, it's that familiarity, the way Belfry interacts with him and how they both strive to get better that keeps him coming back.

"He knows my game," Okposo said. *"He knows my game and he's watched me play more than anybody over the last six years. He just knows the things that I'm doing when I'm playing well. He's able to communicate it to me in a way that's effective for me. I'm able to really take what he says. Most of the time it's two-to-three things per five-game segment, other times it's one. He's able to do that in such a clear way that it allows me to play and really be free and just keep those things in the back of my mind. It's been extremely helpful."*

12

TRAINING-TO-GAME TRANSFER

TRAINING-TO-GAME TRANSFER IS A TERM I COINED A FEW YEARS ago to better articulate to our players the time frame I was expecting for them to incorporate the skills we had taught into their game. It was a process of trying to educate our players that there are some skills you can work on Tuesday and drop in your game on Wednesday, and some that, of course, take a lot longer.

What I was trying to do in coining this phrase is illustrate that some of what you're working on today you'll be able to use, or sometimes you're planting a seed for something else to happen or different. Sometimes there are different types of skills we're blending together; different ways in which you're reading the ice would allow you access to other skills that you hadn't normally been using. It was just a way to create a mindset of immediate transfer and trying to get players to really focus on the idea there's an opportunity here for you to get better now and immediately make changes to your game.

There are three aspects to training-to-game transfer. This concept is a little misunderstood. It's just, "Hey, if you practice, you're going to put this in your game," and it's very vague on the details of what that process entails. What I wanted to do is create a little bit more shape and context to the way I use it, and hopefully it will inspire some other uses.

I use it in three different ways. The first is intentional transfer. This is where you're targeting a particular skill set you're trying to influence or add and put it into the player's game. You're doing it intentionally. The second one is a habit change. You're trying to change a habit and have that manifest itself in the player's game. The third one is a tactical connection. In this one, we're really trying to engage the mind to encourage transfer in a variety of different ways for that particular skill set. It's much more of a competitive advantage exploration.

Starting with intentional transfer, there are three components to it. The first is asset base. We have to leverage the assets of the athlete. We want to engage those athletes, as well. We're always trying to come back to the strengths of the player. Those are their highest leverage points. These are the easiest skill sets players currently utilize that they have the highest amount of belief in, to which we compare other things or attach skills. This is an opportunity for us; if we want to add something, it should come through one of their best assets. We're also just trying to add more of them in their actual game more consistently. There are players who have great assets that they don't utilize consistently in their game, and so part of our intentional transfer is to get them to use their best skills more frequently and have them understand how they can leverage those skills to have more diversity in their skill set.

Another component of game application is your per shift impact. If you want to impact the game in each and every shift, you need to try to find ways to bend the game into your asset base. You've got to try to find a way to have the game played at the speed you want to play it. You want to have it where the puck is coming through you, so you're controlling the game. When you step on the ice, there should be an impact, and you want that to be a consistent impact. So, first, what is your per shift impact, and second, if you want to have a greater impact, what skill sets should you be leveraging?

I also use the concept of the 30-second commercial to illustrate per shift impact. This is a little more for younger players, but it's relevant for everyone. If I look at a shift like it's a 30-second commercial, what do you want to say during this commercial? When we talk about this, it's usually for the benefit of players who are in the process of being scouted. I try to make the point that you just don't know when someone's watching. Someone comes to the game with other players circled on their list, and then all of a sudden you do something in a given shift that catches their eye. While they might want to watch you the next shift, it's only because you did something that caught their eye in the first place. Now they're going to watch you. You just don't know whether they're going to watch you on the first shift, the third shift, the tenth shift. That's why consistency is so important. If you're consistently doing things well and you have a strong per shift impact, then you're going to show yourself in the best possible light. But if you don't understand what your per shift impact is and how to leverage your best assets, then if someone comes to watch you and sees the wrong shift, they're going to get a poor representation of you as a player. What do you want to say with your shift? View every shift like it's a 30-second commercial. That's a mental approach to the types of things we want to do as it relates to training-to-game transfer and assets.

We also look at impacting success rate. We want to change certain success rates because we think they're too low. We look at all the inefficiencies in a player's game and focus on the ones that have the highest frequency. That will give us the greatest impact on that player's game. Most players run about 6 out of 10, or 60 percent, in terms of success rate. They get the odd thing that pops up about 8 out of 10 and they get other things that are sitting around 4 out of 10. For us, we're always trying to do a two-positive swing. If you're sitting at 4 out of 10 and we can get two more, you're at 6 out of 10 and you're a 60 percent player. That's pretty solid in terms of an improvement. If you're already sitting at 6 out of 10 and we get two better and now you are at an 8 out of 10, that puts you among the elite in that area of the ice. Our standard is we want to try to get as many high-frequency elements as possible to be an 8 out of 10 success rate, and we'll create a definition of success that's highly specific. We know exactly what it is that we're tracking and we're tracking it consistently.

The advantage here is adopting the "two to give" mentality. The allowance of failure will be a major factor in reducing failure. The player is not rattled by a single negative result on some asset or some recurring skill set that we've been trying to influence because he knows the goal is not to be perfect. To be 8 out of 10, we need the two negative ones. Those allowances are what allow us to sustain mental toughness. If you're only working out of a 100 percent mentality, what happens if your first opportunity is a mistake? That's going to impact you mentally. It's going to impact your willingness to risk. We've got to get you in a mindset where you're able to sustain failure. The way we do that is we build failure into the success model and give you 2 out of 10. Now, if you're 8 out of 10 in anything, you're elite, so let go of trying to be perfect.

Even though the situations are similar, they're never the same. There's always something that's a little bit different that either helps you or hurts you, so you don't want to be evaluating everything at a 100 percent rate because that's not possible. You want to try to mitigate those mistakes and make them be helpful for you and not hurt you. Where I got this from was Michael Jordan. I wasn't really that big of a basketball fan until Michael Jordan arrived on the scene, and then I was a huge Chicago Bulls fan from the time he was impactful in the NBA, which was his whole career. I remember watching the Saturday game of the week and he wasn't shooting very well in the first half. In the halftime intermission, the sideline reporter stopped him on his way to the tunnel and said, "Hey, you know, Michael, you're not shooting very well at this point, are you going to try to distribute the ball in the second half?" And he said with a kind of a cheeky grin, "I just got all my misses out of the way." *I expect to go on a run* was kind of what he was saying. Sure enough, he comes out the second half and he shoots the lights out. I always come back to that that moment where it really resonated with me. He understood the type of shooter he was. He knew what percentages of shooting he should expect, and when he's below that number he looks at it like it's a positive. He's getting his misses out of the way, and the law of averages is about to be kind to him. I thought that was fascinating and so I use that story all the time because it best represents this whole idea of two to give mentality.

The third component of intentional transfer is manipulating environment. Whenever you're working on intentional transfer, in order to bring that skill set to the game, you should feel a sense of control over the game. You shouldn't go into the game and feel like you have to take what's given. I can tell you a situation is a high-frequency event, so it's going to happen anywhere between six to eight times every game. Now you can you can get ahead of it by looking to control your environment or stack the deck in your favor by playing with expectation. You know how many times this situation is probably going to occur in a game. Now you want to control your environment. You do that first by playing with expectations. You know what's about to come and then you arrange for things to occur, for proper spacing, for people's feet to be in a certain way, to call for the puck a specific time, to manipulate the timing in such a way to control the speed of the game.

You're just trying to control your environment so you can impose this intentional transfer. Essentially, you're trying to bend the game into your assets. You want to put yourself in a position where you decide how the game is going to be played. You decide by using things like leading passes. You turn people's skates so they have a difficult time defending you in space. You can always create more room if you need it. You change checks. If you start off on the left side and you're going against a left-shot defenseman, that's not as advantageous as if you went to the right side and played against a left-shot defenseman. Now it's harder for him to defend in that space. Or maybe you change checks; you've recognized their first guy back was actually the right winger who's not as comfortable down low in defending those offensive situations. This is a great opportunity. So instead of staying with the left-shot defender who is very comfortable in that space, we're going to change checks and play against the right winger who's not comfortable being down in this space. It's much easier for us to bend the game in our favor. Or you're on the rush and know there is one defenseman who's really adept offensively and another who isn't quite as good. He's much easier to manipulate. Or maybe they have a forward defending, and he's not as comfortable doing it. Recognizing and looking to take advantage of those situations is part of manipulating the environment.

The second aspect we look at in training-to-game transfer is habit change. We've identified a limiting bad habit. It could be movement; it could be a mental process as it relates to the player's reaction to this recurring situation. He just doesn't react very favorably because he takes too much speed into it or has the wrong reads. One of the things we try to do is ask a person whether it's easier to learn a new skill or to change a bad habit. Everyone's going to say it's way easier to learn a new skill. What we try not to do is talk to our players about their bad habits. We try to shape every skill we're trying to influence as a new skill. Now, the only new part about it might be how we're applying the skill, but we're coming at it a new way, so the player feels like it's new. Even though we're influencing his habit, I won't say we're trying to change a bad habit. We're trying to replace this skill. We're trying to update it, which implies we're going to be building a new skill set. What we're really trying to do is influence this bad habit. But I want to create a mindset of excitement, and it's hard to get excited when you feel like you've got to drudge down and try to change a bad habit. Mentally, it's harder for the player because he's about to go through a process that's going to be wrought with a high failure rate. He's going to be lamenting all the times he's regressed back into this bad habit. He will recognize times in which he goes into his bad habit, but it has less of an emotional or intellectual impact because he feels like he's trying to learn something new. It definitely fast-forwards the development process by just reshaping how the player views what the development is. Habit change is really important.

One of the things we're trying to do is create automation. We're bubbling this old habit up to the surface to influence it and change the habits that go into it. We want to make it automated. We want to change how the player is recognizing this situation. We want to get him to see things as they occur, be able to anticipate when this skill is going to come up, and then execute it automatically, so he doesn't have to think about it. That's the other thing; if you shape it as a bad habit and then it pops up every so often, the player will bubble it back up to the surface when we should be at a point where we're trying to automate it. So the less we talk about the bad habit and the more we talk about exciting new skills, we're increasing the odds the player is going to go into automation at the time he needs to.

Again, it's asset-based. We want the play to be whatever the habit we're trying to influence is. We want it to be executed with fluidity. That usually means attaching it to an asset. Inside the isolation process of changing this bad habit, we will attach the habit to players' asset base, so it's much easier for them to create fluidity quicker in the new habit because we're attaching it to this vehicle that's carrying the skill through. As it becomes more blended and more seamless, it makes it a lot easier for them to first recognize it and to execute it with more fluidity, which is ultimately what we're after.

The third aspect is tactical connection. With our training-to-game transfer, we're sometimes only focused on how we get a skill set to be applied to create more of a competitive advantage. What other things can we pair this with? What other situations could we explore where this skill set could be more relevant? Effectively, we're trying to engage the mind and get players to start thinking more creatively about the skill blends they're using and how we can scaffold the skill sets in different ways to create new advantages.

One of the things we know is that when a player learns a skill and gets more comfortable with it, he or she is going to want to use it more. So the more situations in which we can apply the skill or the more we can attach it to other skill sets, the more likely it is the player is going to want to use it. The advantages are also competitive advantages: more time, more space, more favorable puck. We're trying to bend the game into that.

We want training-to-game transfer to have multiple applications. Where else could the player use it? When I talk to players, they'll say, "I could see this in this situation," or, "What do you think about using it here?" Those conversations are gold. We want to foster them as much as possible, because you're trying to bubble that up and get the players to start thinking on their own about where they can use those situations. Whatever it is they suggest, I always run with, even though I might not think that's an area it could be really be applied. I go with it anyway, because I want to let the player vet it out and come to his or her own conclusion as to whether that's a good application or not. Sometimes this is where I learn new things. When my brain isn't even going in that direction, the player brings something up and we just go with it. Next thing you know, I start to see where they're going. Now we're in a whole different train of thought, which can be so incredibly valuable to both of us, because now I'm learning from them. I start to understand their mindset much more, and we can start to see more hybrid uses of skill.

Ultimately, we want the player to dictate this skill set so he can not only recall it, but can bend the game in his favor so he can start utilizing it. With recall, pattern recognition is obviously important, but more than that is the pre-check. The more the player's scanning the ice, the more information he's collecting, the easier it is for him to recall or apply this skill because he can see the play developing and knows where the pressure points are. It's way easier for him to start to dictate the play, and that's ultimately what we're really after. Recall is just a step along the way. What we're really after is the ability to dictate the game and bend the game into our favor

We have these three aspects of training-to-game transfer, and sometimes all three are getting engaged at the same time. Let's say we want to work on intentional transfer of a skill set. It directly addresses one of the areas in which you have the greatest frequency and the lowest success rate, so it's something we want to impact. We can focus on that and learn how to manage the environment, learn how to how to leverage your assets, and start exploring how you can have more per shift value. In this, there can be a habit change. We're trying to influence a bad habit under the guise of teaching a new skill. Because it's a bad habit, it has a lot of impact on other aspects of your game. The more we can get this to hold, the more additional areas of your game we can influence.

Everything comes back to a tactical connection. Every time a player steps on the ice in a game, every single move he makes thereafter has a tactical implication. He's either helping his team or hurting his team with every movement. He's either in position, ahead of the position, or out of position all the time. We're trying to find that balance where he's more consistently in good spots, where he can react and create tactical advantages and not be chasing the game tactically because he's never in a good spot to influence the game.

Training-to-game transfer started out simply as a way to shape how important it is for players to understand we can influence something very quickly and use it tomorrow, if we want to. We can shorten the development time. When I was starting this, development was thought of as this long process. The more I became part of it, the more I realized it doesn't have to be that long. If we approach it a certain way, we can fast-forward these processes and these players can start using this stuff right away. It started off as just reshaping the player's mindset, and it ended up being something we use in variety of different ways. To shorten the process, we need to be directly in front of our athlete, but the athlete can impact his or her game or change our perspective, and that alone can create new areas of opportunity for this player to explore.

Right now, training-to-game transfer is a bit of a buzzword, and it's important for us to understand there's a process here. The more we engage in that process, the more we can shorten the time it takes for players to learn something and drop it into their game. If we take the right approach, we can get the players to use this skill pretty quickly. That's what we want them to realize and embrace.

13
VIDEO-TO-GAME TRANSFER

V_IDEO REVIEW IS ANOTHER WAY WE GET TRANSFER WHEN WE don't have the opportunity to skate the player. We're providing suggestions via video illustration. This is an interesting component because in-season video review represents about 90 percent of our business. What we have come to realize is players are capable of making any number of changes to their game. They can do it on the fly basically. They can do it their next game, so it carries the weight of a lot of responsibility to make sure we're providing them the most impactful information we can relating to the highest frequency situations that are occurring in their games. We're constantly conscious of their assets and making sure their assets are being leveraged to the best of our ability and monitoring their success rates.

What we want to be careful with is not drifting into situations where we're talking about things that are coaching-related, like where they should be on the ice and things like that. We try our best to avoid all coaching situations. What we want to do is problem-solve skill execution inside of the recurring situations they're already in. We want the coach and the player's habits and play processing to put them in a certain position. We want to evaluate those positions they're getting themselves in consistently and see which ones have the lowest success rate and talk about different approaches to those recurring situations. We're not saying those recurring situations aren't good, but your success rate is low. How can we improve it? That's how we balance or stay away from the conflict of the way the players are being coached. It really is irrelevant to me how the players are being coached. All that does is put the player in specific situations a lot and then we can pick it up when we see how frequently they're in those situations and begin building better success rates in those positions.

When you're working with video, you have to be very careful that every play in a game is like a fingerprint. What we want to see is the detail inside of each fingerprint. We want to see the differences while keeping in mind that no fingerprints are exactly alike. They've got some similar characteristics, but they're not exactly alike. And that's how plays are. You can be in recurring situations. For example, you could be a defenseman going back for retrieval and could get 10 of these retrievals in a single game. They would be all classified as retrieval. However, each one of them is going to be very different. They'll be different in the amount of pressure the player has on them each time. They'll be different in the puck location of where they've got to go get the puck. They'll be different in the handedness of the people who are coming to attack them. They'll be different in where their puck support is, where their partner is. They'll be different in the communication they get from the goalie. There are just a lot of differences. There are differences in the context of the game, the time and the score, all those things. So those 10 retrievals are all in the retrieval family, but there are a lot of differences between each one.

We have to be careful we don't over-instruct the player in a situation where it's not going to be recurring. If we look at a detail on a player's retrieval and the detail does not impact what we're focusing on, is only exclusive to that particular retrieval, and we spend a ton of time focusing on that one, then we create a high level of awareness on that particular detail yet it really has no transfer to the other nine retrievals. We're doing our player a disservice. This is why you've got to be very careful with reviewing shifts. I make it a strict policy never to review shifts with players. I have come to see too many problems with shift review that I just don't think it's effective. It might have been when we didn't know as much about video or we didn't have the ability to track the game the way we can now.

Instead of shift review, I prefer to work off instance lists. I want to see a list of 10 retrievals. I want to see the similarities. I want to see the differences. I want to see the context. I want to compare the player's reads to each one and determine their effectiveness inside of that one and understand what their success rate is and where areas of opportunities may be. I think that's a really important element. That's why I like to see things in instance lists. I don't want to see things in reviewing shifts. The problem with shifts is you can confuse the messaging pretty quickly because every shift is very different than the last and the details that go into it. Some of them are high-frequency situations, while others are very low-frequency situations. Some are very much one-offs. If you're reviewing a shift, you're going to go through all the different situations, all the different nuances and you're going end up confusing the messaging at the end of the day. You have to be careful of play nuances. Every play has differenct nuances. You have to be careful with how bogged down you are in the details of those nuances.

If it is not a high-frequency nuance, if it's not a high-frequency situation, now you're bogging the player down in a detail of low-frequency events. If it's not going to occur many times, how much value are you creating? We want to have streamlined the messaging to be a situation we can achieve our transfer objectives. The transfer objective is we want to improve the success rate of the player in this particular situation. We want them to have better situational awareness and situational recognition, so they move sooner because they can anticipate the pattern occurring. We want to bend this situation in their favor. We want them to understand how to utilize their assets. We want to understand how to leverage their assets against their opponents and against this situation and understand what things they can do to further improve the application of these assets.

We also want to focus on play principles and skill execution habits. A play principle may be off the rush. Rather than skate down the boards, we may be more inclined to be closer to the dot line. Now when you receive the pass, you can change what your attack line is. We don't want to skate in a straight line and not have the ability to change the attack line because then you become much easier to defend. If you have the dot line when you catch the puck, you can go with a soft catch, crossover catch, or weight-shift catch, allowing you to change the attack line, which is an excellent play principle that allows you to stack the deck in your favor. Just by coming off the boards six or eight feet, you give yourself more possibilities as it relates to manipulating the play to your favor.

With execution habits, if we were talking about the rush, you want to use an angle entry because they're proven to be more manipulative than just a straight perpendicular entry. We want to make sure we're using those angle entries because that allows us to move the D purposely and we want to start manipulating the D as early as possible. We can pull the D off of his line and start stacking the deck in our favor. The transfer objectives are to improve the success rate.

We're going to get there by having the player recognize a situation faster. By executing play principles and skill execution habits, they're going to be designed to lead to a higher level of execution, which is going to be related to improving the player's options at that moment. By running down the boards, the player is limiting their options, so we move them six to eight feet off the wall, put them to work closer toward the dot line and they've improved their options and have more capacity to make a better play. We're not telling them what play to make. We're just saying here's a position or a line you can put yourself in, and if you combine this with an angle entry, that's going to be more than enough to manipulate the play to your favor and make the next play. That's the kind of thing we're interested in with video review.

By focusing on instance lists and focusing on the read component to it, we can start to dial in exactly what we're looking at. Every play is a unique fingerprint there. While they look similar, there is always a difference. There's a nuance. There's something as it relates to the timing, the pressure, the support, the handedness of the people, the spacing, the puck placement. Something is going to be slightly different, which changes the play a little bit.

If we're too hard and fast with our instructions as to what the players should do, we become more corrective and bogged down in details that are not high-frequency situations. The first order of business to determining what it is we should be focusing on with the player's video-to-game transfer is we understand frequency success rates and the leveraging of their assets and then appreciate the fact every play is its unique fingerprint and we need to make sure that we are focused on the play principles and skill execution habits. This will allow them to bend the situation to their favor and dramatically start to improve their overall success rate, which is the transfer objective of video-to-game transfer.

What's interesting is we see kids do this a lot where they'll see their favorite player do a particular move in the NHL and then they get an opportunity and can recognize a situation where they'll look to make those plays. That's video-to-game transfer. Kids can do that and sometimes they do it on the creative side, which I love. The other times you're looking to just improve options, so the player isn't bogged down by putting themselves in low space, low time, low option situations. That's going to reduce their ability to make the next play. At the end of the day, that's what it's about. We need to be able to make that next play.

14

TEACHING PROGRESSION

Now let's talk about working through our teaching progression. The first part of the teaching progression is the research element, trying to figure the player out and study his or her game in a way that reveals what is needed from a performance and development perspective. We want to understand the players and how they generate their success rates. We want to compare how other people are generating their success and keep tabs on the latest players who come into the game.

Every exciting new player who comes into the game changes the game. Each has unique skill expressions, and because the best players are studying all the interesting players, when anyone comes into the NHL with some new expressions or ways in which they create, the better players take notice. That's how the game advances; it's driven by the top players because they're constantly searching for ideas that they can use to advance or create even more unique skill expressions. We want to pinpoint unique skill expressions, which will dictate where we're going to allocate our study time.

We're trying to collect ideas. When I first started, a few of the first books I read were heavy into encouraging modeling other people's success path. My personality is naturally very resistant to modeling. I don't want to follow anyone else's path. However, I did look at modeling to see where I could find opportunity. What I found in trying to pinpoint what everyone else was doing was that it'd be very difficult to model it completely. There are some things you can model and some you can't. You end up with incomplete information no matter what you do. That's why, when I'm looking at other players' success or other people's success, I view it as just where their model is at that point in time. I view that point in time as a platform for me to use as my starting point.

When I do my research on the on the player, that's not the starting point. That's just the preamble until I get to a point where I have a good handle on where that model is. My process starts at that point, and then I'm looking to connect that model or those ideas with other ideas. I'm looking to use that as a stepping stone, and I want to try to take everything a step further.

I'm also looking at the opposite elements. I want to understand what elements the player values, but then I want to look at the exact opposite of that, because over my career I've noticed many of my own insights and breakthroughs have come from the opposite of what convention would be. Early in my teaching process, it was accepted practice for everyone to teach someone to skate first without the puck and then add it in. I thought, *Well, the opposite of that would to teach them to skate and handle the puck at the same time.* I was always looking at whatever convention said and then experimenting with the opposite to see if there was a path that would create either a more effective or more efficient way to achieve the same result.

The other thing I found interesting is the people I was studying had 20 years of experiences shaping their path. For me to try to model it would be impossible, because of course my experience is going to be different. So given those differences, what valuable information am I not going to fully understand because I didn't share the same experience? I know it's a really successful pathway for a lot of people, but I just didn't want to do that. It wasn't for me.

One of the things we do when we are studying is identify the key performance markers. We want to be able to establish the long-term tracking, what the Mendoza Line is. What I mean by that is I want to know where the line is that divides what is considered to be positive and what is considered to be negative. In baseball, the line for batting average competency is about .200, with the saying derived from shortstop Mario Mendoza's poor career average (a slightly better .215). What should be considered a good success rate? We like to work off of 8 out of 10, but in hockey sometimes 8 to 10 is so impossible to get to, like in goal scoring, for example. It's the opposite. If you're 2 out of 10, you're unbelievable. So 8 out of 10 is not relevant for shooting percentage for us. So what is that number for us and does it change by location? The player's total shooting percentage is 17 percent, but in this area it is 35 percent, this area is 12 percent, and this area is 27 percent.

Then we couple the shooting locations with the shooting situations—whether it's off the rush, with traffic, clear sight, or off the pass. All those factors change the way we evaluate what that shooting percentage actually is. There are some shots the player should shoot more often. He should try to manufacture more of those situations, because the shooting percentages are way higher when he's in them. There are other situations where, if there is another play to be made, he'd probably be better off to make it than to shoot. You may want to shoot with more of a purpose to create a secondary opportunity because the odds are so low the primary shot's going to go in. Therefore, in the initial setup of our research we're trying to determine the Mendoza Line, and really understand what a threshold level of performance for us actually is. Then we can properly set goals from there and establish a good fluid understanding of the performance markers. The fluid nature of the performance markers comes from that differences in assets. One player's Mendoza Line is not the same as another's in the same performance marker.

We want to correlate the athlete's own personal performance with the ancillary skills that go along with it and contribute to that number. Whatever number is we're looking at, there's already a set of other numbers that would contribute to it. We want to understand what those numbers are and then have that become a mainstay in our performance analysis. One of the key parts we're looking for when we're doing our analysis is the ability to come up with a snapshot. I should be able to see a series of video clips and be able to know what kind of that number should be. That number should tell me exactly what I'm going to see on video. One should lend itself to the other. The numbers should be an indicator of overall play. If the number doesn't do that or the video doesn't back that up, then I have to start questioning the depth of my research.

One of the numbers we care about most is seconds per play. This is how frequently players get the puck in sequence. I want to genuinely understand this number to the point where I can say confidently that if you're an elite player, this is how frequently you're going to get or should be getting the puck. Any time that number starts to vary in a particular segment or time, it's going to draw me right into the ancillary skills like puck acquisition. Are you not getting the puck off the pass? Why are you not getting the puck off the pass? You're not getting enough forced turnovers? If so, why? Right away that number is a red flag for me.

We also look at instance rates. We might have a defenseman who is defending off the rush, and the high frequency in which he's doing that is counterproductive. We'd like him to reduce the number of instances in which he's involved. We don't want him to be accepting the rush. If he is, that means there's something he's doing early in the sequence that is making him unable to influence the play. If you're on the weak side and the play is coming out and they're able to pass the puck from one side to the stretch guy on the other side, now you have to back up and take the rush. If you're doing that consistently, that tells us there's something going on with your gap where you're not able to influence the decision-making of the original puck carrier as to why he would pass the puck to your check. Sometimes you want the puck to come to your check so that you can influence the play and you can time it with your gap. Though you initially show you have a larger gap, when the puck arrives you have anticipated that, and you can close the gap and be able to contest the puck or discourage the pass through your gap positioning in the first place.

Sometimes we want a higher volume of instances like puck acquisitions per second. Other times we're trying to reduce the number of instances and put ourselves in spots where we're able to influence the play better. But the number we're collecting should raise a question that draws me into an area where I can start looking at a list of clips and start going through them to start understanding what the profile is as to why this number is being achieved. We're trying to determine what competitive advantages the players are going to have. You want a large enough sample size to confirm that is actually something that's worth studying, that the numbers are reliable enough to hang your hat on.

But we don't need that in all cases. All we need to know is there's evidence to suggest what the player's doing is creating an advantage and the advantages are going to be fluid. If it's a trend that is going to create an advantage for a short period of time until the defending teams start to get better handle on it, they'll make the adjustments, and it's no longer an advantage. So if we waited until the study was complete with a high sample size and weren't confident this was an advantage, well, it would have been an advantage for a short window. But didn't really act on it because we were still waiting for the data to prove us right or wrong. We've got to be careful on some of these things. If it is a trend and there is an advantage to be had, we have to present that information intelligently to our players.

Other times it's something that's more long-term. It's starting to sustain itself over a longer time. We can continue to collect the amount of data we need to not only understand that part but also understand the ancillary parts that contribute to it and indicate it's not a trend but actually something that is translatable and sustainable over multiple years or doesn't expire. For example, say a player is in a corner and he is controlling the feet of the defender. Is that a trend or is that is a sustainable strategy? Is it going to create a competitive advantage regardless? Is it translatable? The answer is that it is translatable, because once you take control of the space and can take control of the feet of the defender, it's going to create a competitive event. It's not a trend. That's something we can build a lot of data behind to understand all the ancillary skill sets and the other data that supports it. We can really understand it completely and start building more and more aspects and diversify how our players are able to come at that particular advantage.

Another example might be a saucer pass, where you look at it and say saucer passes are great, but defenders are catching up. They're able to knock down a high percentage of pucks. This might be something that's going to expire as you get to a high enough level. Once you get to the NHL, a saucer pass is actually pretty difficult to pull off. The sticks and the hand-eye coordination of the elite players are so high that in order for that saucer pass to actually get there, it would have to have a lot more pace on it. It's a different type of puck than we would normally have. That's something you have to monitor. Is it something that is sustainable, able to be influenced, and very difficult to defend? Or is it something the defending group can catch up on? We're going to need to evolve and to start building the short-term adjustments to make sure that we understand how to continue to have that as a as an asset and make the adjustments that either hide our intentions or allow us to use that skill more. Maybe you mix that skill in the context of other things. That's another way to keep the competitive advantage moving along and then anticipate the counter-adjustments. What are the anticipated counter-adjustments, and are we ready to adapt once we start seeing them, or are we able to recognize when our opponent has a high level of exposure to this particular play?

We can build more around it. We want to be able to understand and anticipate what these counter-adjustments are going to be and have our players be able to read when they're coming. They can be more diverse and already know what the next generation of that skill set is going to be. We're preparing our players to be able to have a higher success rate and not have a dip while they're trying to figure out how to how to manage the adjustment by the defenders. In the end, there's just a lot of experimentation that goes on in terms of adapting skill and changing skill.

One of the best examples I have of how one thing leads to the next and takes on a life of its own is from when I was working with a player named Daniel Sprong. We were working on his shot, and I noticed something as we were going through the video review on the ice. I noticed how he was shooting the puck was different, and I encouraged him to continue to go down that path even though it was different than where I was originally planning to take his shot. We turned that into what we called the Sprong shot, and two years later it became the core basis of what we used for the Matthews shot.

Now there's different assets of two different players, but the core philosophical properties of the Sprong shot are really what drove the first generation of the Matthews shot. It took on a life of its own, and it's now had several generations of adaptations and adjustments to try to stay one step ahead of the rest of the league. But initially, the core of that skill set was the Sprong shot. Once we were working on those shots with Auston Matthews it really became a staple for him.

One of the limiting aspects of the research element right now is that many people can be skill instructors without having to do their own research. You can just go on Instagram, for example, and follow some people who very actively post there. You can watch minute-long clips of highlights of players executing amazing skills in the NHL. Different skill instructors post any number of things. The issue I have with all of that is it's just a collection of isolated ideas, and the responsibility is on the person who's watching it to then take it to that next level and have it hopefully become something that sparks them into their own research project. The limiting factor is that many are not taking those isolated clips to the next level and doing their own research. If you just take these isolated random ideas and throw them all together in a mishmash, you're not going to understand all that surrounds the intent you're teaching. It's going to be difficult for you to be able to have your players experience a similar level of success. Part of the problem with that type of research is it tends to create a section of skill instructors who can't necessarily teach. It's difficult to teach something when you don't have the context to understand all the elements or all the ancillary skills that contribute to it.

The mindset, the mentality, all those things matter. If we get trapped in that Instagram environment where we're just seeing these quick snippet clips and that's where we're getting our information from, it's a pretty dangerous space to live in if you're trying to learn. You want to learn in an environment that offers much more depth of knowledge and a background knowledge of what's going on in these areas. We're not going to be able to have that, so it's going be difficult to create any real sustainable development.

At the end of the day, we're still bound by the law of the farm. There's still an order. You're always planting seeds, and there is a process that you need to go through to be able to yield the results you want. So much of that is just to be able to have more patience in the process. The research element is so critical now because there's so much to be learned from each player that allows you then to put him or her in a space where he or she can really take off. But if you are looking to shortcut the research process, you're probably going to also shortcut the development process, and then you're actually not creating a shortcut for the player to be able to learn things at a faster rate. That's the struggle with not having a process.

For us, the teaching works as a progression and the progression starts with the personal aspects or the trust factors of being able to have a results-based process. We understand the results and can talk effectively about what we know and can problem-solve inside the truth. I always want my teaching ability to take over. I want my feel, the recall, the manipulation to dictate an innovation strategy for the player in their learning process.

The first part of the feel is you want players to be able to feel through the movements, feel the skill, be able to feel the situations they can recall. You want them to be able to recognize when this opportunity is available. We want them to be able to manipulate the situation so they can maximize their success rates. We want them to be able to dictate the terms, so that it not only does improve the success rate, but they can bend the game in their favor to be able to get the incident rates up to as high a number as you can. You're really pushing the game into their assets. We want to innovate. We want to end up with a signature skill expression. That's the results process we're looking for.

My problem was social awkwardness. I'm not all that personable at times, particularly in situations where I'm not as fluent in the subject matter. I find I'm much more personable, have much better social awareness, and have less social awkwardness when it's a topic I understand. The more research I've done on the situation, the more confident I am on the subject matter. The more effectively I can speak, the more effective I am in my process and the easier it is for me to then quote those results. It makes it easier for me to communicate. If I didn't have that, it'd be very difficult when I'm communicating with my athlete. I'm constantly probing and looking to see what kind of responses we can get. Response to failure, response to success, response to ideas, response to change—all those times you're constantly probing to see what that response is going to be.

You're really trying to monitor the athletes' body language. You can tell in a lot of cases through their body language how they're feeling. Try to get feedback from when they're awkward so we can really understand how they're feeling, because that's the change moment. It gives us a good opportunity to dig into that, and you can force the feedback. If you're not getting feedback, you can force the feedback through struggle. If you create enough struggle, you're going to get feedback. You can either read the struggle or you can start to see it reveal itself, and that's where the truth is going to come out. That gives you the information you need to be able to make the next set of choices as to the development of the athlete.

There's also a power to language. I spoke about this before, but I'm looking to reinvent terms as much as possible. I'm trying to reshape change so the players always think they're learning something new. Which they are, but it's not like, "Well, we've got to change this bad habit." I also want to reshape meanings, what something means to somebody. I want to shape meaning so it becomes more specific to what it is I want to work out or create a better image so the player can really understand what that means and then evolve and update ideas. I'm looking to take successful ideas and evolve them and update them by either combining them with something else or reshaping their meaning, to bring out a certain aspect of their meaning which then changes slightly for the athlete.

Finally, we're trying to produce signature skills. Now, because we're trying to produce signature skills, those become personal terms, and we try to personalize those terms for the player. The best examples I have are the Kane Push or the Sprong shot. Those types of things are important to be able to start reshaping, because now the player's familiar with his signature shot and you can quickly talk about it and it creates an image and a feeling for the athlete.

My teaching progression has several standard elements to it. I use this very similar process, and I do that for two reasons. One is I'm trying to develop confidence in the process in the player. There are two aspects to building trust. In order for me to get where I need to go with a player, he or she has to believe in the process. I have to trust that I can get wherever it is I'm trying to go with the player, that I can really build that success equity with that athlete and that I'm not biting off more than I or the player can chew. At the end of the day, I don't want to be frustrated because we weren't able to achieve what we wanted to achieve. Ultimately, we're trying to get to a training-to-game transfer. We're trying to have some aspect of the training be translatable to the next competitive event, whether it's the next day, the next week, or the next month.

In order to go through that, I have seven stages. I try to begin with the end of an ice session in mind. I know in an ice session where I'm going to start. I also know where I'm going to end. But I don't always know how I'm going to get there. So much of it is reading and reacting to the athletes—how they're responding, how the skill is being built, what they're capturing. I might employ different techniques to get there, but it's going to be one or all of these seven techniques. They could be in a different sequence. What I try to do is get a sense of what the most important element is that I want to convey, the core skill, and then have that be an undercurrent throughout the entire session. So I need to isolate that. That's usually a Category 1 skill, and I'm trying to understand what that skill is going to be and then really give them the maximum amount of reps inside of that.

For example, I want to teach players to be effective off the rush. We're going to go through rush options for this player. The core fundamental skill inside of the rush is the linear crossover, or that change of speed. That linear crossover would be something I'm going to isolate and build up. Then I'm going to start dropping it into situations. I'll show you how I go through that process, but that linear crossover would be a focus for the entire hour. Because it's the most important thing, we've got to isolate it. We've got to really build it up and then we can utilize it as a more effective tool and as a core skill set inside of the options the players may have.

Once we start going into isolation, I think this has replaced for me what you would call fundamentals. The core fundamentals, as have been described by many, are skating, puck handling, shooting, and checking. The problem with that is there are hundreds of skills within each of those. It's just a category, but it's such a big category that it's difficult to pin down. If you asked 20 people throughout hockey what the fundamentals are, each would probably give you these four. But if you asked for 10 examples of skating fundamentals, I think you'd get different answers. That's what I mean. For me, I've gone away from that too broad a term. I've gone into Category 1, Category 2, and Category 3. It's more effective in being able to really pinpoint the most important elements and show what that will require or what we should invest the most time in.

The problem with isolation is you can't stay in isolation. You can't just stay in the power skating component of the linear crossover. If

I just stayed inside of that, then I'm not going to move it any closer to game transfer. The player may become more capable, but you're not training those four skill speeds that I outlined before. Each skill has to be worked in combination with the other skill speeds all the time. Unless I'm adding elements to the linear crossover, I'm just working it in isolation and it won't transfer. It just takes longer. I'm not interested in length of time. I want the player to build confidence in it and start using it in as many different situations as he or she can and get the reps that way with a thorough understanding of how to use it. But if I don't attach a competitive or a tactical understanding of how to utilize the skill or I don't add the competitive component of how to use a linear crossover with the puck to create a competitive advantage against your opponent, if I don't at some point really dig into those options or those elements and combine the development at the same time, I'm just delaying and elongating the development for the majority of players. Some players are on the right side of the achievement gap and they have a capacity to be able to start messing around with that because their ancillary skills that surround the linear crossover are strong enough. For them, this is a tool they can just plug in most of the other skills. But most other players don't have that capacity, so it's very difficult.

That's why I have such a bad attitude toward stations and apparatuses. I don't dislike stations or apparatuses. I think they're very good, but the problem is they're overused and we never really come out of it. If you see someone do a stations practice, they just stay in the stations and there's no real progression. Typically, you'll have four or five stations with a different skill being taught at each station. All the kids get split up and they go to their different station, and not one of those stations builds upon the next one. All five stations should do the same thing, then move to the next level to the next level to the next level. That's the best use of the stations—to work it inside of a progression. But if you have a different thing going on in each of the stations, while you're creating variety, you're not creating developmental progression. You run the risk of losing the reps inside of or restricting the reps to only that station. There's no carryover effect from one station to the next or one set of exercises to the next, which is the building aspect of it.

The same is true of apparatuses. Using apparatuses is all the rage right now. It's probably the best hockey business model I've ever seen. But in terms of its use and contribution to the betterment of development, it has its limitations. At some point, the apparatus becomes the teacher, and as soon as that happens, we're perpetuating the achievement gap. Some kids who are on the right side of the achievement gap would be able to take a look at that apparatus and visualize certain elements of it that would contribute to their development. But the majority of kids who are not on the right side of the achievement gap—who have skill gaps and cannot do multiple things at the same time because a skill set requires them to stay ultra-focused on basic skill patterns—will get stuck in this isolation. The longer we're in the apparatus, the more restricted the player gets. They are improving their capacity, but they're still becoming restricted. They have a skill set they can't use competitively because it's not attached to any of the other skill speeds. You might be able to get to the four skills speeds where they're able to handle the puck and skate, but the other situations in the game and all the other things you would attach to it would be very difficult to do as long as the apparatus stays on the ice. Now, you could do it if you used the apparatuses for 10 to 15 minutes in a progression to build a specific skill, picked up all the apparatuses, and started using ice markings or different types of resistance—whether it be space, people, or opponents—and varying the competitive advantages toward one side or the other in terms of being able to build that mental or tactical component to it. The player would have to utilize the skill he or she was learning inside the apparatus and have to try to find ways to drop it in or maybe manipulate opponents by using those skill sets.

The problem I have with stations, apparatuses, and small-ice games is that we as a skill development community tend to think that's the only way to do it. We just do that to the exclusion of everything else. To me, it's very limiting. Every one of these aspects is outstanding in their own right, but as an exclusive way to teach, they have limitations. So why allow yourself to have limitations when you could go apparatus to stations to small games as part of your progression and you could then utilize the best parts of all of what you're doing? Have the players carry what you're doing in the isolation throughout all three of those drill formats. If they're carrying that isolation skill through all of those things, now you have a chance to create transfer, but it's in the combination of the multiplicity of the ideas. That's where you have the best opportunity to get better.

The first step is isolation. I'm going to isolate a skill in a certain way, and I want to pair it with something else. I might isolate one skill, then I'm going to isolate a second skill, and then I'm going to pair the two of them together in a single expression.

For example, if we took the linear crossover, I would teach the linear crossover, then I would teach the different types of pass receptions—so those are two isolations, pass receiving and probably a weight shift catch or a crossover catch or both depending on how much time I had—and the focus of where I'm trying to go is combining those things together. I'm going to have a linear crossover which takes the player into a place where he can catch a pass inside of a weight shift or crossover, and then pair that with something else. It becomes a single expression. I'm linking isolation skills into a single expression and making the two skills look like one.

Those are also Category 1 skills. I'm going from **isolation (1)** right into **pairing (2)** and blending, then I'm going to go into

shouldering (3). Shouldering is the process by which you're trying to reduce the amount of time between skill expressions. This is how someone becomes fluid or smooth. Those are the two goals: you want the skill to have a smoothness or an athleticism to it.

Most players do things one skill at a time. They're going to stop their feet to catch the pass, then they're going to restart their skating. Anytime they try to do something skilled with the puck, they stop their feet. What we want to do is keep the feet moving independent of what they're doing with their hands, which is the pairing component, and then shoulder multiple skills together.

If you can picture a player accelerating through the neutral zone, he uses a linear crossover to change speeds. Inside the linear crossover as he's changing speeds, he receives a pass. Now that's a skill blend. That's a pairing we're trying to blend together. Now we want to make sure that is a very fluid motion with those three skills. The ability to catch the pass inside of a crossover that's inside of a linear crossover, we want to have fluency and a smooth expression in those three things. I call that shouldering (or reducing) the amount of time it takes to go from one skill to the next.

The pairing is a Category 2 skill. Blending is Category 3. Blending is then taking those types of elements and doing a multitude of different things with them. We want to stack them. Now we're creating a platform to build on. We're building this linear crossover. We've started pairing things with it. We've shouldered a few things so it has some fluency with its ability. Now it has a platform to build other things on it. We could use that linear crossover in tactical change of speed against somebody. We could use it in shooting. We could use it to force the defender to turn and then pair that with a turn. There's a change of speed or a change of direction. That's **stacking (4)**. We start stacking things on top of it, and then **scaffolding (5)** is the building of the ancillary skills surrounding the skill set. It could be inside the linear crossover example. It could be something where there's a play that's made in the neutral zone where we're trying to get the linear crossover, we're trying to catch the pass inside the crossover.

Scaffolding would be a manipulation of the time and space. So as I'm coming up with my linear crossover, I am also paying attention to where the defenseman is, which shoulder he's going, how I can position myself against him. Now, when I get the puck, I have an opportunity to build space inside that crossover. I can dictate and control the space I'm having. That's what I mean.

Or take the exit play—how do I take this and create the exit play that gets me past this forward and into that next movement? The scaffolding is what happens just a little bit before the mentality or tactical implications of what you're trying to do and then what happens immediately after.

Then we go into **sequencing (6)**. Sequencing would be what happens in the offensive zone after this neutral zone play. What other things are going on the offensive zone? What happened in the defensive zone? Maybe this is a play where the center is learning how to position himself off the breakout. He gets a pass in the breakout, he uses his linear crossover to get into change of speed, he runs down the dot line, positions himself against the defender to align his shoulder to get the competitive advantage off the alignment, now he executes a catch off the pass. As he was skating up, he made a pass to someone else. In the time he doesn't have the puck, he moves to set up the next play, so that when he catches the pass, he has great alignment to go with that crossover catch. Now he can get into the offensive zone to force the defenseman into a pivot. Now maybe he has a choice whether he's going to net drive this guy depending on what the speed differential might be and his manipulating of the front and the side gap. Now he turns up into a delay and then he can execute some offensive zone thing. That sequencing is the entire sequence of the possession for his team.

You also have to consider connectedness—how connected am I to my teammates? Did I position myself too far behind or too far ahead? Am I too close or far away? Where's the spacing? Connectedness is the spacing, so you're more marketable to get the puck back.

Innovating (7) is the last one. How can I take this linear crossover and add other elements or take a look at how my assets work inside of this? What are my assets telling me are competitive advantages for me I could then innovate to make it more of a signature skill?

That is a Category 3 skill, which is skill blending. So we go from Category 1, isolating the linear crossover. We then go into the pairing of adding a crossover catch and really understanding how to do those two things at once. We then shoulder it by reducing the amount of time between each skill to create fluency and smoothness. Then we move into Category 3, where we start stacking it and adding different elements to it. We use the scaffolding where we're really working on the ancillary skills and the competitive advantage mentality of what we're trying to do. Then we sequence it. We might change that sequence two or three different ways. Then the connectedness, where are you in relationship to your other teammates? That's critical so you have the spacing down and you're more marketable to get the puck back. Then, is there a signature skill application for you? That's Category 3 blending. Once we have all that built, now we're looking to force a recall. We're going to hide this skill inside of a sequence, so we don't want it to feel like a drill. We want it to look like a more like a game situation where players have to recall or recognize the pattern. Once they recognize the pattern, then they start moving in automation into the movement.

For example, one of the key parts of this linear crossover would be alignment. Can the player recognize when he doesn't have the puck and he's moving through the neutral zone? That's the best time to establish alignment on the next puck. When the next puck comes, he's in great alignment and that puts him in perfect position to manipulate the defenseman. He can start moving him around in a competitive advantage. Dictating is related to the connectedness, where if you're the most marketable to get the puck and you're playing like a spider now, the puck is going to start coming to you more frequently. That allows you to dictate what's going to happen.

The highest level of skill is manipulating the game conditions inside your assets. If you know that this linear crossover is a strength of yours, you're trying to create it multiple times in a game and manipulate the play to your assets. It becomes much more of a competitive advantage for you and your team.

After we get into forced recall, we're going to move into parallel structures. While this is all going on with the linear crossover, I'm also working on the defensemen and teaching them how to defend the rush at the exact same time. While the forwards are learning the linear crossover off the rush catch and all the changes of speed and those rush concepts, at the exact same time I can teach a defenseman how to backpedal properly, what the skating components to that are, so he's not crossing his feet. He's got to learn to skate backward and move laterally without crossing his feet. That's a huge component. I put in this opposing parallel structure and now both sides have been built. The forward side has been built in their linear crossover, and we have the backpedal elements of the defensemen and all their ways of establishing alignment stick position, front gaps, side gap, pivots, pressure stick to puck, denying entry. I'm going to then put one against the other, and that's a parallel structure. I've run two things at the same time, parallel, independent of each other, and then at the end I oppose them. Or I could set it up not as opposing structures, but as a continuous structure or hybrids. I could run that parallel structure with how the center would do it and how the winger on both sides would do it. At the same time, I'm showing the center what his routes might be and the winger what his routes might be. Now it's the continuation between those two things in all the competitive advantages they're trying to create together. There is still a parallel structure, but it's happening together.

They can also be switching roles. At one point I'm learning what the wingers' aspects are supposed to be, and then I'm learning what I'm supposed to do as a center. I'm learning both of those elements, and then I'm prepared to play either role. I know the spacing, the timing, and all the competitive components to it. I know all the linear crossover elements to it, as well.

Another piece to it is asset attaching. Once we get through this process, different assets are going to pop out that are important. We want to connect the asset to the skill, so the player knows how he personally can create more competitive advantage based on his own individual asset. Like in this recurring situation of rushed attack skills and using this linear crossover, what are your specific assets? Are you someone who already has a lot of speed you could use, or someone who's a lot bigger and it can appear as though you're not really moving but you're actually flying by the defender just because of how you're skating? Is it something where you're just really smart with the gap in the spacing and your advantage in the linear crossover is actually in the speed differential? That's how you're going to come at it. It's all different for each player and highlighting how each person can leverage their assets inside this recurring situation.

Then I want to transport any new skills through that asset. Now I start attaching any of the new skills and start putting them inside that asset so players can see the thing that comes the most naturally to them inside of this skill set, and we're trying to attach every new skill to that attachment.

For example, we're going to take a look at the linear crossover component. If the player is not all that fleet of foot and his best asset is actually his mind, then we're going to talk to him about how to use this as a timing principle to put the defenseman in an awkward position from an alignment and spacing perspective. We're going to attach the skill of the linear crossover to that component of his assets. What gets really interesting with asset attaching is when you attach an asset the player doesn't naturally do very well or could be the weakest element of their skill set. So a player has great speed, great hands, but doesn't really understand or doesn't really process the game at a fast enough rate. We would attach the asset of speed differential and alignment and gap, manipulating the front gap and a wide gap to manipulate the defenseman. We would attach all those skills to that weakest component, so that heightens the level of development for the player. He becomes more aware of the different ways he can employ that skill. Even though that's not something that comes to him easily, that's a way for us to be able to really teach that particular element of that skill speed and make sure that's in there.

The last component is shapeshifting. It's related directly to dictating space. It's really also about connectedness. So connectedness, dictating, manipulating, and shapeshifting are all in the same family of what we're really looking to do. There are two types of shapes. There's a support shape, which is what your teammates are doing, and then there's a defensive shape, which is what the opposition is doing. We want to start understanding what both of those shapes are.

Is it a triangle? Is it a diamond? Is it layers? Is it release points? Determine the shape and manipulate that shape to your favor, so you can quickly get into it. It creates a higher level of recognition. Shapeshifting is how you bend the game into your assets.

For defensive shape, what's the pressure? Is it direct pressure on you? What are the release pressures? At your release points, who are the two best people you could pass the puck to? What's the pressure on them? How much recognition do you have of that? Can you manipulate those two elements? If you can, now you're into shapeshifting at an elite level.

Playing between two checks is part of one of the really great strategies of defensive shape. Getting in between two checks and being in that awkward space is time and space and decision-making on the defense, which gives you a competitive advantage.

Understanding shapeshifting is a critical component to each of the other development aspects of our teaching process. It always relates back to the principle that the highest level of expression is in manipulating the play into your assets or bending the game into your assets. By understanding the shapes of the game, you can really process it at a higher level, and that's what's going to give you even more of an opportunity to play the game you want to play. It creates consistency because you can always take the game into your world, and that's just a massive opportunity.

The last part is always developing the transition mind. This to me is the definition of hockey sense—the ability to really understand transition. Early on in my career, I went to a seminar and there was a speaker there from Sweden named Bjorn Kindling. He had studied transition at the international level. He tracked how many transitions there were in a game. How many times does the puck change hands? How much time is it in undetermined possession? How much time is it in uncontested possession? He had this whole thing laid out, and he knew where the places were on the ice that were the most dangerous to turn a puck over that would lead you directly to chances. What I got from that was there is a real value in understanding there are two triangles on the ice. There's a primary triangle, which is at the puck. Three players are engaged at the puck, then there are two people who are off the puck or the furthest distance away, and they represent two parts of the secondary triangle which is linked by one person of the primary triangle. So the primary triangle and the secondary triangle are linked by one person. This is the space of the spider. The spider lives in that space between. The player's in the middle of the triangle, but connects to two triangles.

He understands role changes better than anybody. He knows his role in that group of five and in between those two changes.

That's hockey sense for me, and this is what I call the transition mind or the space of the spider. This is where a really good player becomes ultra-elite in their understanding of this, and it's built on in transition. For the most part, at the puck there are two players who are defending and three players who are attacking, but it's very difficult to have all five attacking and all five defending. Usually there are situations where that is the case, but for the most part because of the rapid number of changes—there are 400 changes of possession in a game—not everybody is on offense or defense at the same time. So depending on your relationship to where the puck is, you might be in the transition space. Our team is defending and you are in a defensive posture, but you're really in a dual position because once we get the puck, you're the best person to pass the puck to create transition. You're in the transition place, the space of the spider. The more you can be in those spaces, that's how the spider becomes elite. That's a really interesting component to hockey sense.

TESTIMONIAL

AUSTON MATTHEWS
on Darryl Belfry

Auston Matthews remembers being intimidated by Darryl Belfry the first time they met. Matthews was barely a teenager, and he and some of other top North American players in his age group were attending a camp Belfry was instructing.

Matthews stepped on the ice with Belfry and quickly realized he still had a lot to learn.

"First time skating with him was pretty difficult," Matthews said. "Lots of stuff I had never done. I think he did it to prove a point to a bunch of cocky 14-, 15-years-olds that were kind of the best players in their area or the best players in their region. I think that was eye-opening for a lot of people."

A few years later, Matthews and Belfry began working together one-on-one. Matthews, then 17, was more confident and was emerging as the No. 1 pick in the 2016 draft, but he was still eager to learn and add to his game.

What Belfry especially wanted to do with Matthews was transform his shot. It was good then. He wanted to make it great.

As Matthews can testify, he did.

"I think he transformed my shot," Matthews said. *"I had a decent shot, but I never had the kind of dynamic skill set as far as that goes as I do now. I think a lot of credit goes to him with his work with me that summer to get it ready to get it to the NHL level and be able to score in multiple different ways.*

"[We worked on] pretty much just everything, different releases. He's usually the one giving me passes, and I think he'll tell you firsthand he's not a great passer, a lot of pucks in your feet and tough areas. I think you can benefit a lot from that because you'll never really get a perfect pass in a game-like situation. Just different releases, different shots, different areas of the ice, a lot of that stuff. I shot thousands of pucks with him in so many different scenarios. It kind of creates muscle memory at that point."

Today, Matthews cashes in with that shot time after time in the hardest league in the world.

"It's more accurate, it's much quicker," Matthews said. *"I think I always had a knack for scoring goals, but it gets harder and harder as you move up levels, especially in the NHL. To be able to have a good shot and a quick release, especially when you don't have as much time and space that obviously you'd like to have, to get it off as quick as you can and accurate as possible, I think that's a big part of what we worked on."*

As Belfry hopes with all his clients, he and Matthews developed more of a co-teacher environment with time.

That was also essential to them in elevating Matthews' game.

"I think the first summer we first started working together I was pretty quiet, kind of shy," Matthews said. *"There wasn't much back-and-forth. It was mostly kind of him giving the ideas and telling me what he sees. He's really a guy who feeds off communication. I think that's something he was looking for from me. As we started working more and more together and I got more comfortable, I was able to give him my input and tell him what I thought, and it almost became a collaboration as far as those on-ice sessions go or video sessions go. It's kind of a bit of a collaboration and bouncing ideas of each other. I think it kind of benefits both of us.*

"For him, he's been around so many unbelievable players and some of the top guys in the world. He's been with Kaner since he was a kid. As smart as he is, I think he's always trying to learn, too. I think he's always trying to add things to his philosophy and how he teaches things. I think there's no better way to do that than when you're working with some of the best players in the world. Obviously they're pretty smart guys and you can bounce stuff off each other as well. Everyone sees scenarios, situations different on the ice."

TESTIMONIAL

JUDD MOLDAVER
on Darryl Belfry

Player agent Judd Moldaver loves what Darry Belfry can do for his players, but there's a respect that goes beyond that.

"We've developed not only an amazing professional relationship, but through our professional relationship we've fostered a really good friendship," said Moldaver, who is part of Wasserman Media Group. "What I love about Darryl is he can be challenged. He can be pushed. He can be asked different questions and respect other people's opinions. He respects other philosophies. We've always had thoughtful conversation not just the on-ice things and individual players' development, but we talk about the off-ice element is just exceptional.

"He offers a unique perspective. I think players really believe in him and trust him. I think he works well to understand that teams have different systems, teams are all in different situations, there are different people. And almost like we do as good representatives, you want to curate your play for your specific players. It's not a one-size-fits-all. I think Darryl's always been excellent at curating and strategizing and taking a player and taking their strengths and enhancing. In time he takes them to areas where players never thought they'd be successful or do certain things and pulls that out of them. I think he's really good about teaching individual skill sets and

optimizing players, but still allowing those players to flourish in a team structure. I think he's got a brilliant mind for the game. I really think he cares about his players. He's really passionate about them."

One player Belfry and Moldaver are especially passionate is Auston Matthews. Moldaver represents Matthews, also known as "34," and Belfry trains him.

"I think it's been excellent," Moldaver said of Belfry's relationship with Matthews. "There's a lot of mutual respect and admiration. What Darryl has done is he's challenged him in a good way. He pushes him and wants him to be the best of the best, which I love, 34 loves, his family loves. I think that's just great. Darryl keeps on wanting to add more layers, so to speak, to the onion, and I know based on how 34 is, he loves that because he wants to keep getting better and keep improving. It's a perfect match because they want the same thing—34 wants to be the best version of 34 possible and Darryl wants that, too."

15

FEEDBACK

ONE OF THE MAJOR ASPECTS OF DEVELOPMENT PROGRESSION OR
teaching progression is feedback. The type of feedback you give
athletes can either fast-forward their development or slow it down.
Over the years, I've approached feedback a variety of different ways
to try to get a sense of what really worked. The frustrating part in
the process was I would find a method of feedback that would work
for one player, and I'd get really excited about how quickly he or she
was able to move through the development process, only to realize
that that feedback was specific to just that person. When I tried to
transfer that same approach to others, the results were mixed.

I tried to dig into this a lot more over the last several years and
start to understand how I could be more effective with the feedback
I was giving. There are a few things I've uncovered I think are really
important as it relates to feedback. Most of the time when you hear
someone talk about feedback, they talk about immediate and specific
feedback as being really important. It's kind of like the how but not
the what. Because the what is so difficult. It's the hardest part. You
can be at the ready to give feedback, but if you don't know what

feedback to give then it can get lost, especially if you're interested in getting immediate feedback. There is an approach you can take that will help everyone. It just comes down to what it is you're going to give. That's where the art is in the end. You still need to know what you're correcting. For me, there are five key pieces to feedback.

The first one is feedback should be sequential. What I mean by sequential is you need to know what to change and in what order to change it. For example, the easiest example is when you're trying to influence someone's skating. Early on in my development, when I was working with a player and noticed something I did not like inside of their skating, I would focus on that aspect. If it was something related to their edge control, I would give specific instructions as it related to edge control. I would talk about the angle of their shin, when and where their weight should be distributed, something related to the lower body. What I realized was when you're making an impact on a player's skating the problem is usually further up the chain. When you teach skating, you teach it from the head down. Most of the problems you may encounter are usually furthest from the feet, even though your focus and the things you're trying to influence are at the feet. That's just the way it outputs. You can influence it by influencing the chain and you can make longer-lasting corrections if you focus on what's going on further up the chain. Sometimes the problem as it relates to the player's edge control has to do with the fact he or she is changing the direction and doesn't initiate the movement through the head or shoulders. Because the upper body doesn't get involved, that's what puts the restriction on the edge. So no matter how many corrections I make on the edges, they're not going be able to hold the correction because you're not attacking the biggest issue precluding the movement.

It's no different than getting body work from a really good physical therapist. You go in and say, "Listen, I've got a problem with my lower back," and they would work on that area but would also be over on the other side of your body working on your top shoulder, for some reason. You wonder, *Why are they working on my shoulder when the problem is in my lower back?* The reason is there's a correlation between what's going on one side of the body and what is ultimately creating the problems on the other side. Even though the pain is in your back, you can draw it back to somewhere else where there is a restriction.

That's a great analogy I think for how we need to be focused on our feedback. You're trying to create a chain reaction. You're trying to influence the part of the chain that is going to create the posture and the position so that the player has the best opportunity to access the body position that's going to allow him or her to skate better. The first aspect is just to have a sequential approach and to understand that the problems you're seeing are often manifested by something that's happening further up the body and in some other way.

When you teach shooting, it's the opposite. You might think, *I'm teaching shooting; that's got to be a lot of the hands, upper body, and all that.* Well, no. When you teach skating, it's taught from the head down. When you're trying to influence shooting, it's taught from the feet up. Usually the problems you're trying to influence are related to the player's feet. The first thing you want to look at is whether there's a problem with their feet, and then you work your way back up the chain.

The second piece of feedback you've got to acknowledge is the difference in perspective. Let's go back to the whole idea of the disconnect between the athlete and the instructor in terms of how they're getting their inputs. The athlete's input is coming from what he's feeling, because he can't see himself. He can only feel what he's doing in motion. The instructor can't feel what's going on. He has no sense of how it feels. He can only go by what he sees. So immediately you have this disconnect, and you're going to need to structure your feedback as it relates to a feel conversion. The athlete feels it as weird, good, normal, or whatever. You have to acknowledge that. Sometimes what should not feel good in terms of the movement quality feels normal to him because that's just his movement pattern. So you have to acknowledge that as part of your feedback. You need to find a way to bridge the gap of the inputs: how you're seeing it and how he's feeling it. Once you bridge that gap, he can understand why so much of our feedback comes in the form of video. It just doesn't lie. It tells the truth every single time. It gives us an opportunity to deal with what's really going on and be able to illustrate what we see. The athlete can see, *Oh, I'm moving in the right direction, but I can see that my body would move better that way or I'm in a better position if I do it that way but it just feels weird.* I have to acknowledge that, and then it gives the athlete more impetus to try to follow this weird feeling path.

The third aspect is you have to be direct. You've got to be honest and learn how to shape honesty. With each player, you have to be very careful with how you shape the honesty. You still have to be honest, but you can't be misleading. There's an art in the delivery, and the delivery is different for each player. You have to pay attention to tone. You have to pay attention to the frequency in which you're creating honesty. You can create some self-actualization in the athlete as well by starting off with a pretty direct and honest approach to how you're seeing the skill being developed and expressed and where you want it to move.

There are lots of different delivery methods you can use depending on where the athlete is in the development process, what she's feeling at that time, what her acceptance level of failure is at that point. A lot of factors go into that. It comes down to feel and really getting to know your athlete. At the end of the day, the direct component to the feedback is that the tone used will be related to your knowledge of the athlete. The better you get to know the athlete, the more you can customize the feedback and the better it's going to be received by the athlete, though you still have to be honest. There are different ways to be honest in terms of the delivery. The art becomes the delivery. You don't want to alienate the athlete. Sometimes you're trying to create a level of anger or heighten the focus, so you're trying to be honest to the point with a delivery that's a little more edgy, and sometimes you're trying to soften the edges. You don't want to misrepresent the feedback. It still needs to be honest. But be cautious of how it's being delivered and how it's being received.

The fourth part of feedback I think is absolutely critical that gets lost in our approach a lot is you want to link the feedback to the tactics on a technical level. You want to engage the player's mind in hockey specifics, strategy, tactics or competitive advantage. If you can link the feedback to the tactics, then you can create a clearer "why" for the player. You can create context. You can create more motivation to keep pushing through a really awkward patch for the player. You can engage or distract the athlete from the fact that he's ultra-focused on highly technical pieces of trying to pay attention to the body. You can over-focus corrections, as well. The player can just be way too sensitive and kind of misinterpret what's really going on with the body if you really focus it. Sometimes you want to distract the athlete from what's going on and get a little more fluidity. You can get that by timing when you're going to engage the mind.

For example, we may be talking about a body position correction of this edge control inside of these turns. But there's another application as it relates to stops and starts or to some transition skill or to making this move 90 degrees and creating this advantage. But if you were to overdo it, so not just move 90 degrees but then start coming back up the ice, having that type of edge control would then open up many options or create even more space or another play. You know you did everything right, and the defender was still there. If you had this edge control and you realized he was still there, you would've been able to create the separation you needed. So again, you're engaging the mind; you're creating further motivation for the player to push through awkward patches and you're also distracting him sometimes from an over-focus on something technical he's trying to correct. You're always linking what's going on with this correction to a competitive advantage, which may spark some other discussions. That gives you another opportunity to further connect with the athletes and see what they're thinking. It might give you some pause for other aspects of the correction that could really take them into another level of development where they're again taking a little more control. If they suggest something, they say, "You know, I could also see this being used here"—boom, right away you move it over there. Let's see. Let's feel through that. So you know they still feel the movement you want, but now it's in a different game context. It's something they're kind of taking control of, but it doesn't eliminate the fact they need to work on this skill. You're not distracting it to the point you know they're losing the focus of what you're trying to correct.

You also have to prioritize feedback. This is probably out of all of them the most important aspect. When I was really focused on feedback, I found that I was giving way too much of it. I was trying to correct everything all at once. Everything was a problem. It's very similar to watching a shift with a player. You see this and you see that. The next thing you know, you have 20 items that the player didn't do correctly. Which one's most important? What should we focus on? Am I overwhelming the athlete with just so much information? How much of this is really important to their game tomorrow? How much of this has a frequency and success rate that it makes sense? There are all those factors that go into it.

You don't want to fix everything and overcorrect. You need to prioritize feedback and allow some things to continue to be wrong until you get there on the list. This is where prioritizing feedback takes you back in the loop to sequence. Do we know what to change and in what order? If we do, then we won't overcorrect. We won't try to fix everything. We will allow for failure and we'll go into a much more deliberate build. We're going to fix this first. We have in this movement six things that are problematic. I'll start with this one, and the reason is because it's the most important and has an impact on two other aspects of the six. So if we fix one, we really fix three; that fast-forwards development. If you understand the sequence, you can get that cumulative effect of correction where you fix one thing and it has a chain reaction. That's why understanding what you're trying to teach is crucial. I'm trying to teach skating, I'm focused exclusively on the edges and the feet, and the problem is probably further up the chain. If I miss that, I'm going to be spinning my wheels. But if I go up and don't even touch the edges at first and just fix their shoulders and get them to rotate through the upper body properly, that could create the chain reaction I need that ultimately impacts the edges, and I never touch them. I've impacted it further up the chain. So again, going through a deliberate build, understanding what chain reaction you can expect from what pieces you influence is going to have a cumulative effect on improving the others.

Sometimes players are on their heels when they turn. The reason is puck placement. They don't put the puck in the right spot. That's where the puck is the most limiting part. You take the puck away, they turn really well. Then you give them the puck and they turn poorly. Well, it's because they don't understand where to put the puck. Rather than focus on all the turning, the edges, the balance, the posture, the lean, the weight shift, all of that, all I need to do is put the puck in the right spot. You put the puck in the right spot, it creates a chain reaction. Everything syncs together.

Understand you don't need to fix everything, have a deliberate build that's related to the sequence, watch a few things accumulate together and fast-forward the development, build some momentum, and then you'll get to the last few parts which are usually the hardest to do. By then, you'll have developed so much developmental equity with the player that it'll be much easier in terms of mindset for him or her to be able to really start knocking those difficult ones off. Then you're trying to balance prioritizing the feedback with self-discovery. You still want self-discovery. You want the player to be aware inside the process. You don't want him or her to be over reliant on you, because at the end of the day the skill has to be expressed automatically and the pathway to automation is through feel. You started off in the conscious. You create awareness. You focus on this particular skill in a way that creates awareness of the impact of what you're trying to fix. You surround it with the ancillary skills to make sure that it's well-supported and then you want to recess it back into the subconscious. You want it expressed automatically, so part of that is self-discovery. That why I think linking the tactics and engaging the mind is so important. It gives you that opportunity to get the self-discovery and add value to those adjustments and kind of riff on some of their adjustments as long as it's reasonably close the sequence. Sometimes it's worth going on a tangent with the athletes in self-discovery and allowing them to feel some different things. You can always refocus them back to the sequence, but you want to allow for self-discovery. It's a critical component, but you don't want exclusive self-discovery again. Too much of one thing is not optimal. You also want to have priority in the order of continuum and the order of sequence, making sure you're understanding that so that the player's not in a self-discovery where they're banging their head against the wall. They're realizing they have problems in their edges and we're over-focusing on their edges, when meanwhile the correction could be as simple as moving the puck in a better spot and then that would sync everything. That's your responsibility as the coach in your feedback.

Perspective is to understand the balance between the self-discovery and the order of change so that you can fast-forward the process. Otherwise, why does the player have you there? You're there to help the athlete be able to touch all the bases in the most efficient way possible but yet still be able to self-express, to link it to tactics, and to feel it. Your job is to heighten the awareness on a sensitive subject for the athlete in terms of what they're trying to change, fully develop it in a way that allows the athlete to convert feel, and then then you recess it back into the subconscious and continue to link it at the same time with the tactics so that their mind is engaged. Now you're seeing the full value of your feedback.

Feedback for me is very personal, and you have to have a real feel for your athlete. Some athletes are really good in terms of their reaction to failure, but that's normal. And then all of a sudden they're not picking it up as quickly as they normally do, and now their capacity for failure is greatly diminished. You have to acknowledge that. You have to read that and find different ways to influence them without overtaxing them from a failure tolerance perspective. Once they get to a point where their reaction to failure becomes counterproductive to their energy, you need to be able to redirect that. Do you redirect that by abandoning what you're doing, or do you redirect it by going through some self-discovery? Do you redirect it by linking it to tactics? I can tell you I don't ever abandon it. I see it through. But I don't mind distracting for a while to get it out of the player's head. Maybe I can find an asset vehicle we can attach to the skill that they're struggling with. You bring in something they do really well and attach it to the sequence so they feel good going into it or coming out of it. That can give you a good vehicle to pull everything around.

I think you know you don't ever want the athlete to feel like you're going to give up on the correction. What you want to do is distract from it and then come back to it and magically, it's there.

Then you go back to the video and you say, "By the way, I know right now we're working on this, but I just want to show you this. This is what you're struggling with, remember that." "Yep, there it is. Oh, geez, that's fantastic, I see that now." That's the magic of feedback. That's the magic of understanding your athlete. That's the magic of doing things from a sequential perspective and prioritizing that feedback. I think if you do those things on a consistent basis and you can find reads inside of it from a teaching perspective, you can dramatically fast-forward the development process through the way you construct your feedback.

16

DUMBING IT DOWN

ONE OF THE BEST ANALOGIES I USE TO DESCRIBE WHAT SEPARATES the really good skill instructors from guys who are still developing their craft is a tree. The really good ones will not just stick to the trunk of the tree. They'll extend themselves out on each branch. They're willing to go off the main trunk, branch out to its furthest extremities, come back, and then start moving back up the trunk and into other branches.

If you have the confidence in your teaching ability to divert and go off into different areas, whether it's the player's exploration, something you see and want to open a different perspective for the athlete, or sometimes just good creativity and riffing between the teacher and the student, that's a separator among skill instructors and teachers in general. As opposed to a teacher who has a rigid adherence to a predetermined curriculum, a set way in which they want to go through that objective and just follow the trunk of the tree like it's a road. They just keep going straight up without much diversion or tangents into different areas. I think the closer you stick to the trunk, the less personal it is and the less you get from that exploration piece, which is vitally important.

Where a lot of this starts, I find, and a real separator among teachers of sport is the whole idea of dumbing it down. It's an over-the-top concern that we need to simplify to the lowest capacity of our weakest player—that that's the level of sophistication we want to operate in because then everyone can be included. To me, that's so restricting and the polar opposite of the things I value, like pushing those limits and encouraging people to push their level of understanding. That's how I get better. Those are the type of things that challenge me. So I find it difficult to just operate at that lowest common denominator without a challenging interest. What bothers me about it the most is the whole idea of dumbing it down. It infers that's also where you're going to stay, that you're just endeavoring to stay in that space. It's an acceptance that this is the level you're going to work at, and then you try to find ways to optimize that level. Again, that's very counterintuitive to the way my mind works. My motivation is I'm going to start in the bottom roots of the tree working into the trunk, but once I'm in the trunk, I'm searching to find the first branch and run it right to the edge of what that might be before coming back to the heart of the trunk and looking right away for the next branch. That's how my mind works. I can appreciate that, particularly in a team sport like hockey, it's important to get everyone "on the same page." But there are ways to do that and still challenge a group intellectually.

Most maddening is when we also make assumptions about someone's capacity without first trying to stretch it in a focused way. Is that assumption based on something the player said or did or the way in which he or she moves through patterns or their drills? Or do we just assume the player just doesn't have the mental capacity to push that much farther and stop trying? My attitude, of course, is the complete opposite. If I see a restriction right away, that becomes my mission, my focus. I want to influence that positively. I'm always looking to stretch, build something, and then see how players react, and then try to add something else and see how they react to that, and then away we go.

Maybe you start to build some development equity with players. Maybe their restriction is just an anxiety. Maybe they're challenged in one or a multitude of the background knowledge areas, which creates hesitation. If I just fill in those gaps or start to create a little more fluidity in their knowledge and a little more structure, that could open their capacity to get a better understanding of what they need to do. And if I can educate, then it might foster questions, and then those questions create a deeper level of learning. Now we've got a connection we can really work off of.

It could be depth of skill. They just don't have the skill or the exposure to the skill, so that creates another restriction. People tend to be projected at the weakest skill set they operate at. They're just using their best skills, so they find their way of doing things and just stick to that, which can be restricting as you move up a level. It just might not be good enough. The depth of skill creates a restriction, which also discourages someone from developing the capacity to stretch too far in the competitive aspects of the game.

You also have all the perception of speed challenges. As you jump up a level, the speed gets faster. The player's perception of speed is also a factor in his ability to process. We assume he's not overly bright, but it could be just a processing speed factor. If I positively influence his ability to process, I can calm his mind down and create capacity for further learning or further expression of being able to understand things more tactically. The game can slow down for him so he can make better decisions.

There's also the element of awareness. Sometimes players don't know what they don't know. If you spend some time trying to probe into what they know or see the sophistication of the patterns they use, you can see what their level of awareness is. You can then bubble some things up to the surface and start working on them.

My point in all this is to say we're still making these assumptions without trying to stretch. If you can make a teaching connection and figure out where the restrictions are and start poking away at that, you just never know where it's going to go. In my opinion, you will uncover a lot more than you originally bargained for. If you can satisfy the speed perception and the depth of skill stuff, then you can really create a capacity for this player to start pushing forward and becoming much better than originally assumed.

You've got to take a look at your approach. It's about understanding what the issues are and then developing an approach. Is it a perception of skill? Is it a learning capacity? Is it their athleticism? Are they just at a level where it's difficult to make these changes on the fly and they have a lot of anxiety when they play? Then you go at it from the skill continuum. It's very granular how you start. You take a look at where the skill gap is in the continuum as it relates to processing in a game patterning issue. They don't see it before it happens. They can't anticipate it. They don't use any pre-check to collect information before the play occurs. They're very reactive, which is what creates the restriction. I just want to get the player to play with a little more forethought. Well, how I do that? They have to be able to anticipate patterns before they're going to happen. They've got to be able to see the cues. If I can teach the cues, and I can teach them how to use a pre-check to collect that information, they can predict where the patterns are, especially the most frequently recurring ones. If I can do that, I'm going to impact this positively in a very short period of time. As for the ancillary skills that go with it, maybe there are some restrictions in those skills. We can build some support structures and start really making some progress here. The more ways we approach the exposure to the skill restrictions, the easier it is for them to add it in. If we can connect the mind to what it is we're doing, then we've really got something going.

Creating the tactical application to skill is the crux of the issue in our effort to dumb things down. We are going to self-perpetuate our hypothesis by over-simplifying. We won't be making any progress on the limitation because of our effort to simplify. We are going to focus in much more isolation. We're not going to be combining the skill speeds. The tactical aspect of skill is one of the major aspects that gets restricted. They're not going to be able to make those connections unless we help them make those connections. By simplifying, we're actually just self-fulfilling the prophecy we had that the player's just not smart. When, in fact, we have made that assumption without any real effort to stretch that player. Because we have made that assumption, we're stuck in isolation, without the benefit of the skill speeds which can fast-forward this sort of development. When someone says they're trying to simplify it or dumb it down, the hair on the back of my neck stands up, because I know what that really means and how that manifests itself in the interaction between the teacher and the player. I see this is just going to be an abyss where the instructor is going to be constantly saying, *See, I told you; see, we tried this and he killed the drill, then we moved to this drill and killed that one, now we get on the ice and he can't see what's going on, this guy just is dumb.* I just don't buy it; my experience tells me otherwise.

My experience in trying to work in some of these areas tells me there is a lot to be gained if we come at it from a different approach. I got invited to work with the Canadian National Olympic Team a couple Olympic cycles ago. I was just going to run a couple of ice times they needed someone to cover. Going into it, my impression was when you work with female players they can be very literal. If you tell them, "I need you to go stand there," they'd just go and stand there. They're not going to take liberties. When I got there and started messing around with it, I chose not to go simple. I actually chose to go ultra-complicated. I tried to do things that were much more about stretching—things I know they had little to no experience with. I was talking about speed behind the puck and utilizing the weak side with speed, making the person the furthest away from the puck the most dangerous player. It was very ambitious. I just didn't know how much exposure I would have to this group and wanted to take advantage of a rare opportunity to have free rein to do what I wanted.

When I got started with this group, I was amazed at their capacity. Once I started to go down this path and open things up, they had a lot of questions. Once they started to understand it better, they started to be able to execute. The execution was not like A to B to C. There are lots of different ways you can express this particular skill pattern. We're not simplifying this. You're going to have to make decisions and those decisions will impact the movement decisions of all the other people.

It was a fascinating process to go through, because I went in with an assumption I wasn't going to change how they thought. I thought they would be very literal, that they weren't going to stretch too far outside of what I told them to do. It was the worst assumption I've ever really made. I came out of the first day just in complete shock that I did not understand this at all, and I was so far from the truth. I was so intrigued. My respect for these women just went right through the roof. They had so much capacity, and I'm talking all of them.

They got going and worked in a lot of the questions. I wasn't half the instructor then I am today, and it was still very much a science project. *Let's try this; okay, they did that pretty well, so let's move to the next piece; okay, let's see how they take to that.* I was really impressed. Even though they were long-time national team players, they were like, *Wow, we've never done anything like this,*

this is interesting. I think they were more intrigued by it. For me, it was just a great opportunity to figure that out. Ever since then, I've been a lot less judgmental about the capacity of the players I work with. I do not allow any outside noise to influence my attitude toward them until I've worked with them myself. Because until I get working with them and we start going through the depth of knowledge, background knowledge, depth of skill, awareness, and we start working through the creativity and start extending ourselves through the branches of this tree, I really don't know.

I try not to make any assumptions without first trying to stretch. I can see where the holes are much more clearly. It allows me to just go in and attack those holes, fill them in like we do with the skill continuum, then we're on to the next. You engage the mind and the players start to really understand what's really going on. You can then start to create a bit more interaction among them. I saw the national team players talking to each other afterward. They were really engaged. It was it was one of the best experiences I've had in my career, where I went into it with a set of assumptions and left with my mind just completely blown.

When we start talking about dumbing it down and simplifying, the approach I encourage is to do the exact opposite. There's so much more to gain. Now, to be clear, you're not just going the exact opposite just to be contrary. You have to have a development plan in place and a method that allows you to travel down some tree branches. If you don't, then that's foolish and will only get you frustrated and perpetuate your previous assumption, and we don't want that. We're trying to break those assumptions. If you put your mind to it and come at it in a reasonable way with a method of how you're going do it, you'll be shocked and really happy.

One of the other aspects of this is just the order in which you do things. I spoke about this in the feedback component. We need to have things work in a certain sequence. If you follow the right sequence, then you can make gains quickly. You can target one thing and have it affect two or three other things. One of the tricks I uncovered years ago was I try to start my development process on the weak side of the athlete. If it's a footwork situation, I try to understand which their dominant leg is and start there. If it's the right foot, we start with the left foot or the left side, the backhand side, whatever it is I know just by watching is their weaker side. The reason I start on the weak side is there is an acceptance of the process for the player. Players know their weak side, they feel it. So they're more accepting of failure, because they already know their predisposition toward their weak side and that it's not as good. There's an acknowledgement that this is going to be a process. They have much more of a correction detail and I can heighten the focus of the correction on that side because it's most needed. I can also have more reps over there. The other thing that invariably happens is it takes a little bit longer to get going. I'm willing to take that time, because I want the extra reps on that side anyway. When the whole thing is done, the rep count is usually at least a third more on that weak side because it takes a little longer to get it done. When we flip over to the good side, the body has a greater ability to take the corrections you've done on one side and transfer it to the other side. By leveraging the weak side, I get more reps on that side, which I need anyway. I have heightened or more engaged athletes, because they know this side is not one that's normally very friendly to them in terms of skill acquisition and when I flip it to the strong side they just fall into it much faster. That also creates a feeling of developmental equity. They feel like they've achieved something.

Now, if I started on the strong side, built it up and it took less time to get it started, and then we went to the weak side and went right to the bottom because it's much harder, we don't get as much carryover because we still have all of that anxiety that goes with being on the weak side. The feeling of just not being as solid, the feeling of not having that stability on that side, it's much harder to build. They went from getting it fairly quickly to taking a long time to just get it psychologically. It's just a less ideal place to be. Almost every time, nine times out of ten, I'm starting on the weak side because I just feel like it's the best approach to development mentally and relationship-wise between me and the athlete. I'm trying to build that trust with them.

I used to miss this next piece because I was too anxious to get to the next part. I would start on the weak side, build it up, we'd finally get it where we want it on that side, a functional knowledge, and then we'd flip over to the strong side. On the strong side, they really pick it up quickly. All the correction pieces just fall in place on the other side, and they get a good high-level proficiency. Now I'm done. Well, no; I'm not done, because now what I want to do is leverage their excitement toward it. They're feeling good, and I flip it back to the weak side. What happens when I flip back to the weak side? They carry that positivity, that feeling of accomplishment into the weak side, and it starts to feel more natural. You never really get total balance between one side or the other, but they have much more of a positive feeling about both sides. I don't do it very long, just a few reps to kind of check it over to see where that's at again. They feel a lot better in their mind and feel a greater level of capacity between both sides.

That's a major part of my teaching process. It's always starting on the weak side. I still think the order of the skills and your development is important. If it is something the player is struggling with, the order by which you structure your feedback, the order in which you're teaching is so important. If it's a skating piece, then we want to start from the head and move toward the feet. If it's something with the puck skills, we want to start with the feet and work our way up.

It's really important we acknowledge where it starts. If we're working on skating, it starts with the head and the eyes and then the shoulders, the T spine, the hips, the knees, the ankle. These are the major points of emphasis we need to influence. If we notice they're really struggling with the upper body turn and we identify the T spine has restrictions, then of course we work on the head, eyes, and shoulders to influence that, and then get that to create a whip effect with the hips or leverage the impact of what we're doing inside that twist so they can feel they're creating some automation in the lower body. Now we have something.

It's the same with the puck skills. Maybe they have a lack of range. So the right range can be influenced by weight shift and by putting themselves in a better posture. So you don't have to really work on their hands or having a sliding bottom hand to start, which is kind of difficult depending on the type on the player. We can get more range through weight shifts. So instead of banging our head against the wall with the sliding bottom hand, we start with the weight shift range. If they feel a greater sense of the range through the lower body, then we start adding the upper-body elements into it and then really getting into the hands, but that's much later even though we know it's a hands thing. We don't like how much grip they have on the bottom hand, it creates too many restrictions, and so this is what we focus on.

Being able to identify the order you should be teaching is a great way to help when you're trying not to simplify. You're trying to actually engage in and make things a little more complicated to see where it nets out. I would encourage every instructor to find situations where they have a bias or an assumption about the player's capacity going into it and come up with a process that makes sense logistically and from an order perspective. You're going to work through a continuum. You want to tackle this, and not just haphazardly. You're going to give this a good chance and stretch them well beyond what you originally thought and see what happens. If it's anything like my experience, then you'll see there are players who will react in such a favorable way that it'll make you want to do it more and more. That's what we need. We want to find the players are more capable than our assumptions are allowing them to be.

I'm always the greatest source of restriction for the athlete. It's not the athlete. As long as I believe that, it will allow me to take these type of risks with my athletes. Because if I think I'm the problem, then I'm going to try to do my best to get out of the way of their learning and I'm going to be much more supportive, engaged, and come up with a better process. It just challenges me to be better. If I get to become better and put them in a spot where they have a chance to get better, they're going to see that by the variance of my approach. They're going to see it by the type of content I'm providing to them, and that's going to create an excitement for them. Enthusiasm often makes the difference. I can influence that enthusiasm by not treating them like the lowest common denominator with our approach. I'm going to believe in them. I'm going to believe in myself. I have the right process. If I don't have the right process, I need to adjust that process to really dial it in and give them every opportunity to expand their mind. In doing that, I expand my own, too.

17
PRACTICE DESIGN

I WANT TO DIG INTO UNDERSTANDING HOW TO GET THE MOST out of the training sessions. I had quite a few questions that needed to be answered when I started designing practices. The first question I had was who is the focus on? I have a group of 20 players, and I need to know who I'm teaching to. Can you teach to the entire group? If you can't, then how do you decide who to teach to? You certainly can't teach to everybody at the same time. Everyone has different needs. Do I teach to the top? Do I teach to the bottom? Do I teach to the middle?

Another question I had to answer is what am I actually teaching? What's the content? What should I be teaching, and how should I be teaching it? What's the methodology? What are the important aspects of a solid training session? How do I deliver my message? What are the communication pieces? How do I engage the listener?

The last question I had took quite a while for me to really understand, and that is which is more important, me and my teaching ability or the vehicle I use to deliver the message, in terms of the drill? How important is having the right drill in my teaching?

If it's really important, then where do I get these drills from? How do I connect them into what I'm really trying to do?

It took many, many years for me to answer these questions because I couldn't find these answers in any of the books I read. I basically had to start with a single question and try to answer that question the best way I could.

The other problem I had was everyone was doing similar things in the same way. That made it difficult. There really weren't a lot of differentiating components. It was difficult to assess who was more effective and why. My best learning strategy became trial and error. I had to try a bunch of different things and throw some stuff against the wall and see what stuck. But a lot of it was also teaching myself to be more self-aware and using video, too, to help understand more about what was going on.

So the first question, who am I teaching to, didn't take as long to figure out because it was crystal-clear who everyone else was teaching to. Everywhere I went or everyone I talked to, they were all talking about the bottom of their group and how important it was to them to have the weakest part of their group become stronger. They felt they were only as strong as their weakest player. They could only progress at the rate of the people who represented the bottom. It made no sense to them to get too advanced if the bottom couldn't do it.

My luxury in all of this was I was in private business, so I could do whatever I wanted. My only real consideration was I needed the clients to want to come back. I had to be careful that I was teaching the right part of the group and the people felt fulfilled enough in what it was I was doing. I needed them to want to come back the next time, so I could sustain my business. But at the same time, I want to be different in the sense I was able to produce results at a better rate than what they could currently get elsewhere. If everyone was teaching toward the bottom of the group and could only progress at the rate at which they were improving the bottom, then naturally, I have to focus at the top. For me, it was real simple. That was one of the first opposite things I did. I just found the answer in the opposite of what everybody else was doing.

I was lucky because when I first really got going, the player I spent the most time with was Nathan Horton, and he was clearly the top player at his age group. He was the best player, the best athlete. Everyone wanted to skate with him. My whole goal initially was let's just make Nathan Horton intrigued by development. Let's make him want to come back for whatever reason, and everyone will want to skate with him—because who the hell is Darryl Belfry and why would anyone want to skate with that guy? There really wasn't a reason for anyone to want to skate with me, so I needed to have a reason. Nathan was the best one. Basically everything just became about him. I went into every ice session striving to improve his ability in some way or at least intrigue him in a way where he would be challenged and would want to come back. I really didn't give a second thought to anyone who was at the bottom. My attitude was very much, we're going to teach him, we're going to make sure he gets better, and then we're going to hope that whether it be by osmosis or just by the general environment we're going to drag everyone else along and see how that goes. It was fascinating, because the more intrigued he became, the more engaged the other top players also became. They were really challenged and they wanted to continue to come back. The kids who represented the middle of the group actually did make a tremendous improvement, even though the focus wasn't on them specifically. That's how I started. I just started with the player with the greatest learning capacity. Nathan was my focus.

Once I started getting more groups without Nathan present, I would try to do the same thing. I would look for whoever the best player was and I would focus on that player and evaluate what I could do to make him better. I would have a drill I felt would challenge that player, and what I found unexpectedly was, unlike Nathan, this player wasn't the best at everything. He was the best overall player, but as we went to different skills, there were other kids who were better. I had hypothesized this one player was going to be the best because initially he appeared to have the most capacity. But when we went into a specific skill set, he wasn't actually the best player. Another person who might have been in the middle of the pack was actually the best at that particular skill. Then we moved to the next skill set, I would realize, *Oh, well, it's not that guy either. It's another guy who's actually better.* What was very interesting to me was when I got into these groups where it wasn't clear who was actually going to be the best person, it became this moving target throughout the group. It became interesting to see who the best player was at whatever we were doing. I could run my pacing of the development through whoever that moving target was. When I was with Nathan, he was largely the best player at everything, but when I went into other groups, it was very much a moving target depending on the skill set.

Once I started a sequence and knew what it was we were trying to teach, I began to focus on what that player needed, and then I'd see another player emerge. I would pivot and start pushing that next player, which would then drive the pacing of the group. I was always just trying to get the pacing to whoever had the most capacity for that particular skill set at that time and push that player. That became a fascinating experiment for me, and I still use it to this day as a major part of my approach.

What's interesting when you do it this way is there is very much a *lead, follow, or get out of the way* type of attitude on the ice. We talk about having accountability a lot with our players. We want everyone to be accountable to their own development. We want to have a great work ethic. When I would watch development sessions or team ice times, I would watch the best players very intently to see their approach, and a lot of them were genuinely bored because development was targeted for someone who was way below their capacity. They were clearly capable of pushing the envelope further. They were doing things that were very mundane and had no real development value for them. They were not going to be stretched in this ice time. The stretching was occurring way lower in the lineup, so they were bored. One of the things I really strived to do was make sure they weren't bored. If I was challenging the best players, it just had a way of driving engagement throughout the entire group. Some kids were kicked into the deep end of the pool and fighting just to stay above the surface. Other kids were refining a skill or adding pieces.

Everybody was engaged, and I found that to be really interesting because at that time I was also trying to drive the group's emotion myself. Not only was I challenging the top of the group, but I was really demanding performance. I was so animated. I had full engagement not only because I was barking at them, but also because I was challenging every player. The realization that came next was when I was challenging every player, I didn't need to bark at them. That took a long time for me to realize. I genuinely thought I was the driving force, then I started to realize later on I really wasn't. I didn't have to be the emotional pulse of the group. I could transfer the emotional pulse to the group to the fact that everyone was accountable to the development. They were all being challenged. The teaching or the learning process could drive the emotion of the group. When I stopped acting like I was the emotional pulse, I started to show support where it was most warranted. So players who were standing out because they were ultra-engaged, asking questions, you could tell they were really close to acquiring a skill. I would zero in on those kids and I would try to push them over the top. The content was first driven by whoever was the best player, but my focus inside of the teaching component of that drill was then focused on the kids who were emerging and you could see the momentum starting to build. Those were the kids I would focus on to make sure they got it. It was interesting because I could really reach a lot of kids personally that way, where initially I just focused on one. Everything was just driven through that one player, to the exclusion literally of everyone else. I realized I could have the content make its way through the group and could support different kids as they would earn my attention by their focus and by just how hard they were pushing to acquire the skill.

One of the other skills I learned was I could level the playing field with new content. Early on, I focused on teaching a skill I knew someone would be good at. As I got better as an instructor and skill analyst, I realized I could present a skill that no one's seen before, and the entire group would be learning. We don't know who the best player is going to be. Let's present it, start the development process with it, and see who emerges. I found that to be a fascinating process because when you level the playing field you just don't know what's going to happen. It's really cool to see. Sometimes you would hypothesize *this kid's going to get this quickly,* and then he doesn't. Another kid picks it up quicker, and you would not have expected that. I love the whole idea of leveling the playing field because when you don't know who's going to emerge, it challenges the whole group to really be focused on the task. It's like a race to see who can learn it the quickest. Some kids have more advantages to learn it because they have background knowledge on this skill set. They have way more depth of skill, the ancillary skills that surround this particular skill, and more capacity, so that gives them a leg up in being able to acquire the skill faster. But when they all start, they are even in terms of their exposure to the skill set. They don't understand where it would be used in a game. They don't know how to how to execute the nuances of the movement. That all creates a little bit of anxiety for everyone. They're now trying to learn.

What was interesting was we had a large number of kids who were top players who really struggled when we leveled the playing field. When there wasn't someone who was emerging as the person to follow or the person to chase or if they weren't the best player, they just shut down. I had no real frame of reference for that. Once I started to learn how to level the playing field with providing this new content, I would be really disappointed in some of the kids because I wanted them to dig in and really try to learn the skill. If it was something that didn't come easily to them, they didn't want to do it. Their reaction to failure was just so poor. Their mindset was, *This is going to be over in 10 minutes, so I'm just going to fake it and once it's over hopefully we'll go on to something I'm good at.* That was the feeling I got about these players' attitude. Of course, that didn't sit well with me, and that's what inspired me to try to make failure cool. I really wanted to dig into leveling the playing field. I wanted that to be a major part of what I was doing. I was always presenting new skills to these players that they had never seen before. They were hybrids of different skills that made it look like they were new when really they were two skills combined in a different way. They would know both of the skills individually, but they just didn't know them once I shouldered the skill or combined them. That's when I came up with a motivational tactic which was basically to present something new and skate by the best player and jokingly say, "Man, you really suck at this." It was a way to draw the line in the sand as a challenge. Like, *You're not really good at this, wow, I'm surprised.* It was also meant to humble the group—none of you are any good at this, let's see who's going to dig in and get better. I found that that helped a ton.

We had this mantra for years. We still do it sometimes where I come across a situation where it can have real value. It was interesting at first to see how some kids would take to it. Some kids don't know me and have never really been on the ice with me before, and I present something, no one's really good at it, no one's really picking up, and I'm like, *You guys are awful, I know you're supposed to be the best player in your team but you've got a long way to go.* It became a running joke or a badge of honor as they moved through. I would say things like, *There's really good, there's good, there's bad, there's awful, and then there's you.* The situation was, *This is where you are, I'm pretty sure you've never been here before, but today you are here and you've got to move through all these stages to be good, so good luck.* Again, it's all about delivery. I tried to have the delivery of "you suck" have an endearing quality, where it was something that was fun for them. I used it in every ice session for the longest time, and now I sprinkle it in when I think it's appropriate. The relationship building is just awesome to see as you help this player move through the stages and see him finally get the capacity to really express the skill properly. Now you're able to say, *Wow, you are awesome, I didn't believe you were going to get this today and look at you, what a great job.* All those ways you can connect with a player, the little things you can say that really push it over the top, can make such a big difference. I love that.

The next question I had was what am I going to teach and how am I going to teach it? I was really interested in doing things that were different or coming up with skill sets that were distinct from what anybody else was doing. So that was easy. I was trying to learn what to teach from the games. I was watching the players in my research and analysis, and that's really where I was getting the content.

Then, I asked myself, how do I teach this? I need to build my own drills. That became clear because obviously there weren't drills out there for the skills I wanted to teach. I had to figure out how to build drills, which I'll get into in the next section. But this was a really interesting process, as well. There were really six elements to the idea of practice theming, which became my way in which I wanted to do things. As for how it was born, there was a standard practice format that most everyone I would watch would follow. The initial drill was a standard warm-up drill that had no relationship to what they were going to do with the second drill. So whatever skills they were focused on, there really wasn't any carryover into the next drill. Then they would go to the third drill, which had no relationship by game situation, skill expression, or really anything to the previous two. The coach would do eight drills and not one of them had any relationship to the other. Yet every coach would talk about reps. You need to have high reps and you need to give the kids many opportunities.

The real focus was actually the per drill work-to-rest ratio. The premise was to get these kids moving and to get them hopping and popping so you could maximize the number of reps they could get in a given drill. I became this pseudo expert at work-to-rest ratio. I would look at every drill or teaching exercise I was trying to do and find different ways to challenge myself to improve the work-to-rest ratio. If I had 20 kids on the ice, I would put them in four corners. I would send the whole line to do a specific skill sequence at once, so now I could have the work-to-rest ratio, at worst, 1:4. But I thought, *Okay, wait a minute, I can do better here.* I could do opposite sides at the same time. Now I'm basically 1:1. I would start off with each corner doing it one at a time. Then I would do opposite corners to improve the work-to-rest ratio and maximize the reps. I did that for years. I really tried to manage and always be conscious of work-to-rest ratio.

What I didn't realize, and started to figure out once we were inside the practice, was the players were not really executing what I wanted at a high enough rate inside the eight minutes I had allotted for that particular drill. They didn't get it in time, so I needed more reps on that in another drill. I would come up with a variation of the original drill I was doing to make it look like the second drill was a different drill. Maybe I would do it from a different format. So

I'd start four corners and then I'd move it to four blue line stripes, so the pattern was basically the same, they were doing exactly the same thing, but it looked like a different drill because I just moved the line to a different spot. I was trying to trick the kids all the time and hide the reps. They didn't realize they were doing the same thing over and over again, but they were, because I needed more time. Then I started to think, *Wait a minute, sometimes this skill goes to three drills, and it's still really not solid.* So first I had to evaluate my teaching approach and make sure I'd given them every opportunity to learn or that my teaching process was fair for them to acquire the skill. I also needed to find ways to have the key things run as an undercurrent throughout the entire practice. Let's say it's a retrieval situation for the defense and I'm interested in the pivot. I don't want a crossover pivot, I want more like an open pivot, what most would call a mohawk pivot. Maybe I don't like the way the players use their stick inside of it, so that's what I'm trying to influence. Rather than do one drill on that, I would have that as a part of every drill we would do the whole practice. One of the things I started do is whatever it was I wanted to do next, I would just include that particular part of the skill at the beginning of the drill execution. So, this drill is going to start with a retrieval and then you're going to do this, this, and this, and this is how the drill changes, or it's going to end with it. This is the new drill, you're going to do all of that first, and then at the end you're going to do that retrieval, so we get another rep in at the very end of it. I would use a lot of those as continuations when they would start the next play. It became more continuous. I use my undercurrent reps, which is what I call that, the entire practice. I use that to be the bridge to the next rep to start the next drill sequence.

That became a really cool way for me to have unique drill designs because I could manipulate the drills in a distinct way. No one was really doing that stuff at that time, and it allowed me to have the highest rep value. This is really where I separated myself very early on in my career. Let's say the first drill is an eight-minute drill on retrieval techniques. A player could come on the ice with me, could do that retrieval maybe 10 times, now I move to the next drill, he does it another 10 times. He uses that skill 10 times in every drill for the practice, so if I run 10 drills, he is getting 100 reps. I'm getting 10 times the rep count of this particular skill than anyone else who's teaching because they're not linking the drills or skills with an undercurrent, so if all things are equal, my kids are going to learn 10 times faster than everyone else. That's what helped me get a lot further ahead as it related to practice-to-game transfer, because I had high rep numbers. I could get the rep numbers wherever I wanted depending on what I was focusing on. That was a huge separator for me, because everyone was talking about reps, but they were going at it from an eight-minute perspective and trying to maximize the reps to the exclusion of teaching and correction. They only budgeted eight minutes for the drill, so there is no time for correction. I felt like I could take my time teaching the drill now. I didn't need to be in an all-out sprint to try to get this done because I had 100 reps to work with. I didn't need to fix everything at one time. I wasn't confined by any time constraints, because I knew I had 100 reps with this for this kid. I can take my time and build it properly. I can add the corrections in and pace it much easier. That was a major part of my development early on.

Another aspect of practice design is skill peaks. Using skill peaks is a great opportunity to really get into what we call drill runs. Let's say I wanted to work on breakout skills. Instead of doing one breakout drill for 12 minutes, I would do three five-minute drills. I would spend 15 minutes on it, but I would have three different drills that were contributing to what I was doing or building the skill in some way. I could also set up what I called pacing, which is essentially trying to build toward a peak. In knowing I was going to do a three-, four-, or five-drill run on a given topic, I could really explore all the different types of skills inside that topic. I knew I had more time, so I could add a lot of variability to how the players were expressing the skills and the way things were being added. For example, you're going to go first. You're going to carry the puck. The second time, you're going to catch a pass. The third time, you're going to carry the puck, move it, so you give a puck, then you're going to get a puck back. Then you acquire it off the pass, then you carry it, then you give it, then you get it back. Then you make a play or generate a shot. Then you retrieve it. Then you make another play. Now you've executed the skill maybe three or four times with all different types of acquisitions at different speeds at different rates at different pass angles. All the exposure to the skill and the variability of the exposure to the skill was so high. So that's another real trick to learning, is you want to have the player exposed to the skill at a multitude of different ways. Skill variable coding was part of the building process.

Then I needed to create stress. I could create stress by pacing with speed, mental stress of space, or both. Then I could create competition, which helped create a game situation in which this skill was going to be expressed and you were now also being defended. Now you've got to express the skill inside of a physical space being closed, speed being changed, and there's a possibility you're going to get knocked over, so there's a competitive element to it. That helped create skill peaks, which I was basically able to build to game speed or game conditions.

The next part of the design strategy was hidden recall. As I was doing my skill peaks, I realized I was adding so many pieces and layers to this particular skill in an effort to change the look of it or to add variability so the players didn't get bored and didn't catch on they were doing the same skill for an entire hour. I wanted to hide it. I would build the skill to a certain competency level and then I would have the drill situation hide the core piece, so they wouldn't know where that skill was going to be. They had to find it. They had to manifest it and or they had to catch the timing just right because they had this skill and this skill, and then the core skill was in the middle. Then they had two more skills, so it's a five-skill sequence. The skill I'm really targeting is hidden in the middle. Now you can't mentally be focused on all of them, so because you're distracted, it gives me a better evaluation tool to see how far along this skill is. Did you just regress to your habits? Is the new habit holding even though you're not focused on it? It gave me a great evaluation tool. I use hidden recall a lot to evaluate how well I'm doing in the teaching process.

Once hidden recall starts, now we're looking for forced recall, which is a fantastic tool. It's basically a challenge to manufacture the skill application inside of a drill. This is where I think we missed the boat in our small games. This is why I've gone to great lengths to really study small games and look for opportunities to have much more of an impact than just having a game and letting the game be the teacher. That's not for me. I like the player to be challenged to have to find a way to manufacture this skill situation inside of a game. The game is, of course, free-flowing. It has varying degrees of speed, pressures, time, support. Now you have to take this one thing I've been teaching you and you've got to find a way to put it into the game. Don't just play, transfer.

For example, let's say it's shooting off the pass. We've been focusing the whole practice on all the techniques related to shooting off the pass, all the footwork, all the pass receptions, all the different timing, all the different routes you can use, all the different ways in which you would separate yourself from the from the puck support or the defensive pressure, all the little push-offs, all the little body positions. Then we would talk about offensive seam and weak side availability and timing, occupying the space you want to shoot from, all the things that really matter as it relates to shooting off the pass.

We've been building this thing up. Now we get to a point where we need to put it in a game. In setting up the game, I create a rule that you can only shoot the puck off the pass. Now you've got to find a way inside of a game to put yourself in these positions to acquire the puck off the pass. Are you still finding those habits and looking for those things, or are you just standing in a spot waiting? What is it you're doing in this way that's going to either confirm for me or give me pause that you've acquired the skill? That's forced recall. I'm forcing you to recall the skill in the context of a game and you have to manufacture it.

This is a game-changer, and this is how I believe small-area games are best used. It's when you've gone through a teaching sequence on something and then you set up a small-area or a modified game in which you challenge the players to use those skills and manufacture them under game conditions. That, to me, is the best utilization of a game rather than just doing a small-area game because we've gotten to the end of the practice, it makes sense, and it will be fun for the kids so you just let them go. You're not doing anything to influence the achievement gap. To influence the achievement gap, you have to level the playing field by challenging the players to manufacture moments and see if they can dictate the terms of the game

Once I got through that, I realized there's an opportunity to stack the deck. The stacked deck element is another underutilized teaching tool I think is absolutely critical. It's used in some ways, but to me not to the degree in which its value would suggest you should use it, and that is when you're structuring your drills. When you get to a place in the drill set where you're trying to evaluate where the skill is, you create a competitive environment which favors one person. Let's say you've been working on stick handling and you're trying to go through the triangle of the defender and build this triangle development. You've worked on all the changes of speed. You've worked on the alignment. You've worked on the stick handling skills. You've worked on all the deceptions. You've worked on all the escape movements. The players have experimented with different skill combinations. Now you want to find out what level of competency they're really at. So you create some type of one-on-one drill while you stack the deck in favor of the puck carrier. You don't make it an even match. You make it so that the guy who is learning the skill has an advantage by putting the defensive player at a competitive disadvantage by starting him in a bad gap. Maybe you start the defender on his knees so he's in recovery, or create a speed disadvantage, or start at a bad angle. Whatever it may be, you put him in a spot where it's going to be easier for the offensive player to execute. As he gets better, you start to reduce the competitive advantage and make it fairer. Ultimately, it ends up at 50-50 and the guy who executes best wins. What you're doing is trying to build confidence in this skill, because the players aren't going to use it if they don't believe they're good at it. You've got to manipulate the success rate, and you can hide it in these stacked decks where they believe they're way better at it than they actually are. You're just trying to get them in game conditions to execute the skill and you just give them a little bump, a little bit more of an advantage.

You can do that through the drill design like I just described, or you can do it through strength of competition. For example, let's take a kid in the middle of the group who is a good player and acquiring the skill at a pretty good rate. You're starting to zero in on him because he stands out by how much progress he is making. So what you do is pick his opponent for him. At first, you pick a player who's weaker than he is. You put the weaker guy in a defensive posture, which is a competitive disadvantage, so now your player has every advantage to get better. You put him against that guy for two or three reps and you gradually reduce the advantage until he's winning even when the deck is stacked a little against him. You gradually slide the advantage scale for him with each rep. Then you switch the drill and bring in an opponent who's a better player. Once he has gone through the competitive sliding scale against that guy, then you challenge him against one of the best players on the ice. So he's gone through the stages of working through the strength of competition from someone he's better than to someone who's about his level to someone who is better than him. By the time you get to the third stage where he goes against someone who's better than him, he wins at a high rate and now he's thinking, *I didn't even think I could beat that guy.* Well, you stacked the deck in his favor, but he doesn't necessarily know that. You're essentially controlling the pace at which we're building confidence through a drill designed to give him an advantage and the strength of his opponent. The player starts to find success against better players because he has the confidence in the skill because you manipulated the scale. You helped him along stacking the deck, and that gives you a chance to really build kids and stretch kids. This process could play out over one session, a few weeks, or the entire season. It depends on the growth rate of the player's skill set and how much confidence the scale is providing him with each success.

You can also stretch players by putting them in situations where you're stacking the deck against them. Let's say you're one of the best players. I would put you in a competitive disadvantage in acquiring the skill. I would have the defensive pressure be right on you, an even match at best but more likely giving you a problem to solve right away. Maybe you have to start on your knees, or maybe your back's turned to the play and the pressure is going to be emerging so you've got to turn and then execute it. There are lots of ways to stack the deck against a player. Whatever it is, I'm going to make it so it's way harder for you. You now have to execute at a much higher level. You've got to be right on point. You've got to get the timing to get the spacing. That's stacking the deck against you to force you to employ different skills to solve the competitive problem.

The next design strategy, parallel structures, is a more recent one. I started doing this over the last maybe six or eight years. How a parallel structure works is I'd do, let's say, a five-drill run on a given topic and then once I've built it up, I've gone through all the stages of its acquisition and I'm satisfied with it, I'm going to stop that development at a point. I set it aside and leave it alone. Then I'm going to do another drill run to build up a second component. Then I'm going to weave them together at the end. So I build up one, build up the other, and then they come together whether they're meant to be paired or whether they're meant to be worked opposite, or sometimes you can do both in sequence.

For example, I could have a defenseman who's learning rush defense. This defenseman needs to care about his gap. He needs to care about his footwork, his backpedal patterning, being able to defend going forward, stick position alignment, timing, contact, puck separation, escapes, all that stuff. So he's focused on that, and I've got a five-drill run I'm focused on. At the same time, the forwards are working on rush offense where they're focused on changing speed, alignment, manipulating defensemen's feet, attacking through the triangle, delays, net drives, hesitations or any play that gives them a stutter-step type of thing, all the stick handling and deceptions that go with that, all the escapes, and I build that up for the forwards. I build them separately and then bring them together at the end and let the guy who learned the most win. Who acquired the skill the fastest? That's the guy who's going to win. I then start stacking the deck to create advantages and disadvantages on a rep-to-rep basis to challenge and provide opportunity for players to push it further.

The last strategy I've explored most recently is drill rules, where you control the drill just by having execution rules in place, but no set patterns. The players are free to create the play, but they need to weave in the drill rules. For example, I may have a line rush drill where I've provided the group with five entry and attack options. I then tell the group that they can't do the same one twice, so they have to pay attention to the reps before them so they don't duplicate. This concept could progress to where I provide them multiple drill rules. An example may be an offensive zone rep where they can organize the play any way they want, so long as they change sides twice and shoot off the pass from the seam. The way or part of the zone in which they change sides is completely up to them. How they create the shot and the passing angle they choose is completely up to them. They have to read off each other and manufacture the play, incorporating the rules into it. This type of drill design, especially when built into team concepts and games, is a way to leverage the hockey sense of the group.

When you look at these seven strategies, you can use them by working backward. I can understand what I want to teach. I can have two things I want to accomplish. I can then figure out how I'm going to stack the deck. I can figure out where I want to use the forced recall. I can look at how I'm going to sequence the skill, so I know where the hidden recall opportunities are going to be. I just have to figure out the skill peaks, how to set up the pacing and the variability and the mental stress. When I figure all that out, ultimately I'm really paying attention to the undercurrent reps, because the player is going to get 100 reps or more on this. So I want to make sure that's dialed in and my focus in terms of the teaching technique and holding him accountable is going to be on that particular skill set. That's a major part of what I love about what I do.

The next part, which is really important, is the communication piece. How am I going to deliver this message? How is this player going to learn what I am intending him to learn? How am I going to connect? How am I going to drive the message? How am I going to engage this learner? This the major part of my process. I'm trying to shift my role between me and the athlete, whether it's with a group or an individual. I'm trying to evolve it.

At first, I want to start off as basically the director. I tell you what to do and you do it. It's very much 100 percent the teacher is driving the situation. Then I try to move a little bit more to a collaborator role, which is more 50-50. I acknowledge I saw something with the player. I ask him about it, get some engagement and some feedback, and then try to incorporate his ideas into what we're doing. Then we start taking a look at their ideas and start running with those ideas more. Now I've become much more of a facilitator of what it is that they're trying to do. It's more 80 percent student-led. I'm there if they have comments about how it feels and questions about where they need to go next, or how they can make it better, or what other situations they can see it in. I just follow that path and facilitate by coming up with the drill, by coming up with the teaching techniques, by pairing it with whatever else. I create the environment to allow them to do what they need to do.

Ultimately, I'm trying to become the co-teacher, where I'm learning just as much from them as they are from me. That to me is the ultimate relationship between the athlete and the teacher. That's what we're aspiring to be. That's my objective with the communication. I want to move it through those stages. It's not to say once you become a co-teacher with a player you're always a co-teacher; your role changes with the competency of the player in all the different skills you are working on. So the relationship changes and it's new every time. It always starts with you as the director and then you move your way through, trying to get to the co-teacher environment. But once you switch skills sequences you're trying to build, you start back at the beginning. You don't just leverage the fact that you've been a co-teacher. You're just trying to keep reaching that goal with everything.

Then you have all the feel-based learning, which we've talked about quite a bit. All learning is brain learning, and we have to be conscious of triple coding. Triple coding is having the ability to communicate verbally and have the person understand it visually, whether it be demonstration or through video, and then ultimately, regardless of what it is you're doing, it has to be coded in an athletic expression. That's where it's got to get to. You always have to be conscious that it needs to go through triple coding and ultimately has to be converted to an athletic expression. They can't just understand it conceptually. If they can't express it athletically, that conceptual understanding isn't going to help them when they get on the ice.

I stopped using a coaching board, where you draw the drills, because I wanted that part of the triple coding be brought up to the surface. If you don't use a coaching board, you just start describing the drill verbally. As an example, I'd say "So, the next drill, everyone's going to start in the corner. The first player is going to come up to the blue line, you're going to turn toward the boards, so make sure you get the dot line when you come up to the boards, maybe throw a weight shift in. Now you want to turn toward the boards. Make sure you're protecting the puck. Now you're going to come off the boards, re-establish the dot line, you're going to make a dot-to-dot pass to the guy on the far side, and he's going to shoot. Now, when you're the guy on the far side, you can't just stand on the dot, you need to time it, so make sure you're surfing up near the top, then you find your way into the spot, but know the puck's going to get to the dot and then he's going to shoot it. Okay? Ready, go!" Of course, there are two or three kids in the group that know exactly what you're talking about because they can follow that. Then there are other kids who have no idea, because that's just not how they learn. But it is part of the coding process. They're starting to hear terms along the way. They may not know what's going on. That's not really the goal. The goal is not to let them know what's going on. The goal is to get them to hear the terms multiple times because that's going to be part of the coding process when we get to the cueing inside the physical part of the movement. The athletic expression is still going to need correction and code. You're going to be correcting it through verbal feedback. All you're doing is presenting terms, and some kids are going to understand it completely. Now, if you see a kid who has a confused look on his face, and you'll see a few of them, you skate over to him and tell him to just make sure he gets a dot line and turns to the boards. That's the most important thing. What's the dot line? All the dots are in a straight line down the boards. I'm not really saying go up the boards. I need you to get on the dot line. You start on the boards, but then you've got to get the dot line because I was going to give you the space to turn. *Okay, got it.*

One of the big things we have to remember is if the player doesn't understand and can't follow the drill I just described, that doesn't mean he's not smart. He is very smart. He just doesn't learn quickly that way. What you want to do is just highlight the terms you're using that are going to be part of the teaching techniques. So when you get into the cueing inside the skill, maybe this kid's all feel-based and doesn't really learn quickly by listening or watching, so it's all kinesthetic learning. He still has to be corrected, and he's still going to need to know these cues. That's why you want to do that verbally. Now, if you go to the coaching board and start drawing, and he doesn't learn that way, over time he's just going to tune you out. You can see these kids, they're not even looking at the board. You're not trying to embarrass them by saying they're not paying attention. But you can tell there's a kid who's not really cued in when you're talking, so as you're going to the corner you would skate beside him, and say, "If all you got out of that was the dot line, that's all that matters."

The next piece is the way you wanted him to turn. Do you want to use a hook turn? You want to use a slide turn? You want to use a regular turn? Do you want him to use a stop turn or a jab turn? Do you want him to use all different ones? That'll be part of the queuing process once he gets going. Then there are all the puck protection pieces. You know he's going to want to put the puck to the inside, where you want it to the outside. But you're not going to get him anywhere unless he's in the right pattern. So you've got to tell him as long as you get the dot line, that's great.

That's why I'm so adamant that as part of the learning process we have to recreate situations that allow us to use the natural geography of the ice—the dots, the circles, the hash marks, the lines—and the terminology—the dot line and the seams, the corners, the offensive blue line, the defensive blue line. When you use those elements, it allows you to improve the triple coding. But if I just put a bunch apparatuses around haphazardly and I have them go, I'm missing a huge queuing opportunity for transfer. That's not to say you can't use apparatuses, but you've got to pick these things up and start using them in some other way. You have to start using the geography of the ice, so you can have that become part of the coding process. Because if you don't, I'm going to win. I'm going to be able to transfer this player much further, much faster through the development process than you can because I'm able to do the things that allow him to create the connections to the game situations. He can use it at a way faster rate, which means he's going to be able to use it tomorrow if he skates with me because I'm going to take him through that process. That's so important. That's why triple coding and feel-based learning are so important.

The second-to-last part here is to try to hold the struggle. Once I get the player in a struggle, I want to keep him there as long as possible. The way I do this is I will force the athlete to chase me around for a correction. I'll get him started in the correct order in the development process, I'll make a couple corrections, and then I'm going to leave him alone. The reason is because I want him to have more self-discovery as part of the learning process. I don't want to be standing on top of him all the time and have him rely upon me to make all the corrections. I do want him to feel things and make corrections based on what he's feeling, have that self-expression, and then come over to me to confirm his corrections are correct. That's the relationship I'm after. A good player is going to stop doing what he's doing, come over, and say, "Hey, can you come see what I'm doing here and let me know if I'm on the right track?" Now I've got an engaged student. I've got a kid who's ready to pop because he's so mentally engaged in what he's doing. He's working on self-discovery and having the balance between instruction and self-discovery occur inside the development process.

That is such a critical component. We don't do that enough. We either overcoach them or undercoach them. We say the game is taught by playing a game, put them out there three-on-three, drop the puck, let them go. Well, a high percentage of players are not going to get any better by that because you're perpetuating the achievement gap. What I want to player to do is have some self-discovery and then some instruction and then self-discovery and then instruction. It's a balance of going back and forth and having that become a critical component, because it's going to raise questions. The player's going to be much more actively engaged in his development. We get this really positive exchange and relationship between the student and the teacher. The teacher is not overcoaching, because at the end of the day we're trying to become co-teachers. I want to learn from him as much as he learned from me, and that requires an exchange of ideas. The player has to be comfortable talking to you to be able to get this dynamic, and so getting him in the struggle forces him to come see you to ask if he's on the right track. "Hey, can you watch me?" is my favorite thing that comes from the player. That tells me that he's really engaged. So holding players in that struggle is really important because it allows self-discovery.

Then there's the language factor. How am I focusing on the language? How am I using the cues? What types of words am I using? How am I creating the language? How am I expressing success to that player? Am I putting a glass ceiling on top of this thing? Am I making it so that however good it is, it can always be better? I need to be mindful of my verbal cues, making sure I'm not putting artificial or unintended ceilings on development by overexpressing my enthusiasm over a breakthrough. A drill ends and I say, "Okay, that's great, it's perfect, so that's done." Meanwhile, there are 10 more levels we could get to, and I've put a ceiling on it.

The last question I had was what's more important, my working of the drill or the drill itself? Can I just get the perfect drill and not have to worry about it? Can the drill alone teach the player, or how important am I? This varies. I do think there are drills that lend themselves better to the acquisition of skill, but players still need you. They still need feedback. You need to vary the feedback, but you need to let them problem-solve. We want that self-discovery, but we need the player to learn and you have to be teaching and working the drill. I think that's a really important piece. There are really no magic drills.

The way I come up with my drills is I have a game situation I'm interested in influencing or a skill that can be used in multiple game situations, and I just pick one to start with. I work my way backward to the lowest level of skill expression to the highest level of detail. That's the thing I'm focused on inside that expression. Then I build it up. Look at the whole, break it down into its parts, and then look to rebuild it to end up whole again. That's my exclusive approach to building drills. I don't have any drills I write down. I don't have any magic drills that teach this or that. I always look at it like a fluid situation that's going to change by the way the player's going to express it, his assets, all that stuff factors into how I'm going to build the drill. That's why I don't really keep any of them at the forefront.

In the next chapter, I'm going to talk about the actual designing of the drills and how I come at it. At the end of the day, I view myself and my eye as a critical component of players' development. I have to be actively working the drills. The drill design is less important as long as a drill satisfies the movement capacities of what it is we're trying to work on. That's all that matters from the drill design perspective. What does matter most is how active I am in the teaching process and the whole idea of correction and self-discovery and working that balance to try to move through the relationship. Progressing from being a director all the way through to co-teacher, that's really the most important piece. We miss that when we just throw an obstacle course down, go three-on-three, and just let them go. If you're not actively working the drill to provide the player with mental engagement or you're not moving your way through that teaching relationship, I think you're missing a huge opportunity to have massive influence on their ability to transfer from training to game.

18

DRILL FORMATS

The first time I realized I needed to understand drill formats and drill design was when I had forgotten my plan. When I first started, I wanted to have my plan all written out so I could save time drawing on a board. In an earlier chapter, I described my flip chart with the rink diagram, everything color-coded, all the lines drawn, all the descriptions laid in. I just literally flipped the chart so that I could describe it and move on. I was trying to shave time to be able to add reps. That was fantastic, until one day I was rushing out of the house, got to the rink, and realized I didn't have my flip chart. So there I was, with really no plan, just trying to remember what had been on my flip chart.

In not having my plan, I could feel my awareness heightened. In the perspective change, there were a couple things inside the practice as I got going that I didn't see when I was just sticking to my plan. I noticed things I didn't think were going very well, and so on a whim I started to change a few drills and make up new ones. It wasn't overly sophisticated, but it was an effort to spend a little bit more time on that particular element I didn't like. That started me on this path of being able to adapt. I still needed a plan, but I didn't need as fixed a plan as I had previously, because I knew I could pivot and go into other things. That was really empowering.

One of the more important aspects of my development was when I spent almost five years in Brantford, Ontario, as a coach mentor for Brantford minor hockey. I was basically trying to set a curriculum. While I was trying to set that curriculum, I was trying to do some coach development, which I thought was really important. In many respects it was before its time. There was still a lot of pushback to doing it. The organization is built on volunteer coaches. The coaches have jobs and families and don't have a lot of time to be indulging me with my stuff.

Despite a valiant effort, it reduced down to being a different face at practice. As each team would get rotated into my schedule, I'd email the coach to ask what types of things they would like to work on, so I could prepare. Sometimes a coach would write back with a bullet point list of things they were struggling with as a team. It was typically very vague, with the usual topics of having trouble getting out of their end or having trouble on the power play. Some were more detailed than others, but for the most part, if I did get a response back, I didn't find it overly illuminating and it didn't really give me an opportunity to do the preparation I thought I needed.

There were guys who just didn't get back to me, so I'd be trying to gather information about the team in the time it took the Zamboni to resurface the ice. It'd be a novice single A team and the coach would be worried about breaking out. I remember thinking, *I can't be doing five-man breakout stuff with a novice team. I need to focus on breakout skill development.* So I was thinking about how I was going to weave this in, and I needed to figure it out in mere minutes.

Once I started there, I realized I had my own limited drill bank. I had a bunch of drills I knew and liked, but they all needed to be adapted every single time I went on the ice with whatever group it was. The drills themselves were never quite right for that age or skill level. I could be on the ice with a novice team followed by a midget Triple A back-to-back, all ends of the spectrum and everything in between, so the drills would vary every single hour I was there. I had to adapt to make them age-appropriate, skill-level appropriate, and fun.

Initially, I couldn't have felt more uncomfortable. At first, my focus was to just run a good ice time that moved well. The focus became just passing the sweat test. I was a different voice for the coach on a couple things from my perspective that were different from what they'd normally do, and everybody was happy. But I wasn't happy. I'd be driving home frustrated because I just didn't feel like I had enough range and adaptability and my drill set was just not sophisticated enough. One of the things I did during that time was try to build a drill structure format where I had a way to run an ice session. That gave me a lot of adaptability and an immediate remedial plan. If I didn't like something, I knew where to go. I also needed it to be able to follow the skill continuum, which I was working on at that time and trying fit into what I was doing.

Once I found something I really liked, I wanted to incorporate that. But I didn't want to get so married to it where I just believed that was the only way to do it. I want to stay open to best practices. So as soon as I found something that was better, I would adopt and utilize it right away. I was always looking to add to my skill set, and everything I was doing was subject to evaluation and updating. Nothing was set in stone. Everything was fluid. That way I could add new tools and new ways of doing things.

All the stages I went through ended up being about a 15-year process. Initially, I was just looking for varying formats and an ability to draw a drill instantly off the top of my head. I wanted it to be that I could just be given a topic and figure it out. I would know the level the kids were at, and I should be able to immediately come up with a drill that would address that from an age-appropriate perspective. I needed to be that automatic.

I also needed to understand and be mindful of work-to-rest ratios. I didn't want to have long lines of kids standing. I needed to be able to move the ice, so aesthetically it should also look good. The ice is moving at pace, it's got energy, it's got enthusiasm. We're using the whole ice. We're not stuck in a single corner with 15 kids when we have the entire sheet. I needed to be able to manage that part.

I also wanted to progress it through game situations. The coach would say, we've got a novice team and we need to work on the breakout. I can't just set two defensemen and three forwards up at the red line and dump the puck in and teach them different breakouts. That to me was counterproductive. I needed to build it up into stages, starting with two-man situations, then progress to three-man, then move to four-man. I needed to find simple ways of creating progression for the hour but getting it more into game patterns. Depending on the age group or performance level, I could add some pressure, maybe work up to five-on-two. I just needed to have the capacity to immediately understand how to set up these drills on the spot.

As I moved forward, I was trying to match the drill structure to the teaching objectives. What are we really trying to accomplish, and does the drill structure lend itself to that? For example, something like angling is an individual skill that has tactical implications. The angling just gets you there; then, you have to try to take the puck away, so you have all that you can dig into as, well. But I couldn't just do a drill. I had to make sure I had a drill format that really matched what I was doing. Is this something I want to isolate at first? In what time do I want to teach it and move it to where there are a lot of high volume of reps?

I could use more of an assembly line–type drill and then create some resistance, or maybe focus on the takeaway part of it. I could do the takeaway part in pairs, and then I could bring it all back into an assembly line where there's more of a continuation—you angle, you take away, you finish with a shot, and then you make a pass to the guy who's skating for the next guy to angle, or you pick up a puck and you're the one that gets angled and taken away. It creates this assembly line that generates a high volume of reps in a short period time.

I could have it be a situation where we have three roles. You have the puck carrier, the guy who's trying to take the puck away, and then a pass option. The drill would move you through all three roles. If you started as the puck carrier, you would get the puck taken away from you, and then you become that guy, and then the guy who got the puck passed to him becomes the original puck carrier, so you move your way through each of those roles.

These are all different formats I had percolating in my mind. But I wanted the drill structure to match the teaching objective, and I needed a good decision-making structure, because I was trying to do everything off the top of my head. How do I know what drill format to use? If it's something I'm trying to build more, I'm moving that through stages. Is there a rough format I could use to run if something went wrong where players didn't capture what I wanted and inform where to go next? I needed a structure that gave me an ability to make decisions while allowing me to have a lot of versatility and variability in what it was I was doing. The time I spent in Brantford was invaluable in my teaching development. The need to build drill structures that gave me an opportunity to make drills up as I needed them was the skill I needed to learn to do that job. Once I became proficient in that skill, it has been something that has stayed with me my entire career. I use that skill every day I'm on the ice.

The last five or six years, I started really moving through the teaching roles. I really felt like that was a critical component. At first you're the director, then you're the collaborator, then the facilitator, and, ultimately, the co-teacher. I wanted to set up my drills to mirror these teaching roles. I was progressing the kids not only through the content, but through the relationship with me and their reliance on me as the teacher. We'd gradually move toward teaching each other. That's ultimately where I want to end up on different skills. The next parallel I was always trying to match was that the drill structure had to have a lot of variability and a lot of opportunity for me to be able to pivot for different reasons.

To start off, everything was way easier for me when I understood game situations. That was the best part of Brantford, because whenever I would ask the coach what his challenges were and what the team was doing well, he would always relate it to the game. *In these games, our kids don't protect the puck well enough, so we're on defense all the time or we get into good areas and our kids just don't shoot the puck well enough. It takes us a lot of time to score. What do you got for scoring, Darryl? We have a hard time getting out of our own end. We get pinned in. We're very susceptible to an aggressive pinch. We can't problem-solve the pinch. Our wingers just aren't strong enough. What can we do with that off the forecheck? We pride ourselves on having a strong retrieval game, and we don't forecheck. We don't get in on it fast enough, our support is too late. F2 is nowhere to be found even if we do get the puck stop. We're susceptible to a team that that uses their D partners. Whenever they go D to D, we really struggle with rotation. We need to work on rotations.* These were all the variables that could happen in just one night.

I was always trying to figure out, *Well, what is this game situation, what would that look like at this particular level, where else could this type of thing be used?* If it's puck protection, we could do that everywhere. I could do that in the defensive zone, in the neutral zone, in the offensive zone, off the rush, in small space. There are lots of things I could do with that. Then I could start to pinpoint the undercurrents here. What's the underlying message that we want the coaches talking about? Forechecking, well, the premise behind forechecking is pursuit and angle, so we're going to focus on those two things. That's going to be an undercurrent. That's going to run all the way through. Puck protection, well, that's body position and puck placement, so that's important. A little bit of awareness, maybe some reverse hits, we could put all that into it. The team doesn't pass well enough, so there's timing, puck support, passing technique. We can have that as the undercurrent. There's also pass receiving. Maybe the passer is okay, but the pass receiver doesn't take good angles to support the puck or doesn't understand the casting component of being able to use their stick to soften the catch. Maybe there's just a whole availability situation in that the younger they are, the less understanding of movement off the puck they have. Maybe there's a real value in what we could do off the puck.

Then, what are the key details? I understand the skills I want to do, but what are the details inside of it? What about angling? Well, there's stick position, there's the actual angle that we take. How can we elongate the contact opportunity here? What can we do with our stick? What can we do on the takeaway? What are the details with this whether we stick lift or stick slap or stick press? How are we doing this takeaway? What are the escape routes inside of that? Maybe there are two people coming; what's the interaction between those two? How are they reading off of each other? Is there a way to simplify it? Could we go old-school where you have the rabbit, the hound, and the fox? The rabbit is the guy with the puck who's trying to get away, the hound's pressuring, and the fox is reading the play and trying to anticipate and time his support. Is there a way to articulate the rules to these players in a way they can understand? What are the details? How can I communicate those details?

When I was in Brantford, I never got into parallel structures. I wasn't that far in my personal development. It hadn't revealed itself to me up to that point. It was a big enough bite just to understand how to set up and run the sheet and be able to hit the target areas and still pass the sweat test. Later on, I started understanding parallel structures and that became a big part of some of the questions. Like, can I do two things at once? Do I need to run them opposite of each other, or can I run them together where it's a sequence and we're building two different things, but they're expressed together with good shouldering? Where could I build the peaks?

Sometimes I did go on drill runs where I'd have three or four drills. Usually the coach would ask for two different things, so I would teach two different things. It was rare for those things to go hand-in-hand. It was usually like, *We struggle on the breakout and we have problems on the penalty kill,* so I would be doing things that were breakout-oriented for a drill run and then we would pivot and work on the penalty kill concepts. But how do I build the peaks? I needed to have the energy spike at different times to keep things hopping and popping for a little bit, at least, without getting so slow where it's too teaching-oriented and the kids leave the ice without passing the sweat test. Now everybody is unhappy.

I also had to determine who the top players were. This was something I carried over from my Nathan Horton days, understanding who the top player is and what top players' assets are. Is it just one guy, or could it be two or three? What are their assets? That would allow me to understand which kid we could start zeroing in on to push the whole thing along. Then, ultimately, I focused on relationship building, making it fun and creating a real connection inside the teaching, where I was relied upon.

In the early days, I wanted to be relied upon. I wanted all eyes on me. I wanted the respect from the group, from the coach. I wanted him to respect what I was doing and be like, "Wow, that was awesome." I needed all of those kind of affirmations. That was all relationship building and how I was moving the group through and what kind of a handle the coach had on his own group. Whenever I was there, I wanted to be the best ice they had. It had to be significantly better than what the coach was capable of doing on his own, which was tough, because there were some outstanding coaches who had been coaching for years and years and knew what they were doing. So whenever I came out there, it was a little intimidating, because I didn't have the same kind of experience that way. I knew how to teach, but I needed to be able to make an impact and have the coach's takeaway be that having me there was worthwhile.

The drill formats were a live document for me. I kept adding new formats as I started to understand them and started to mess around with them and use them for different purposes. But it really starts with an isolation. That's the very first thing. Which drill formats can I use to create an isolation? We used to use the continuous butterfly drill format a lot for edge control and all the skating components, as a warmup of sorts. You'd start with the kids going from basically top of the circle to top of the circle, down the middle of the ice, and executing something. It could be the inside edge with a puck. Then they'd make the turn, either direction at the top of the circles, and come back down the boards or the outside. Then you'd have another skill, so maybe it would be inside edge on the way down and outside edge on the way back. Then they'd make the turn at the bottom and come back down the middle, so the way the ice is moving looks like a butterfly. There might be some spacing problems because kids aren't moving at the same speed, so there's some trying to navigate out of the way. Once you understood the group or the group undersood you, you could pivot. As they're going, you could be just shouting the next thing. You could let them go for two or three reps doing outside edges, long strides, some crossover or overspeed work, and then switch to going backward. You could just be standing there telling them what to do. You could add pucks, you could add passing; there are tons of things you can do. I used to love that format, because again I felt like it had a lot of variability. I could do different things with it. I could slow it down. I could speed it up. I could isolate. I could teach from it.

The end zone line, for us, was a straight power skating format. Depending on how many kids they had on the ice, they would try to have groups of four or five lines, and four or five kids in a line, so 20 kids total. If you had more kids, you had to add more lines. Now you've got six or seven lines across the goal line and you're just progressing straight down the ice doing certain isolated movements. I remember watching power skating situations where they would stay in that line format the whole time. It was literally a whole hour of just going down the ice doing one thing, getting some corrections, and coming back down the ice doing another. Their entire ice sheet would be worked off of those lines. It was very controlled. You could see everything going on. You could move the best kids to the front of the line. It really was a simple format that was good for isolations, whether it was starting kids in the corner and using the icing line and then maybe the blue line in their end. You have two groups. One's in one end and one corner, one's in the other end and the opposite corner. They go across the goal line, up the boards, back across the blue line, and back in line, working in a square. You could also do all the lines. They go up across the goal line, cross the ringette line. We have the ringette line in a lot of Canadian rinks, so it's a good line to be able to use for teaching blue line, red line, blue line, ringette line, icing line. I've also used the dot lines both across the ice and down the ice, but those are good isolation formats where you can run a lot of kids through in a short period of time and you can isolate whatever skill set you want to work on.

Then you have pair skills. I liked to use pairs to start getting the work-to-rest ratio going. Sometimes you have a group of 20 kids on the ice, 10 in one line, 10 in the other. By the time it accordions around the rink, the kids are standing in line a whole lot. Even though you can get a lot of kids moving, there's still a lot of time in between as they wait for that centipede to come back to the end. So I have found using pairs is a better way to create high reps; I go, you wait, then you go, I wait, and we're doing different things, which could also add a bit more skill blending.

I used to do a lot of catch-and-turn stuff where there were some techniques I really wanted to work on the turn. I would do it off the pass. I could also do it through puck protection setup. Pairs were a really good format, and I could use multiple skills in a sequence. I could have partners go, and I could tell them, "You're going to do three skills. You're going to start off with one skill. When I blow the whistle, you move to the next skill. When I blow the whistle, you move to the next skill, and then you switch roles." If I had multiple things I wanted to work on that were components of what we were doing that day, I knew I could go to this pair and knock them all off in a very short period of time with a high rep rate. I could see which the weakest one was and then isolate that, if I wanted to, and put it into a line or an end zone line or something. By isolating it, I could make sure that we did the extra work on it and then move on to the next thing. That's what I mean about the corrective value of it. You could use a drill format just to evaluate where the skill is at before you pull it back into isolation to work on it, build it back up again, and you plug it back into the overall structure of what you're working on. If you had like a small group, this would be like the role rotations we went over.

Role rotations are another good way to get a lot of reps in varying situations and to work through a parallel structure while the kids are learning the same thing. There's an offensive component and a defensive component and a playmaking component. By learning all three of those things and adding turns or stops or protections or whatever it is, you can do a lot of different things inside of those role rotation drills. Then you have triangles, which you can do a lot of with three guys and teaching rotations. I used to do this a lot when we were teaching forechecking. Forechecking was often the interaction of at least the first three guys in the primary triangle working off the secondary triangle. How does it work between the D, F1, and F2? How does that interaction go? It could be F1, F2, F3. It could F1, F3, and the D. It could be just a high triangle. Or, if you're working on offensive concepts, when I was doing this there was lot of 1-2-3 principal of attack, so F1 would take the puck wide, F2 is driving the net, F3 is the high man. I could create a lot of interactions within those situations, and work in the pass and follow and weave components, with having them in threes.

I used to do a lot of squares, which were especially great when I wanted to do multiple pucks. For a passing situation, I would have the pass go through a square, and while the puck was going through the square, I'd add a second puck. So now the puck has to move twice as fast. Your accuracy has to be up. There's a little more automation to it. All the errors or holes in your game will come to the forefront when I add that second puck in a square. We did also a lot of understanding how rotations work. It's a square but you only have three guys. You're always rotating your people to be able to manage a square. We called it L support. You were always trying to keep a strong L everywhere you were going, but it had to rotate and change. All those pairs and small groups were a good format I could use for a variety of different things.

There was an element I called fours. Fours are like four corners or four blue lines or opposite corners, but the two groups would be on opposite corners at the same time. This was great to really manipulate work-to-rest ratios and pace. We did a lot of overspeed training. I wanted the kids to basically skate two circles: skate one circle one way and then do a figure-eight and skate the second circle the other way. We used a lot of overspeeds to really work on their crossovers, but also their edge control at a high speed, posture, and the way they handled and controlled the puck at a high rate of speed. You send them in a pack. You send the entire line from the corner and they have to do the circle immediately in front of them, then do the center circle or the opposite circle beside them, and they're just sprinting. It's all-out, and you have all these spatial things where you're in the middle.

I remember one of the things Nathan Horton did that I love was come out to ice times where he was the oldest player. Early on in my career, the first thing a lot of parents wanted to know about the ice time was the age group and the skill level. They wanted their kids out there with the best possible players, which I understood. But Nathan often liked to be out there with the younger players. What he would do is he would put himself at the back of the line. We'd send the whole group from a corner and he would be trying to weave or work his way up. Let's say there are five kids in the corner, and he puts himself last. As he goes from one circle to the next, he tries to see how many kids he could pass. He would do that on his own. It had nothing do with me. I never talked to him about it. I didn't even know that someone would even want to do that, but he would. He would then do that with his own age group, which I always thought was really fascinating. There was a lot of tight space and being able to handle a puck in high-traffic areas.

Then you have the four blue lines format. I would do this a lot when I wanted to change the drills format but not the content of what we were doing. We would start and do these figure-eights skating in the corner and then I would just say, "Okay, move to the blue." They'd move up to the blue line thinking the drill is going to change, and now I just have them coming from the top down. It's the same thing, only I come from a different place. Instead of going from the corner up the boards and then around the circle and then over to the other corner, they're starting at the blue line, facing the end and moving inside first.

If I was doing some type of defensive move or forechecking skill set, I would have them come from the middle as kind of an inside-out forecheck, with all the same footwork and stick position but like a figure-eight coming from the top down. But it was a good way to change a format without having to change the context of what we were doing with the drill. That just maximized more reps. But from their perspective, they were doing two different drills. If I was really good, I would be able to articulate what the difference was for those really smart kids who picked up on the fact we were doing the same thing. I would create a different focus so I could appease those kids and make sure they weren't getting bored thinking we're just skating circles the whole time. Meanwhile, that's what we were doing, but I needed to refocus and redirect their energy.

Sometimes you'd use the four blue lines and then you'd put the defensemen in the middle. This would be a lot of your one-on-one type drills, two-on-one, two-on-two. The players would start at the four blue lines, maybe all the forwards at the blue line and then the defensemen in the middle, and they'd be accepting a rush in some way. There are a multitude of ways you can get into that. That was a really good drill format for me.

Instead of putting the defensemen in the middle of the center circle, you could also put them on the boards at the red line. So the four corners had the kids at each blue line and the defensemen were at the red line, also against the boards, leaving the whole middle of the ice. It just gave them a chance to rotate themselves in as we needed. A lot of times, the defensemen would be on the half wall, the forwards would be at the four blue lines, and the defensemen would start at the opposite hash marks and work a breakout behind the net. Someone would come down from the weak side, and that's where your pass outlet came from. We could do all kinds of stuff. Starting at the hash marks, the defensemen would jump up to the top the circle, pivot backward, retrieve the puck, use a little deception, take the back of the net, and make an outlet pass to a forward coming down the dot line. They've got to get the pivot, the shoulder checks. Then they'd catch the break, go fast, and make the next play. Then you can send them down toward the other end where the other group was going, creating a one-on-one against the opposite line, or they could turn it back and come back. There's again a lot of variability in how you could do that. These were great opportunities to maximize the work-to-rest ratios. It could be two groups that pass each other by an imaginary line that split the ice in half in the opposite corners, like lanes on two sides. That was a way to maximize the work-to-rest and get more kids moving at the same time.

I also had stations. When I first started, I did stations like everyone does stations. There are five stations on the ice, and in these five stations, you do five different things. This coach is teaching one thing, then you move to the next station. Over the years, I started to get frustrated because I wanted to run a sequence, and it was very difficult because no matter what, only the group that started in the right spot would run through the proper sequence. Then you'd have a group that started in the complete opposite wrong spot, the fifth spot, and then moved to the first, second, third, and fourth spots. Then you have the poor kids starting in the middle. There was just no way to really set up a five-station or multiple-station format and have it be progressive in any way.

What I started doing instead was having five stations, but everyone is doing the same thing. Then, when we change drills, you can change locations on the ice, but now we're in a new progression only. We're adding something. There are all kinds of different things you can do where in this station you're doing it this way, but everybody's doing the same thing. It could be that in station one, you just establish body position, cut through the hands. Station two is being able to use more of a chuck in your puck protection. You get your arm out and you're trying to chuck to get body position. In the third station, we move into a turn, so it's the same thing: get body position, and now you have to turn to escape. The fourth station might be that you're catching a pass, and as you catch a pass, you've got to go right into protection. Then you have some manipulatives you're adding into it, maybe an offensive stick check. In the fifth station, now you have free rein to use all the skills that have been presented to you in a short period of time. So that's five stations, it satisfies the work-to-rest ratio, but instead of all five stations doing five different things and rotating without a change to progression value, they all do the same thing and I just add a new detail each time there's a rotation. That's where I started to go because I want the progression. I didn't want to just be doing five random skills.

It's also important to incorporate situational changes. Let's say I wanted you to learn use of escape moves, so I would move that strategically into different things. You're on forehand side in the corner, then you rotate to the backhand side on the corner, and now you're off the rush and using the neutral zone space. There would be a way in which you're doing the same thing but you're moving it around the ice to illustrate it can be used in multiple places.

To this day, it agitates me when I see people running stations and doing five different things with no relationship between one thing and the next. I like using stations, but I like it to have a logical progression and compound the rep count.

A common format we use a lot is splits, where we have half the defensemen working on their thing and the forwards working on another thing, and then we bring them together. This is the start of parallel structures, where the defensemen are working on how they can stop the forwards, the forwards are working on how they can beat the defensemen, and then eventually you bring them together to see who learned the quickest.

Then you have all your timing stuff. There are three elements to timing. You want to arrive at the right time, at the right place, with the right amount of speed. If one of those pieces is missing, you have bad timing to the degree that piece is missing.

Working on timing and spacing is so important. You usually use a lot of assembly line drills for this type of thing, where you're moving up the ice and doing something in relationship to other people, so you can't go too fast. If you go too fast, you're going to be too early, and you'll have to slow down or stop before the next group is prepared to accept the play for their part of the assembly line. Then, you move into their part, and when the play comes back around, you jump in and do their part, and then you move to the next piece. Assembly lines were really good to teach timing and arriving at the right place at the right time.

You can also do role change rotations inside of assembly lines. It's like the drill I described before with the three players, but you'd use more of a three-line situation. So it's not just three players; it's three lines, with players moving from one spot to the next block to the next block and doing three different roles inside the execution of the skill set. I like the role changes a lot because the defensemen are so active in games now, jumping in the rush and getting involved offensively, and the forwards have to cover for them. So you have defensemen who fill lanes normally reserved for forwards and you have forwards who now have to fill spots normally reserved for defensemen. Having a functional understanding of each is really critical and will lead to greater levels of success.

Inside these timing drills, you can teach different patterns, such as rush patterns. You can do it off the breakout. You can have it go from the defenseman to one forward to another forward, finishing with a shot. The forward who shot now becomes the defenseman, who rounds the net to make the first pass to the next guy, and off they go. You can run those patterns any which way and you can make them up on the fly. You don't have to have a drill bank of those.

The next one was a real breakthrough for me as it relates to assembly line drills. One of the best parts of an assembly line is that it's continuous. I wanted to be able to take any drill and make it continuous. The way you do that is you create some level of a transition concept where you start the next play in the next direction. It's usually that I start as an offensive player and then become a defensive player to make the next play, or I start as a defensive player and I move to an offensive player to start the next play for the next group. Typically these things go up and down the ice one end to the other.

The other way you can use continuations is to actually continue the drill in a new format. It could be a play that starts off the rush and then you throw a second puck in that works the play down. So there are two objectives: a rush objective and an offensive zone objective. This is beneficial because you can teach players how to manufacture or take advantage of spatial problems. Invariably people are going to arrive late, arrive with bad timing, have poor sticks, have poor angles. So you manufacturing advantages or even do things that dictate the terms that allow you to take control of space. Second pucks and continuations can be a natural way you can teach those types of things as on your way to game situations.

The next format is shifts or slide-ins. You have these situations where you know it's a continuous two-on-two drill on the four blue lines. The forwards from one end are attacking the defensemen going in one direction. As they pass center, the next two forwards slide into their spots, while the defensemen win the puck, make a play to those forwards, and move out. As they're attacking on the other way, the defensemen who were in leave, and the new defensemen come out. So players are sliding in and out of the drill to keep it continuous, but it's much more hockey-specific. They're coming from spots that are more recognizable as it relates to rush play, for example.

You could design an end-zone drill where the players slide in from one side to the other. One thing is happening on one side of the ice, and soon as that's done, the puck goes to the other side. This group that was just on one side is out; the on the other side of the ice starts, and so on. That's how it creates a continuous nature. Shifts or slide-ins are all really important. You can do it in transitional components. You can do it with players waiting for the next thing to arrive. They get into position early and then they're just waiting for the puck or the play to arrive and then they activate. It's a good way to keep the whole line activated.

You're then moving toward small-area games. I've gone away from putting the nets in different spots. I tend to keep one net where it's supposed to be, and I want the players to use the ice geography as part of the competitive aspect we're working on. If this is going to be a game situation, I want them to use or have the ability to use the references of the ice geography—the dots, the circles, the lines, the crease, the back of the net. All those things I think are really important. I know there's a lot of value in creating more of an open free play where people have to jump into space learn how to play off the puck. I get all that. I don't think you lose that when you move the ends. The only problem is if you have multiple goalies. How am I going to keep this goalie busy? Well, to me, the answer is to send him with an assistant coach or goalie coach to work on his technique and rotate in and out, so it gives him a little more instruction time while you're focused on working the drill. We tend to want both goalies to be involved in the drill, and to do that we've now become, to me, over-creative, limiting the possible transfer effect we could get had we left them in situations where they're able to utilize the lines more effectively.

The ice geography is always an important consideration for me as it relates to smaller games. I try to stick to that as often as possible. If I'm working on a small-area game, I might do two or three games in the time we'd normally do one. But the first one is more open. It's side-to-side, we're using both goalies, we've got nets creatively configured in the zone. Eventually, those nets come out and we have one net where it's supposed to be with the ice geography, and then away we go again. I cannot emphasize this enough: the key for me for small-area games is that they need to be in relationship to what you're working on. It's one of the final steps along the way before you can confidently send this kid home and feel like he could use the skills you were working on in his game tomorrow. He'll be able to recognize the spacing, the timing, the ice markings, the way he can manipulate the situation to his favor to be able to execute the skill you want him to work on. In the end, it should feel a little bit like a game, and yet he has objectives that are manipulative he has to add in to be able to capitalize on the development process.

At the end of the day, I'm interested in a couple different things. I'm interested in being able to use any combination of these practice formats I've described to build a logical progression. I want a broad enough range of drill formats that I could come up with a drill on a given topic on a moment's notice and it would satisfy the direct needs of what it is I'm trying to teach. The objective is that at a given juncture of the practice, if I needed remedial work in some way, I could pivot and go into an isolation or a small group or pair to be able to build up that skill set. If I needed to I could spend a little more time on it, then start progressing it into a more advanced drill structure which is a little more game-like. Once I get into the continuations, the shifts, the small games, I'm looking to try to drop what I've worked on into game situations and be able to figure out the timing, the spacing, the competitive advantages, the manipulations, the ways I can dictate the sheet and puck support, the multiple player effect. I want to be able to get to all that. But if something goes wrong and I don't like what's going on, I have a way I can pivot. Let's say I don't like the puck support or the spacing. I can come out of the continuation drill I'm working on, go into stations, and work on getting a little more situational understanding. Or I could go into pairs or triangles or squares. It could be something like a real individual skill that needs to be isolated, something like a puck-handling component or a skating component. I can go right into an isolation; maybe I go back into lines or something that allows me to really focus on those skills, get those details down, then start working it back into the sequence. But this format I'm describing is how I want to move this along. This is my methodology, and then I have every level of flexibility inside this particular model to give me an opportunity to push toward training-to-game transfer.

19

BREAKING RULES

ONE OF THE THINGS WE WANT TO BE DOING IN SKILL DEVELOPMENT is taking a look at the long-established skill rules and figuring out how to use those rules to our advantage, evolve them, or break them. We can make it appear as though we're going to execute a skill in the exact way it's normally done, and then have some type of adaptation where we break the rule to gain a competitive advantage. So breaking rules is really one of the last objectives of skill development. We don't want to be abiding by the rules for everyone as it relates to skill execution. If you do what everybody else does, it's going to be very difficult for you to achieve any level of deception. Obviously, a ton of skill execution has to do with being able to do multiple things at the same time and hide the skill execution inside of something else.

It's difficult to be great if you're the same as everyone else. There needs to be an ability to find ways to become different or have a unique expression of that particular skill. What we want to do is take a look again at the core evaluation tools of frequency and success rate. We go into areas where there's a high frequency of use with a low success rate and try to determine why. A lot of times, a player is just adhering too much to the skill rules.

What are some examples of these rules? One of the popular ones right now is under-handling. We don't want kids over-handling the puck; under-handle the puck if you get it. Under-handling does have some indisputable advantages for everyone. It's just that if you continue to be the player who always under-handles, then you're going to be predictable, and it's very difficult to be good if you're predictable. You can use the under-handle to your advantage by making it look like you're going to under-handle and then have some type of an over-handle at the right time. Figuring all that in, slightly breaking or bending a rule of play that's common for everyone is a way to create uniqueness.

If the last objective is to start bending and breaking some of the rules to create deception or different expressions to make you much more difficult to defend, then the first objective is to establish projectable habits. You still want to be technically sound. You want to have excellent depth of skill, which creates some ancillary skill understanding that gives you much more of an opportunity to acquire or adapt skills because you have so much fluidity of motion. From that, you must be able to leverage your projectable habits to create skill blends. Then, once you have an ability to do that, you can start messing around. This is where we start progressing our relationship with the player and start moving into the more advanced aspects of our roles. We want the athlete to start teaching us. We want them to start talking about situations that they come into frequently with lower success rates. They're creating some level of feedback for you to be able to work. Often it's best to start listening at that point, and then you can start becoming more of a facilitator and ultimately a co-teacher in that environment. You can kind of see what happens, but we really want to start following their path more.

One of the best techniques to start bending the rules in your advantage is mirror skills. We want to make something look like it's going to execute a particular skill but at the very last second, you're going to adapt, or mirror, it. For example, one of the better mirror skills you can use is a shot fake. The best shot fake is one that appears to have every characteristic of a shot and then at the last second, just before you would release the puck, you adapt. But all the way leading up to it, all the body language, the foot position, the way you're going to approach the technical execution of the shot is exactly the same. That's called mirroring a skill. So depending on what technical skill rule we're trying to break or adapt, we still want it to look like that. We want to have those same properties because that creates predictiveness for the defender. What he's doing is preparing himself to defend something that's not going to happen. That's really what we have. That's the art of deception. Mirror skills is one of the first places I like to start with the breaking of some of these longstanding rules.

Then, ultimately, we want to break the rule, and we want the advantage of having this skill expressed differently or adding one more movement piece or pairing another skill that would be relatively unexpected at the end of it. That's the best way to express the skill. Become an expert at the rule so you have the greatest capacity to adapt the rule. You've got to be careful because you don't want to just go rogue without the core basic skills. Because you're not creating deception there, either. You're just doing something completely different. It's better in my mind to follow the rule until you get to the end of it and then start to adapt it.

The real restriction in being the same as everyone else is you get the same predictable defense. People learn how to defend certain things, especially if they're highly repeatable and everyone is doing them. We can box ourselves into poor execution because a defense is more prepared, and it puts more pressure on us to have the highest degree of execution just to get by. You want to be able to leverage the fact the defense is prepared to defend a certain way and turn the predictive nature of the rules against the defender, but using the rule to mask the adaptation we will utilize for our competitive advantage. By being the same, you lose your deception and become predictable. A lot of times, we use the same defensive principles to teach offense. This is one of my big arguments in hockey and has been for a long time: I feel like there's such an emphasis on coaching defensive play that we tend to teach offense using defensive principles. We'll say, "Well, you know, defense controls the game," and the reason we can confidently say that is because we teach offense using the same principles as defense. One feeds into the other. It's a bit of a rouse for me to suggest that offense doesn't ever control play, that defense controls everything. But it becomes more believable when you're teaching offense to abide by the same defensive principles and that's where it becomes a little self-perpetuating, which has always been a big frustration for me. We want people to execute at the highest level and we want as many kids as possible to be able to do that on our team. The problem with all of that is it becomes asset-deaf. We lose the individuality of the expression of skill. We lose the assets that each individual player is bringing into it, which can be what you're actually beginning to leverage at the end of that particular skill. As you make it look like you're going to do something to mirror the skill, if it becomes asset-oriented the player will be able to adapt it very quickly.

The other problem with teaching everybody to do the same thing is it's just arbitrary. It's an arbitrary rule that's based on the execution of the average. I work with players who are among the very best in the world, and they're far from average. Now we're going to apply a rule that's good for the average to the ultra-talented, the ultra-skilled, the top one percent. We can have them abide by the same rule or we can encourage them to use these rules to their advantage and then at the end of the skill execution they're going to adapt the skill in an asset-driven way and put their signature on it. Now you have something that's truly unique. It has all the properties of deception that really gives them a greater advantage than they had going into it. That, to me, is what we should be taking a look at when we're dealing with the top players.

We have to get away from adhering to what's arbitrarily used to encourage the average. Let's use that to our advantage as we're dealing with the top one percent. Ultimately, what we're trying to do is create a personal expression of that skill after it's been mirrored to create our tactical advantage. We're going to do it in a way that has a personal expression. We call innovating in this way signature skills. It's something that is a signature to you as an individual that capitalizes on and expresses your assets in the best possible way. We also use the term benchmark. That's an outstanding skill someone else has that we might want to leverage. We want to learn that skill, understand it, and then convert a benchmark skill to a signature skill. That's ultimately what we're after.

When you're dealing with the top one percent, these are the type of things you should be considering. That's why the last objective is to break the rule we want. We want to use the rule to our advantage. We want to create a high level of predictability, and at the last second we want to be unpredictable with a high degree of execution inside our asset base. If we're able to do that, we are now giving our best players the highest number of tools to have an even greater impact.

We talked a lot about under-handling. Another rule is being centered in a turn. From the time people are really young, they're taught to turn with both feet. The weight is relatively evenly distributed, maybe it's a 60/40 split on the on the inside foot outside edge versus the outside foot inside edge. If you're really good, that's probably where you are, but both feet are relatively even on this particular turn. What we want to be able to do is start using more hook turns. It looks like a turn, but we're able to gain speed out of the hook turn. It kind of looks like you're turning as I'm defending you. I can see you're turning, but your turning execution has asset base principles in it that allow you to create a competitive advantage. That's what I'm after. The rule for you when you were growing up was get both feet on the ice, get your outside edge, get a 60/40 split. But as soon as you do that, you're in a deceleration. For the 90 percent of players who, when they turn, have their weight either evenly distributed or on the wrong foot to carry the speed, they have to wait until they get through the end of the turn to add speed. They're slowing down and their weight distribution means they're locked. That's a competitive advantage for the elite. They say, "You know what, I have better skating ability than that. Even though I currently turn like that, I need to adapt this skill, so that I can create more speed coming out of the turn or I can make it look like I'm going into a deceleration and then I get into an acceleration." That's a competitive advantage. That's a signature skill. That's a way in which we can take one of these commonly taught rules and adapt them to make them our own.

The other one that's really interesting is body contact. The first thing you're taught is that when someone's going to hit you, make sure you get your shoulder and hip against the boards, so the impact gets distributed down the boards and lessened. Which is great until you actually get hit like that; then you realize it still hurts. The other thing is if my timing just isn't quite right, I'm a little bit off the boards, and I take the hit, now I get hit twice. I get hit by the guy on one shoulder and then I crash into the boards on the other shoulder. Now I'm getting crunched, so that's not good, either. What we do to adapt is teach players not to get hit. Here's a kid who can skate and has good awareness, but maybe he's undersized and it just doesn't make any sense for him to be taking contact. So let's learn the contact angle lines and change a line. You're going to look like you're in a position where you're vulnerable because you're in the danger zone of two to three feet off the boards. That's the, *Oh my God, don't be in there because if you get hit there, that's really dangerous* zone. That's not to say it's not. It is dangerous to be there, but we're going to take the fact that this is considered a dangerous area and we're going to turn that into our advantage by using change speed. We're going to invite people to come into contact. We're going to change the contact point with a spin off the check.

We don't just teach that to everybody, because that's how the average player gets really hurt. It's for the top kids who are not average. We say to them, "This is a skill that everyone is taught right now, so this is a rule we're going to break. We're going to make it look like you're in a vulnerable position and we're going to capitalize on your ability to understand the awareness of where you are on the ice. You're going to invite people in here and going to make them look silly the first time they try to hit you. You spin off, they go crashing into the boards, and they're not going to come quite as hard the next time. This is how you're going to survive. This is one of your advantages."

Now, there are going to be situations where it's a little bit more of a 50-50 puck. It looks like you're going to win it, but narrowly, so you don't have full control to manipulate. You're going to have to protect yourself yet again against the boards. So you only use the rule when it's advantageous to you. You're going to break the rule when you have a chance to create a competitive advantage. That becomes then the mindset.

Our goal is to push every player out of the average. We don't want to teach everyone standard skills. That's just a baseline. That's our starting point. The real objective we're trying to work up to is to break the rule. But you have to do it in a certain way. To me, what makes it advantageous is you don't want to just to have a firm departure from the skill altogether. You want to create predictability for the defenseman. They start to think they know what's going to happen because everyone does it the same way. You need to leverage that, mirror the skill, then, at the last second, we make our adaptation and create our competitive advantage.

20

THE SICKNESS

THE SICKNESS STARTED ALMOST IMMEDIATELY FOR ME. IT'S AN all-consuming, 24-hour obsession with the game of hockey and the players I'm working with. It's an insatiable obsession to learn more about the game, about skill, and about teaching—anything possible to improve my skill set. I am all-in, and there are really no days off, no minutes off from being involved in it, thinking about it, or having it there at the back of my mind regardless of what I was doing.

There's really not a lot of balance that goes along with that. That's why, when I first met my wife, one of the things that that really jumped out at me and what I really loved about her was she really didn't know anything about hockey in the beginning. She hadn't been exposed to the game at all before meeting me, and therefore she wasn't that interested in talking about the game. So being with her was a great mental break for me. To be able to spend such meaningful time with her in a way I didn't have to think about hockey was just a really nice and healthy distraction.

But, of course, over the years after we got married and got to progressing through the next phases of our life, I continue to carry this obsession with me all the time. I would say her primary role is to provide such a great distraction to alleviate some of the sickness or this all-consuming focus, which in my mind is necessary. In order to become good, you need to be obsessed.

So for me, my focus was on the players. I was watching video. If I wasn't watching video, I was looking for ideas or trying to take down any ideas I encountered. Before there were iPads and smartphones, I had a notepad beside my bed. I would wake up in the middle of the night with an idea and a couple times I would just go back to sleep, thinking I would remember the idea in the morning, but of course I wouldn't. After a few of these frustrating moments, every time I woke up in the middle of the night, I'd feverishly scribble down all these thoughts on the notepad so I wouldn't run the risk of forgetting what could be a great idea.

I don't think that's uncommon. If you're trying to become great at something, you want to be uncommon amongst uncommon people, which is a great quote I got from David Goggins. He really believes if you're trying to be uncommon amongst the uncommon it requires an entirely different mindset. I've noticed that among the great players I deal with. It's been something I've focused on all the time.

When I started my career, I didn't have a backup plan. I was all-in. I figured if it wasn't going to work, then I would figure that out afterward. I pushed all my chips into the middle of the table. There was no turning back. If it didn't work, then I would start over and try something different from a completely different perspective. But while I'm doing it, I'm completely immersed.

The sickness for me was born from four fundamental belief layers and support system. The first layer is the difference between becoming elite and having a job. I never cared as much about having a job in hockey or making sure I was getting compensated financially for any work I had done. Even now, I do a lot of stuff without any expectation of being compensated. I value becoming elite more than I value having a job. I've always felt like if I became elite at what I did, I wouldn't have to worry about compensation, because I haven't really met too many elite people who don't have a job. I was trying to be that person who was all-consumed in pursuing greatness. The money would follow.

My focus was on developing a process. The process had to support a different way of thinking. It had to produce repeatable results but be adaptable to each player and produce better results than others do. So that's a very difficult process to find. There are a lot of things that need to go into that. It requires a tremendous amount of thought. So if I'm focusing on chasing down a dollar, then that pursuit will impact my decision-making and my focus. I've made decisions at different times in my life based on money and not based on trying to be elite. Every time I made a decision based on money, it ended up costing me in the long run. It cost me opportunities that were right around the corner, if I would have been more patient. As fate would have it, every time that compensation package was way higher than what I had originally settled for. Now, there are times in my life we're literally eating SpaghettiOs out of a hardhat trying to get this done, and it does require a tremendous amount of sacrifice. It requires putting off financial gain. That's a prerequisite for me in the pursuit of becoming elite.

I read a ton of books on trying to determine your worth and get paid the right amount. When it was all said and done and I reached the top of my profession, I was compensated very well. I think that's part of the process. But there were times where I slowed down my process because I was too interested in squeezing out a buck, to the exclusion of trying to be elite. I took jobs or responsibilities I knew were mindless for me or, worse, situations where I had not even a high enough prospect to personally improve, and I just did it for the money. There are times where you have to do that because you have to find a way to earn, especially if you're married and have kids, and that's very different. But there are ways to balance that, and it took me quite a while to figure it out. I tried to take some financial shortcuts, knowing this wasn't going to be something that pushed me closer to becoming the best at what I do. I look back at those things with anger and frustration that I allowed myself to fall into those temptations.

The more I focused on being elite and the less I focused on having a job, the more I became elite and the less I had to worry about having a job. The jobs would come to me. Both jobs I had in the NHL I didn't apply for. I was approached by someone seeking me out because of my reputation, the players I've worked with, and the results I've achieved. It's based on the fact I've become elite at what I do. The jobs will come to me. I firmly believe that. It's been a mainstay for me for the longest time. But when I first started out, I chose to do a lot of pro bono work in an effort to learn and get better.

My second belief pattern is I'm only as good as my next idea. This is a belief I've carried with me for my whole career. It's about the next idea. My last idea was really good for that particular player, but that's it. I'm only as good as the next one, so I'm always searching and chasing the next one. It's a never-ending quest for a breakthrough of a different perspective. It could be vocabulary, wording or phrasing. It could be looking at what the opposite is or going against convention in an intelligent way. It could be finding a way to leverage a player's best assets. It's all individual; every day is different and every player is different. There is no shortage of these challenges. It's just a matter of seizing an idea and being able to recognize it when it comes and vet it out. I just need it to be a little bit more effective than the last one. If it's been the previous way to generate results, that's what we have to be focused on. Those tend to lead to little breakthroughs and, eventually, bigger ones, because it changes the mindset gradually. It takes you into a whole different world and opens a door to possibilities you wouldn't have seen had you not been open to the first ideas.

The other thing that really dovetails with this is the training-to-game transfer concept. You learn something, use it tomorrow, come to me again the following day, and learn something new. I'm only as good as the next idea I can put in your game. If I'm trying to work off this training-to-game transfer and I can find ways to reduce the amount of time that it takes for you to acquire a skill you can use actively in a game, then the next time you come you're going to be looking for the next thing, and I need to be prepared to provide that opportunity. If not, that will reduce your view of my effectiveness. But if every time you come you get a new a new way of thinking, a new skill, or anything that improves you the next time you're in competition, you're going to want to come back. That's the pressure I put on myself, and that's an important part of the sickness. It helps me stay on edge, but it's a sickness. You're trying to always stay one step ahead and put pressure on yourself to be able to deliver that next best idea.

The third layer is that the teacher is the student. I'm always the student, and I'm my best client. The best research I've done is the research I've done on myself. I'm always the student trying to learn from the players. They're the ones who are the geniuses, not me. I'm the one who's trying to observe what they're doing and trying to understand it on a granular level that will allow me to then build it out and take it to another level. I try to take their genius and add different ideas to it that create opportunities for uniqueness or build awareness that this is an underutilized advantage. It's a hidden ability that could produce better results if utilized properly. That's my job. That's my role. But in order to do that, I have to be constantly learning. I've got to be able to find something I've learned every single day that's going to contribute to the betterment of my athletes.

The last layer is that there are no shortcuts. There are no marketing tricks. There are no network schemes. There are no social media tricks or overexposure that are going to give me a shortcut. I see people in in player development taking what I would consider to be shortcuts to find their way into the NHL or find their way with different players. The problem is you're going to need to produce results. That's what we do. We are in the player improvement business, and the player needs to be able to make a tangible improvement during their time with you. If they're not able to do that, they'll find someone else. That's why I say I'm my best student. I follow the same path I'm trying to impart to our players. I'm trying to build my background knowledge, my depth of skill, and my level of awareness. The Triple Helix I use in reference to teaching our players is in direct parallel to the way I'm approaching my own career. This is one of the better things I've stumbled upon. I try to take the same authentic approach building my own career as I do developing these athletes. There is no shortcut to that. It's hard work. You roll up your sleeves every day. You have to watch the video, do your own research.

I have people who do research for me now, but I still do my own. We still build our own systems. We're still looking for the next best idea. That's really important. It's a focus on the process that leads to results. The research is critical. I have to do the research. Every day we have to be researching. I have to know more. My advantage has to be I know I'm more prepared. I understand this player better than he knows himself. That has to be my advantage. That will lead me down a path that will give me original content. It'll be unique ways to teach, unique ways to communicate, unique expressions of skills and ability to collaborate with the athlete in a way that pulls out the most creativity. That all comes from the process. If the process is not building into extraordinary results, then I need to re-examine my process.

I get anywhere between 20 to 30 requests every year around March or April from college students looking for internships. When it wasn't that many early on, I would respond to everyone. I would call them and ask, "What do you want to do?" The whole thing was just looking for a summer job that would give them an opportunity to make some money and to learn from me. My attitude was that I'm in a never-ending quest for new ideas, so for every minute I'm spending trying to teach you what I'm doing, I'm taking away from my own learning, which I'm going to be relying on once we hit the season.

My fear was I'm going to get that done, then they're going to go back to school or move on to the next thing. I always struggled with this. When we started getting so many more of these requests, I started to ask myself what it was I really needed. If I was going to bring one of these people on, what do I want? Well, I'm only as good as my next best idea. That's what our quest is every day. That requires someone with a capacity to think outside the box or have original ideas. What I would do is tell the person, "If you want to work for me, I need you to come up with a new idea. When you have a new idea, just send me that idea. It doesn't have to be good idea; it just has to be different. Teach me something I don't know. Give me something to pause to think about. That's all you need." I just needed to see a capacity to think differently, which would then spark me to be able to send them on projects, much the same way John Stevens did for me. It's like my bias against shortcuts. College kids are trying to acquire work experience in a field, and I'm someone who has a bias because I did so much for free and was so willing to do it just for the opportunity to learn. And that's just not this. That's just not the perspective or objective. It was just really hoping for one kid to say, "Oh yeah, that's great, I'll show you my idea, I have these ideas in mind," and that would start a great relationship.

That's how I started with Brett Vancise. He's my longtime assistant. He started with me when I had made a terrible decision that cost me dearly. It was the worst professional decision I've made in my career. I was at the lowest point of my career, and I met Brett. I was in no position to even pay myself, let alone pay him. So he came on with me and worked for upwards of six months without pay. He was just trying to learn what we do and find a way to contribute with the trust that at some point, things would turn around. Ultimately, they did, and we were able to forge a great working relationship. He is now an invaluable component to what it is we do with the level of precision and research and way we track players. He passed the ultimate test in terms of working with me and the way my mind works, and he's able to contribute at a level beyond expectation and create a model for us that allows us to do things differently and reinvent ourselves at different times. In 2019, Brett himself did 2,200 player performances. That's an incredible amount of research we're able to capitalize on. That's a level of intellect he's collecting he can share with me that gives me the tools I need to be able to do what I do.

When someone starts with me, they really don't have any value to me. The value is only realized on the on the backend. At first, it's a pure deficit. The time I have to invest is to the exclusion of time I should be spending on something else, so I'm working on a deficit to try to bring someone up to speed with no guarantees they'll have the capacity to provide a level of ideas that will move the needle for us positively. It just isn't worth the time and energy for us to do that moving forward unless the person can show a capacity to create original thoughts. That's really what we need. It's not going to come from an internship necessarily. It's going to come from someone who is passionate about new ideas, is creative, and has a mind full of questions they want to have answered. That's what our search is for.

When I went through the experience with my mentor, Bud, he said he was going to be with me for two weeks and then stayed with me for 20 years. He invested in my ability to teach and became a really close friend of mine. I always thought during that time, *I hope I'm going to be able to find a kid like me.* A snot-nosed kid from Ridgeway, Ontario, or from some small town like me, who doesn't have any real hope to do anything of any real value but has a tremendous desire and willingness to do something, or who would be in a position to be different in order to be successful. There was no chance for them to be the same as everyone else and have any level of success, which was basically my plight. I wanted to try to find someone like that and then be the Bud for that person. Now, as I look at it, why would I do it for just one person when I could write this book or be involved in the education process of a lot of people through my experience, and perhaps I can impact many more? Even though I may not spend any time with them personally, they could read these words and become inspired in some way, and that's the push they need to start thinking about things differently. Then they can begin to innovate and start to create value in our great game in a way that pushes the needle forward for player development.

If that's the case, then perhaps the best way I can honor the people who invested in me as that snot-nosed kid is trying to find a way to be different, because I had no chance to be successful in any other way. If I wasn't different and I wasn't better, there was going to be no chance for me. I had no backup plan, so I had to be all-in. That's how the sickness was developed and has been maintained, and it carries with it a healthy and sometimes unhealthy fear of irrelevance. If I go too many days without really uncovering something different, I create a lot of anxiety for myself, because this is what I need to have going forward. That's what's going to maintain my relevance among my players. I fear they're going to outgrow me, and I can't have that. That's just something that burns inside of me.

I'm always going to be able to stay one step ahead. As much as the sickness creates problems in terms of balance, it is, to me, a rite of passage in order to be great. You just have to be all-in. You have to look at things from a totally different perspective. If you are, then at least you give yourself a chance. But if you don't have the sickness, it's going to be really difficult to achieve any level of greatness.

TESTIMONIAL

ADAM NICHOLAS
on Darryl Belfry

Adam Nicholas struggled to catch Darry Belfry's attention the first time he approached him.

Nicholas wasn't discouraged. He knew it wasn't the right time or place. The second time he had better luck with what began as a Twitter interaction.

"I said, 'I got something to show you,'" said Nicholas, who runs Stride Envy Hockey and has a number of NHL clients. "He goes, all right, here's my e-mail. So I sent him over this defensive skating progression that I had done in a video DVD package, teaching like how to keep a tight gap through using your feet. He's like, 'Wow, here are my thoughts, this is what I think you can do better with that, but this is the first time someone shared something with me that I never really thought about.' So that's how we kind of connected. Because I wasn't just trying to take his stuff and then show him things that he was already doing through my lens. It was more along the lines of me showing him things that he might not have thought about, and that's how we got a connection. That to me truly explained and showed me he really is an unbelievable teacher."

Since then Belfry and Nicholas have been working together, and Nicholas finds himself continuing to learn and evolve under the guidance of Belfry.

"I really fell in love with the process which he always challenged me to improve everything I did," Nicholas said. "Nothing was just good or okay, let's run with that and then just kind of burn its course with it. It's like, okay, we're doing this now, let's add to it, let's build it, study this and let's see if we can take this and move it into specific areas so that we can really enhance it and move skills along and not just get stuck or have a shtick. I feel most other skills coaches have got their shtick that they live off of rather than just being the best in every single possible area so you can provide every player with the most unique experience when you're on the ice them in terms of learning and teaching and maximizing the players' ability. That's what he did."

Nicholas has witnessed as Belfry has continued to prove people wrong about what's possible in player development.

"When I first started, there were a lot of people in NHL front offices who weren't very keen on Darryl because of how outspoken he was about player development on Twitter," Nicholas said. "They just don't truly understand player development like that, and what Darryl is trying to get across is how to teach players to really maximize their assets. So many players want that, they crave that, but yet there's nobody in the NHL that can really give it to them. That's what Darryl is trying to explain, but nobody wants to hear that. You know they don't want to think a development coach can influence a player's success. They say they do, but they don't really want to believe it. And that's what Darryl is. He's good at proving that, proving I can help you."

21

TEACHING SKILL IS A SKILL

OVER THE YEARS, I'VE LEARNED THE HARD WAY THAT TEACHING skill is a whole set of skills in and of itself. The one thing I came to understand is you just don't wake up one day and become a great teacher. It takes a long time to acquire teaching skills, and there are so many elements of teaching skill you have to become fluent in. What I realized was that in becoming a teacher, I began to see a parallel with my skill acquisition. The process of my acquisition and how intentional I was trying to become in learning and experimenting with skill development and all the teaching elements was a very similar development path as the players I was teaching.

A player doesn't wake up one day and decide to be an NHL player. It takes a lot of time. It takes a lot of work in the Triple Helix I've been describing, acquiring the background knowledge, the depth of skill, the awareness. It's the exact same thing as it relates to learning to become an effective teacher. You have to acquire background knowledge. You have to have a wide range of depth of skill, and you have to have awareness in and be intentional about not only what you're teaching but what you're learning.

The interesting dynamic I came across was while I'm teaching, I'm also learning to teach. I'm taking in information from the athlete. I'm watching his or her response. I'm evaluating my performance. I'm learning to teach, and that creates a higher level of skill for me for the next time. I've become more intentional about my own skill development that I know I'm not as fluent in. Maybe it's becoming a better communicator. Maybe it's changing the vocabulary. Maybe it's teaching a particular skill. Maybe it's learning the actual skill, so I can demonstrate it properly. All those things I'm becoming intentional about and trying to learn become part of my depth of skill process. While I'm then teaching that to my athlete, I'm also learning it at the same time. That where this co-teaching really takes a life of its own for me and is relevant all the time. It's the actual goal of teaching. It's to be learning while you're teaching, whether you're learning from the athlete or learning your own skills of teaching. I never really looked at it that way until about 10 years ago, and then when I started to become more intentional about the skills I was trying to acquire I started to realize that's exactly what it was.

You might say, "There are hundreds of concepts in this book I want to learn to teach, but where do I start?" My approach would be to be intentional about learning one of the skills and then try to get this reciprocal relationship and awareness between what you're doing and how it's being received. Start that process the way the Triple Helix entwines itself together. You're not going to be able to learn all the skills all at once. You have to be intentional. You have to see which ones are the most important based on your own current skill set and start to fill in the gaps. Become intentional about the way you learn those things, but integrate it as a multi-dimensional process so you're taking in a lot of information and creating this reciprocal relationship between yourself and the athlete. While you're teaching him or her, you're also learning how to teach, and it's just a fascinating dynamic.

I was also trying to develop a calling card for myself. *What are you good at? What is your thing? How do you influence skill?* People would ask me what I teach, trying to figure out what my specialty was, and I never really developed a specialty. I teach whatever needs to be taught. I have to research it. Once I pinpoint what it is, I have to figure out how I'm going to influence that in a positive way. I have to learn how to teach what I'm going to teach. It's a never-ending process for me. I have to be the expert at whatever it is I'm teaching for that player. Then the next player comes out the following hour and he needs something different, and I need to switch gears and become an expert at whatever that player needs.

When I was coaching and we were starting off with our teams, I began with these kids at eight, nine years old and worked with them until about the time they were 15. By the second or third generation of those players, I had learned quite a few things about the skill I was trying to teach and what I was trying to influence. One of the things my mentor Bud said to me was if you can skate and pass the puck, you can play at any level. Those became two real staples of our delivery to our teams. We want to be known as a team that skated well and moved the puck well. If we did those two things really well, that would translate the best for those players to move on when they were leaving us.

What was really cool was there were several instances in which an opposition coach from the other team would come to us and say they were out somewhere and saw one of our players in a camp or playing for another team in a tournament and knew right away that kid was a Playmaker because of the way he skates. It wasn't just once but several times people had come to me. The difference back then was we were teaching a ton of crossovers. We really valued kids crossing their feet. It created a difference because so many kids were and still are skating in straight lines. So much of the instruction from a power skating perspective you could get at that time was very stride-oriented. We, of course, were trying to be different, and so we went right down the crossover path. That became kind of a calling card for me for a long time. People knew based on their experience of watching our kids who was a Playmaker because of the way he skated.

It was my first exposure to having a calling card as a teacher. Then, as I got further down the track, I started putting together some of these pieces. I was really trying to embody the idea of teaching the three skill speeds together at the same time, speed of hands, speed of feet, and speed of mind. I was really trying to link them all together as a coordinated effort of the learning process. And if I was teaching skating, I was going to do it while teaching puck skills at the same time. I was going to do it in recurring situations that would happen in a game, so the kids would have a better ability to understand what we were doing. I was linking tactics to skill. I felt like that became my calling card. That's what we do best.

There's a great Brayden Schenn story. When he went to the World Championships, there were a few players on the Canada team I had worked with previously. He stepped on the ice and started doing his warm-up. One of the players skated by and said, "You started skating with Belfry, right?" They could recognize the types of things I was teaching. They could see that in in themselves, so I thought that was interesting. There are a lot of players in the league who would ask me if I worked with particular player. I would say yes, and they would say, "Oh, I could tell." The calling card is not what I say I'm going to teach, but it's how it's expressed in my students, which others can then see. There's a uniqueness but also a common link to the types of things we're teaching that's different than what other people are doing or how other people play. You can recognize it right away, and I think it is a tremendous consideration as it relates to learning to teach. It takes a long time to develop that. It takes a long time to learn what your actual calling card as a teacher is.

Of course, you don't want it to be too limiting, but at the same time there has to be a reason why people come to you. You're going to come to me because my training-to-game transfer rate is extremely high. I can teach you something on Tuesday and you're going to be able to use it on Wednesday. I'm going to be able to link the tactics to the skill, which is a separator for you. It creates a skill that separates you from everyone else, and it's also a skill that separates me from everybody else. Again, it has that kind of dual thing where it's a co-teaching environment.

One of the other things I wanted to do early on was answer the question of how much time it takes to teach skill. For the longest time, people were under the impression that it just took forever to learn skills. My experience was very different. I felt like I could make an impact very quickly. I felt like if I was even more well-researched and had an even better understanding of the player's ancillary skills and refined my teaching process to become more efficient and more effective, I could continue to reduce the time it took to teach skill. I was constantly looking to be different and better. Part of being different was doing things in a new way to produce results either better or quicker for the athlete. They could learn it faster because I was so dialed in with those training-to-game transfer rates. My progressions were on point, and I could overcome the bridge skills and any physical challenges the player had. When I started to take responsibility for the learning process, which was another critical component to this, I knew I could transfer that skill the next day. It creates a burden, and that burden is something I welcome. There's pressure here for me to really try to perform and become even more dialed-in and efficient, to read the athlete better and become more effective in what I was developing.

There are several skill sets I think are really relevant to teaching skill. It takes a long time to acquire these types of skills. You have to have time in the field. It takes years to develop a presence and develop an understanding of being able to be watch a player so intently and know what to do next with that athlete. I think that's a critical skill. You have develop an eye for skill. Being able to read video is a skill, but just being able to watch a player execute skill on video and know exactly what you're looking for to be able to see the details inside the movement is a really difficult skill. And when they're moving quickly, there are really subtle differences. You have to be able to either see it in real time or see it on video. Because if you're going to make any kind of meaningful impact on skill, it's going to occur through movement. Hockey is expressed in movement, so if you want to make an impact, it has to be rooted in a change in movement and the linking of the movement. It's the movement, but it's also how they think. So can you impact how they think and how they move concurrently inside the skill expression? Then they have to be able to read and recognize when these situations can occur or manipulate and dictate when these situations can occur to really be able to make that impact. Being able to develop an eye for what it is you're actually looking for. How do you even know when you're watching the player what's wrong? If you do know what's wrong, do you know what order you should teach the correction in? If you know the order you can teach it, do you also know the ancillary skills that surround it so that you can pick which of those skills you can use to transport it through the development process? That takes a long time to really understand. That's why it's such a difficult process, a never-ending learning process. That's why I say the co-teaching and learning is so critical. It's so important you're in that loop with the player you're teaching, when the player's learning and you're learning how to be a better teacher. Being in that loop is constant; it never ends.

With deconstructing skill, can you take a look at a skill and deconstruct it into its pieces? Can you understand skill gaps and why a player has this skill and this skill but is missing another? You need to isolate and build that up and put it back in to be able to strengthen the chain of those five skill expressions. Understanding how to deconstruct skill, re-teach it, put it back, plug it into situations, and link it to the mind has been a lifelong process for me, for sure.

That's just the skill part. There are all the other components. I can watch a player. I can diagnose exactly what's wrong. I can see it clearly. I can see the skill progression. I could understand conceptually how to build a development plan to execute that. But if I can't deliver a message the athlete can understand and I don't have a relationship with the athlete where I can leverage that trust and I don't understand the manipulation of success rates to build developmental momentum, that whole human side of delivering the message is a whole other platform I have to learn. Otherwise, I can know whatever I want to know, but if I don't have a medium to communicate it in which the athlete can both understand it and then express it exactly the way I want it, then what are we doing it for? You're going to get lost. I could know the most and still get the least done because I don't have the leverage of the relationship and that capacity to accept responsibility. When you listen to coaches or skill instructors, you can tell their experience level by the level of responsibility they're willing to accept in that player's development. If you don't have a high level of experience in coaching and teaching and don't have those experiences of being able to transfer skill and the confidence that comes with it, then when someone says something about the player, you're going to point out the restrictions and say he's not smart enough, not athletic enough, doesn't have enough skill. You're going to have a laundry list of reasons why this player cannot learn a skill. He wasn't born with it. He's not instinctual enough. He's just a practice player or just a game player—

whatever the reason you're going to have for why he wasn't able to acquire this skill in his time with you. But you're not going to put it on yourself, you're going to put it on the player. *It's the player's responsibility. He has a restriction. What do you want me to do?* The longer I did this and the better I got, the more responsibility I was willing to accept in that player's individual development. I'm at the point now where it's entirely my fault if this doesn't happen. If the player doesn't learn the skill in a timely fashion, it is 100 percent my fault. I obviously didn't approach it properly. I misread it. I didn't do the proper progression, whatever, but I'm willing to accept 100 percent of that responsibility. Ten years ago, I would have probably accepted maybe 50 or 60 percent of that responsibility because there was so much skill I didn't have. I didn't have the capacity to accept the responsibility. You need that capacity. You need a skill set in order to accept that responsibility.

That's why I think the burden of transfer is huge to become a teacher. Once you know you can do it, now it's a burden. If you know you can teach or influence a skill today for the player to use the next day, that's a burden. And you have that burden every time you go on the ice. You now have a responsibility with that player. In my case, it's a paying customer who is coming there to have me influence his skills, and I have a responsibility to be able to do. I have the ability to do that. I need to be able to impart it on that player, and the player needs to be able to express it and understand the specificity of that development to a point where we could then track the ability to transfer that particular skill. It's about understanding the details enough to be able to recognize it and then educate the people I'm teaching to be able to recognize it so they know when they're doing it.

There's nothing better for me than getting a text from a player who says, *I was thinking about you on the bench today because I was trying that particular skill and I knew you'd be happy* or *I*

TEACHING SKILL IS A SKILL

knew you wouldn't like that one. That's awareness. I'm teaching the specificity of understanding exactly what is going on in that athlete in that situation. They can recognize it and that creates that level of awareness. That's part of the burden that I just need to be able to accept. But to have the burden, you have to have the skill set and the ability. That takes time.

Developing a teaching process like the Triple Helix is a critical part. I remember years ago, I just wanted to be busy. I was sitting there waiting for the phone to ring. I wasn't in any demand. Then, when I became in great demand, I remember my dad saying to me, "Be careful you're not too busy to think." He must have seen how important it was for me that I was constantly coming up with new things or doing the research. I feel like if you get too busy, you're not going to have that. I did get into stretches in my career where I was too busy to think. I wasn't learning as much because I wasn't thinking. I wasn't reflective. I wasn't an active participant in the learning aspect of the co-teacher relationship. I learned to become a better teacher, and because I'm a better teacher, I re-teach the athlete in a in a better way to produce better results. Now I continue that loop. If you're too busy to think, then that becomes a problem. Over the last few years, I've done a better job of scheduling time to really be reflective and make sure that I'm not too busy to think.

Again, like the parallel process of player development, the teacher is the student, and the Triple Helix is the most important element of that and really understanding that whole circle of the development process. Right now, we're in a very interesting time where coaches' reaction to skills coaches is kind of where analytics was a few years ago and strength and conditioning was years ago. There's an acknowledgement in the coaching fraternity that there's value there. It's trying to figure out what the value is and the role skill development can have on a coaching staff. It needs to be integrated into the fabric, but the skill development coach has to be diverse and has to be able to follow a path and enhance a team's ecosystem. It's tremendously difficult to really integrate yourself into that fabric. We're still not there yet. The burden is on the skills coaches to create meaningful work to have an impact on the players and have a speed of transfer that allows the coaches to have confidence in them. The coach's responsibility for me is to be open-minded and able to recognize the impact or recognize the process and be curious. If the coach is curious and provides interesting projects for the skills coach to be able to prove the burden of the meaningful work, you can create a really cool relationship. But it takes time, and we're not there yet because we don't have enough skill development coaches doing meaningful work. So it can be viewed by coaches as very isolated. It's almost like summertime work. We have a lot of work to do and we need more and more people in this community of skill development to start taking the next step to be able to find our way with meaningful roles and create an impact at all different levels, not just the NHL level. There's a need there, and it's just trying to get more of us finding ways to become more meaningful, more impactful, and create a better speed of impact so that coaching staffs can better see how it can be integrated.

In order to do that, we need a process. We have to do a better job of analyzing players and coming up with better systems to analyze players to be able to prioritize the acquisition plan. What skills does this player need, and how can we impact that? What order should it be impacted in? Do we know if we teach one thing it could carry over to five or six things? Do we understand the ancillary skills, or are we just like a beaver trying to fix the dam? Or do we understand we can build things more holistically or by leveraging assets a player might add to carry the new skills? We need to create better relationships to where the player has more trust and we can reward that trust by creating more impact in that athlete quicker. We can build that developmental equity which gives us a chance to really take some shots with our development because we can leverage the success rates. Because we understand that whole process, we leverage the relationship to be more effective. We can execute the teaching process and make sure we know the teaching progression. We can adapt and adjust quickly as the player is acquiring the skill. We recognize it and can start moving on to the next. We're not scripted, but we are still process-based. We're not flying by the seat of our pants, but we're not following a script that is going to be limiting to the athlete, either. We create a great feedback loop, which is becoming more and more and impactful.

You are the teacher. At the end of the day, the teacher teaches. The drill doesn't teach. The skill doesn't make it on its own. You are the teacher. You need to teach, and you need to create an environment that allows the feedback loop to begin and the athlete to ultimately take responsibility of his or her own development. With transfer tracking, do we know how much impact we're having when we watch the games? Is the player better? If so, where, and how did you impact him or her? Can you quantify that? Because if you can, then we really have a great teaching process. We get away from schticks and people doing limited development because they're not willing to analyze or study the game. We have to study the game. The more we do that, the more it gives us a better opportunity to have more depth of skill, more background knowledge, and ultimately more awareness, so we don't get stuck doing limited items, which transfers the responsibility onto the athlete. We want to be in a situation where we're acquiring more and more teaching skill so we can assume more and more responsibility for the development of the athlete. I think that's critical.

That's why, for me, teaching skill is a real skill. You just don't wake up one day and all of a sudden you're a skill instructor. It takes years and years and years. It takes a ton of intentional development. You can know a ton about the game and skill development, but you're going to have to intentionally do something to become much more effective so that we can continue to make great gains. The more we accept the burden of coming up with great research that leads to meaningful work, the easier it's going to be for us to have a greater impact and more speed of transfer that's going to be amenable to and accepted by coaches and players at all levels.

22

BURDEN OF GREATNESS

ONE OF THE GREATEST PRIVILEGES I HAVE HAD IN MY CAREER HAS been working with players who have the burden of greatness. These are players who are expected to become the best in the game. Every year, they have the burden of battling for that title. It doesn't sound like it's that big a deal. There is a long list of players who could win a scoring title in any given year. There are many players who could lead a team to a Stanley Cup in a given year, but there are only a select few who have the annual burden of competing to be the best player in the game. This is a player who has to win an MVP. He has to win a scoring title. He has to win a Stanley Cup. He has the burden of that career checklist. There are a lot of star players in the league who are unbelievable players, but they don't have the burden to be the best in the game. It's a never-ending weight they carry with them as long as they play.

What I found when I work with these players is they think very differently. The difference between their thought process and the process of even a superstar player is marked. It's different in the sense they have an immediate feeling they're responsible and carry that responsibility. They're responsible for their team. They're responsible for their linemates. They have to find ways to make other people better. They know the pathway for them to achieve these goals is through the development of the people around them and their ability to work effectively with those people.

Now, what I've found is if they're able to win a Stanley Cup or an MVP—or both—very early in their career, it becomes very different. For a player who's already done it, it's different in the sense that the fire burning to try to do it again burns even more, but the box is checked so it becomes a different mindset. It has a never-ending quality to it, but there's a confidence about him he continually leverages. These players are different from a player who has the burden but hasn't done it yet. There's an anxiousness and urgency that goes with that if it doesn't happen early. It's very distinguishable when you spend any kind of time with them.

The NHL is very much situational. Whether it's linemates, opponents, game situations—everything is tactical. It's a very situational league. Because of that, to slay the burden, you have to find ways to overcome your situation. The NHL is very much a defense-focused suppression league and in a lot of ways it's risk-averse, although it is getting better every year. But in order to overcome that suppression mentality, you have to earn those liberties through your results. You have to find that balance between having an opportunity to play with the risk necessary to be special while being responsible in production—and you have to do it against the game's best. You're playing against the best people every night and you've got to find a way to produce. And it's an expectation, not a hope. The expectation is you are responsible for winning. Part of overcoming your situation is you have to be able to produce with any type of player. Every team's situation is different. Every team has different assets. Some have very good offensive skill in the top six. Other teams have to divide that skill throughout the lineup. Some teams are competing for championships. Others are battling to become contenders. Every situation is different, and you have to be able to produce in less-than-stacked situations. There is no escaping how critical it is to find a way to elevate your group.

So it's a twofold burden. The first part is you have to be the reason your team is winning—and your team has to win. Those two things go hand in hand. In order to do that, you really have to elevate people. You've got to find ways to leverage your hockey sense. You have to provide situations in which other people can be leveraged inside of your hockey IQ and processing speed. You can walk them into a play, go to situations or places on the ice they can get the puck in better spots. But you're the one who understands where it should go, so you put the puck in places where they can do it. And you have to adapt. You've got to adapt to your team's system. You've got to adapt to your linemates and recognize where the growth opportunities are.

This is where it gets interesting, because I find the guys who have won early have a clearer ability to recognize and seize opportunity. They understand the difference between a possession puck and a puck they can attack with, and they're a little bit more patient. That comes with the experience of having done it, having won a scoring title, a Stanley Cup. Once you've done that, then it's a drive for more. They have much more clarity, where others will take more chances on pucks and look to convert attack pucks that are actually possession pucks. This is the balance between seizing the risk to be special while still being responsible. The difference lies in the evaluation of the quality of the puck and what you can do with that possession.

That's the value of playing the game in sequence. There's a puck you know is a possession puck, so you just make a possession play, move to the next play, then move to try to get the puck back in a situation where you can attack. So rather than having each individual puck graded, you look at whether it's a possession puck or an attack puck and try to create a chain of events that converts a possession puck into a second or third possession that is a puck to attack with.

How are you acquiring the puck—loose pucks, off the pass, forced turnovers? It's way easier to attack when you're getting the puck off the pass. But the lower in the standings your team plays, the harder it is to get those types of pucks, because it's probable you will be playing a much more conservative style and with players who don't have the offensive capacity or encouragement to make plays in certain areas of the rink.

Can you turn a lemon situation into lemonade? This goes part and parcel with the burden of being the best. At the end of the day, this player takes it upon himself to be responsible for influencing winning. When the game is over, the first place everyone's going to look is at you and what it was you did, so you have to find a way to produce every night. Put yourself in a spot where you're going to be able to influence the opportunity for your team to win. That's a fascinating burden borne by just a few players in the game. When you spend any kind of time with these players and hear how they talk and the things they care about and the things they're interested in, it's a different world than for any other player.

One of the other interesting components that goes along with this is being able to assess positive and negative impacts in players. We talk a lot about positive impact on a line or when a given player is on the ice, and what we need to understand is the facilitation process of the possession effects. The possession right now is largely defined by a shot proxy. It's a proxy of possession numbers. But sometimes the players who generate personal shots are a restriction to playmaking and shot quality. So someone has a positive effect in generating shots, but is also a restriction in generating quality shot attempts. So where's the balance between generating high-volume shots and generating high-quality shots? There's a tipping point where you're going too far to try to create so much quality that you're not getting any volume. Then there's the other end of the spectrum, where you're creating so much volume that you're not really generating any quality. Somewhere there's a balance, and that's really what you're trying to find, but someone is facilitating those possession effects. This is where we need to be—finding people who are positively impacting those possession effects.

I think we need to acknowledge negative possession effects. There are players who are positive in our proxy of creating high-volume situations who have negative effects on the opportunity to actually create production. These players struggle to understand the value of multiple possessions in a sequence. They just get the puck and shoot it, causing another loose puck, which can reduce the ability to create quality at all. It creates a 50-50 that we may not be able to get the puck, so it's a waste of possession. We know the quality of a possession improves with the number of times that star player gets the puck in a given possession sequence. We want the best players on our team to touch the puck two, three, four times in a given sequence, because they're then influencing and facilitating the puck possession effects. They have an opportunity to facilitate it because they touch it multiple times. The environment that surrounds their possession expands and improves each time they touch the puck. We need to be able to influence how often those players are getting the puck.

We talk a lot about players who can win pucks, but they've got to be able to win the puck and make that next play, and the struggle is finding guys who can do the latter. What happens is these players who have a burden to be the best have to adapt to the players they're playing with. If you have a guy who's an elite puck retriever, he needs to be able to make the next play. If he's not capable of making the next play, then he has to move into positions where he can make it easy for that player to give him the puck, even though it might not be an ability to attack right away. He might have to add another play into the sequence. The good news is we have the puck. The bad news is the work really starts at that point. We're trying to create a second, third, or fourth possession in that sequence to give us an opportunity to generate a truly dangerous attack.

One of the real burdens is the personal performance in a team game. Everyone is responsible for generating top-level performance inside the team. That's the objective, but that's not how it plays out practically. There is one person who has the burden of having his personal performance related to the team game. The team results are assigned based on that player's performance. It's a very different set of expectations. It is a burden and responsibility, and we have to acknowledge that burden exists. We can help facilitate these players to have better opportunities to fulfill that burden that's unique to them in a given team.

On a team level, everyone is responsible to do their job. But what if your job is to decide the game? That the plays you make decide the outcomes. You're the one who makes those critical plays at the critical moments. You've got to be able recognize those moments. You've got to have a feel for the game and play with such detail, and that detail is what moves the needle. You need to have the feel for when the game needs to turn and recognize a moment for impact and where you have a chance to threaten. There's a weakness in the defense where you could perhaps decide the game in the first period. There's an opportunity to attack and you must seize it when it presents itself. You just don't know when that opportunity will come. But when you see it, you'll know it, and you attack and you look to decide the game with ferocious aggressiveness. These are guys who have high levels of experience impacting games. They've been responsible for this for quite some time.

They've had moments in which they've missed, and they have a great ability to reflect. They have tremendous detail in their ability to recall the way every play happened in the game. They can assess those situations, and they know when they missed a moment. Maybe there was a moment in the second period where the defenseman broke his stick, or they had a line out there for an extended shift—a clear competitive advantage to take control of the game—and they missed the opportunity by being conservative. There was a quick two-on-one that happened in the middle of the second period, the only odd-man rush that occurred during the game, and that was an opportunity to score they missed. Any two-on-one in a big game could be that chance that decides it, because you might not get another one of those opportunities. These players have an ability to recognize those moments. They know when those moments are and they attack. They talk about those moments more than anyone else. They talk about missed situations in which the game could have been decided earlier. They talk about obscure moments like a line change opportunity where they had a fourth line caught out there and they came on fresh and they just let them off the hook with a poor possession. There are many situations in a given game where there's an opportunity to be aggressive to attack, and these players recognize those moments. They don't always take advantage of them, but they know where they are and they're constantly assessing them.

One of the more interesting examples of this level of memory was a clip of LeBron James in the NBA Finals in which he recounted the last eight possessions of the game. He was lamenting a missed opportunity to win the game, and the reporter asked him about a given play. He went back seven or eight possessions and detailed each one. Everyone was amazed by how much detail he could remember for every single possession. He's not the only one. The players who carry the burden of greatness have that level of detail and ability to recount given situations. They're extremely reflective. These players learn from their mistakes and from missed opportunities. They talk about these moments in games they aren't even playing in or even in other sports. They try to train themselves to recognize and know every detail. They know the positioning of every player on the ice. They know who they're playing against, who they're playing with, what the play sequence was, what should have happened, what they could've done to correct it. A lot of this is in hindsight as they're recounting it. But when these types of mistakes are made, they know what was supposed to happen and they're always looking for ways in which they can become more effective in those situations. Sometimes it works where they're able to decide the game because they recognize the moments. They execute well. They've prepared their linemates to be able to seize those situations. Other times they're still a work in progress, but even then, they still understand every detail. This level of recall and detail may be an indicator of future capacity to be great.

It's fascinating how they see the game differently. They value different things. They understand the game on a very micro level. They understand the strengths and limitations of everybody on the ice. They study the game. They watch their opponents play. As a result of how different they are, they are also misunderstood, particularly early in their career. I've seen these players labeled as selfish, or as guys who can't win the big game or don't execute or have a hard time elevating their linemates. They get accused of having something missing, and this is what will prevent them from being great. The truth is they will be great. They'll find a way. They'll figure it out because they're so intentional about greatness. They see the game from that lens.

There's really no chance they won't be misunderstood. Any player who has this type of ability to have this burden where they have the opportunity to be the best player in the game is going to see the game differently, so their teammates have a hard time identifying with them. Coaches have a hard time identifying with them. They're really different in every way. It requires a lot of thought and inquiry to try to understand them. I've had opportunities to spend time with players who have this burden, and I find myself asking more questions than offering anything. It's truly a situation like no other.

The first thing is to understand how they think. Try to see these differences of how they see the game and the things they care about. They'll come up with a detail you didn't even notice; you'll have no idea what they're even talking about. They'll talk about the handedness of the weak-side D and how it made all the difference in him being able to defend a passing lane a certain way. The fact he had that handedness meant he could have taken advantage of him on the other side—these are the details they understand. They're highly reflective and they're typically very sensitive to the greatness burden. They understand it. They accept it. They relish in it, but it is a burden to carry every day, some of them all the way to the end of their career.

They also know the team system, inside and out. These players are sometimes accused of going rogue and either not knowing or adhering to the team system. They know it inside and out. They can describe every detail. They know every responsibility of every player on the ice. They know their teammates. They know who their opponents are. They know what the opponent's system is. The reason they're so interested in it is that's how they create. Their best success is through the predictability of others. Because they understand the predictability of positioning, they know where the opportunities are. If they didn't know the positioning or they didn't care about those things, they wouldn't see where the opportunities are as clearly. They're looking for every advantage and every opportunity to attack and put themselves in a position where they can decide the game. So every detail matters.

I always find it interesting to hear these players often accused of being hard to play with or having difficulty in a team system. My experience with them is very different. As it is, I get to hear some of their innermost thoughts of how they view the game. When they talk about opportunity, it is related to the predictability of where people are, which is directly related to the team structure.

The reason I find I have the most success with players who are the best in the world and have these burdens is they have what I call the luxury of improvement. They have the ability to improve because they have the luxury to try different things. Players who are the closest to making the NHL, like just breaking through the AHL, have the hardest time making big gains because there is so much risk that goes with change. They've worked their way up to being on the doorstep of making the NHL. Now you want to ask them to make all these radical changes? It's very unsettling for those players to make any changes, because they feel like there's too much risk if it didn't work that they would perhaps slide back further away from making the NHL. So they're much more conservative at that particular time. If you're going to make big gains with them, it has to be in other areas. For example, you could make big gains with them on a penalty kill, because that's not an area of the game in which they've typically spent a ton of time. They have a lot of growth opportunity there. They can make some big gains defensively for sure, but offensive gains and gains with the puck and skill components are really difficult for them to wrap their head around, because they're just that close and they feel one mistake with the puck could prevent them from achieving their dream.

The people who are well-established NHL superstars, guys who are regularly competing to be the best player in the world, have the most luxury for improvement. My best work comes with those great players. They have the most consistency in their habits. The best players in the world are the best players because they do the same things over and over and over again that lead to the highest rate of success. They have a real trust in the repeatability of their process, which is different than most players. They have a great feel for what's working for them and what's not and have a real willingness to transform any area that has a low level of efficiency. That's where I started with frequency and success rate as my two guides, because it's built on these players. They understand frequency and success rate. They want to have the highest level of trust in the repeatability of their process. If that repeatability is not leading to success, they're willing to change any and everything to try to improve that in the slightest way.

But the thing is all the improvements have to be specific to their game. That is the secret sauce of development as it relates to these elite players. They are interested in something that's highly specific. It's very difficult to work with these players if you don't study them, if you don't know what those repeatability factors are, the things leading them to success. It can be very difficult to make a meaningful impact, because they have such a specificity toward what they're trying to target and what areas of their habits they're trying to influence to make sure that they put themselves in the best possible situation to be successful.

What's clear about these players is there are levels to being a star player in the NHL. There are a lot of star players in the NHL who become superstars, and there are a lot of superstars who are unbelievable players who have great careers, but they're not at the level where they have the burden of being the best. That type of player is very different from everyone else. There are stages to that development those players have to go through, but it's still fascinating. I'm not sure we acknowledge it enough. There are some players who have to think differently because the expectations they have for themselves and the expectations others have for them to leverage their skills to influence winning is different than everybody else.

ACKNOWLEDGMENTS

"When the student is ready, the teacher will appear."

—Buddhist Proverb

Perhaps no other statement I've ever come across rings more true than this one. I have experienced this many, many times and have been fortunate to have had many great people lend me the next most important lesson that I needed to propel me to the next level of thinking...which opened the door to the next level of my personal performance.

What I find most interesting in reflection is how many people there actually have been. It genuinely feels like everyone had a hand in shaping how I think, and I'm amazed by the timing of their arrival in my life, how pointed and relevant their lesson was for me to learn at that time. There are too many to list here, but I feel any book that I would write on teaching has to acknowledge the key influencers who shaped how I think and the crafting of the tool set.

It all started with an 11th grade teacher, Mr. Laing. I was very much an angry kid wandering aimlessly when Mr. Laing told me I was crazy if I didn't choose a path in teaching.

To my mentor, Albert (Bud) Chenard, who came into my life at the perfect time, with a consistent message that "it doesn't matter how much you know if you don't build a vehicle to deliver the message." Bud is responsible for fostering so many of the early teaching tooling and the courage to blaze my own path. A genuine investment of time, care, and belief that carried me through the hardest times in the quest for relevance.

My co-teaching philosophy unknowingly began right at the beginning with Nathan Horton. I was a kid trying to teach a kid, and Nathan's ability was a confounding riddle to me that I obsessed over. He taught me a lifetime's worth of insight that is in the fabric of what I do every day.

There were many pivotal decisions that let me down this path. The most critical of those was the decision to leave coaching the St. Catharines Falcons in favor of focusing full-time on being the Coach Mentor at Brantford Minor Hockey. This fast-forwarded every aspect of my career in every way possible. Soon after I arrived, I met Larry Stevens, who was coaching Brantford, and we became great friends. Larry was instrumental in encouraging me to take full advantage of the opportunity for growth. His entrepreneurial mind and innovative spirit helped me countless times to continue to look for new ways. He also introduced me to his brother, John Stevens, who was coaching in the AHL for the Philadelphia Phantoms. John started me on my research path, which has been a 25-year process that has become the backbone of everything I do and everything I continue to uncover. It is my passion that I invest in every day.

Unbeknownst to me, John's Phantoms general manager was Dean Lombardi, whom I would spend nearly four years doing research projects for while he was the general manager of the Los

Angeles Kings. Dean taught me how to think. He challenged me to evolve from just collecting data to formulating an opinion and advocating for a position based on what I've learned. He taught me the value of digging into the research data with a process to uncover more questions. To use the data collection to create a never-ending loop of discovery. Dean Lombardi is a genius whose questions and contemplation were so unsettling and nerve-wracking that they created a desire to come to L.A. the next time with something (anything) of more value. The stress of trying to uncover something useful reshaped how I think. I can't imagine a more meaningful gift you can give someone than the opportunity to think differently. Dean gave that to me in every possible way.

Kyle Dubas and Sheldon Keefe, whom I met during their Sault Ste. Marie days. Kyle brought me to Toronto. What can I say about what it means to have a meaningful role with the Toronto Maple Leafs? I mean, the quest to win a Stanley Cup in Toronto is a lifetime opportunity, and the spirit of collaboration combined with the faith in my ability drives me every day to uncover the small percentages of improvement toward the ultimate prize.

Finally, Patrick Kane, with whom I've undergone a career-long journey from when he was eight years old to, now, a true co-teaching relationship. Patrick is a hockey genius; it's so fitting that the one who has the most to teach me is the one I have the longest relationship with. The best part of our relationship is the length of the collaboration, throughout all stages of the development of his personal game structure, which is the ultimate opportunity in player development. To be able to ride shotgun every step of the way and learn the process by which he interprets the game, how his skill set must lend itself to how he plays, is a once-in-a-lifetime opportunity. How do you thank someone who's entrusted you with such an opportunity? I don't have the words, other than to say, "Thank you."

Every teacher will tell you the relationships with the kids is what makes it all so special. They teach you more than you teach them. This has been my experience. Every player seems to offer something of a different challenge, and the uniqueness of each of those experiences creates an excitement that keeps the passion burning hot.

At the end of it all, I've realized that I was my own best student. My career is a reflection of the people from whom I had the privilege to learn. I am the very challenge of innovation, creativity, problem-solving, and empathy that I tried to be for the players I was entrusted with.

Thank you all, as you all have contributed to this book, which hopefully inspires many other coaches to think differently, take the insights that I've gained to the next level, and evolve well beyond what I've been able to uncover.

In teaching, ours is the opportunity to uplift, inspire, and enable...and in turn become uplifted, inspired, and enabled.

—*Darryl Belfry*

GLOSSARY

ACHIEVEMENT GAP: In the context of hockey, I use this term to describe wide disparities of skill acquisition opportunity due to preexisting skill capacities.

ANCILLARY SKILLS: The skills that are supporting to the main skill and help make up the entire execution system.

ASSET ATTACHING: Utilizing a player's best skill to help build a skill in development.

BRIDGE SKILL: When a player has a long-term restriction that will make consistent execution challenging, we intentionally build a set of compensations to accomplish the execution of the skill and overcome the restriction. Once the restriction has been alleviated, the player is left with both the original skill and the skills used to build the bridge, leading to greater depth of skill.

COMPETENCY BIAS: A distortion of what we feel is good based on the ability to perform in a limited pool.

COMPETENCY SPECTRUM: The range of ability of all the players skating on the ice at a given time.

COMPOUND POSSESSIONS: As a player acquires the puck multiple times in a given possession sequence, the quality of the possession (time, space, opportunity to attack) also improves, compounding the value of the possession opportunity.

COMPOUNDING EFFECT: When directly and intentionally influencing a given success rate, that improvement consequently leads to improvement in other success rates.

CO-TEACHER: When the student teaches the teacher as much as, if not more than, the teacher teaches the student. A symbiotic relationship.

DEVELOPMENT EQUITY: The confidence the player has that their teacher can help them learn and apply new skills and concepts directly into their personal game structure.

DRAG EFFECT: When the pace of the ice session is driven by the top players and it spontaneously elevates the contribution of the bottom tier.

DRILL RULES: When the setup of the drill is not a set movement pattern, but rather a specific set of rules that must be adhered to and goals to be achieved in the rep. The pattern and order of execution belongs to the players.

ENERGY SPIKES: Purposely employing a drill format that will infuse energy into the practice. Adding competition or reducing the work:rest ratio are examples.

FINGERPRINT: In the context of hockey, fingerprint is used to describe the uniqueness of every play which, while similar, are never exactly the same.

FORCED RECALL: When a collision course is designed for the player to run right into the target skill and they have no choice but to execute it.

HABIT SEQUENCE: When a player strings two or more of their habits together for competitive advantage.

HIDDEN RECALL: When the target skill is buried in the middle of an execution sequence, sending the skill into the subconscious and its expression quality by the athlete in a hidden situation will provide clues to the player's state of mastery.

ICE GEOGRAPHY: The ice markings that serve as landmarks and distances.

INSTANCE LISTS: A collection of a category of events in a list to view for purpose of study.

INTERDEPENDENT SKILL: A skill that is deeply connected to other skills.

ISOLATION: Teaching a single skill expression in one context.

LEAD FROM BEHIND: The time when the player assumes more responsibility for their own learning and you provide a supporting presence to their initiatives.

LEADING PASS: A play made by a player that intentionally leads their teammate into the space they want them to go in for the next play they have in mind.

PARALLEL STRUCTURES: When the teacher builds two skill packages independently of one another, then brings them together in the end either as opposing or complementary elements.

PERCEPTION OF SPEED: Every player on the ice has a different feel for how fast play is moving.

PERSONAL CONTEXT: A player's perception of themselves in comparison to a group.

PERSONAL GAME STRUCTURE: The collection of frequently utilized habits, tactics, and skills a player uses every game that, when studied, can accurately depict the lens by which they make decisions and play the game.

PLAYER ASSETS: A prominent, high-utility skill a player employs that leads to a high level of success and confidence. It is a skill that can be attached to and/or leveraged with other skills.

PLACEHOLDER SKILL: A skill that can be utilized at one performance level, but the positive effect it has at that level will diminish in the levels above and will need to be replaced with a higher-yielding skill.

PLATFORM SKILL: A technically sound skill expression that other skills can be attached to and stacked on top of.

PRACTICE PEAKS: The point(s) in a practice where what you have been building reaches the highest expression.

PROGRESSION SEQUENCE: An entire set of levels of execution, meticulously added one element at a time.

SCAFFOLDING: The analogy of building a new level. In development, the term is used to illustrate a mentality of using the previous platform to build the next level up.

SHAPESHIFTING: The way in which a player purposefully controls the movement of both their support players and the defender for competitive advantage.

SHOULDERING SPEED: The time in between the execution of two skills in sequence.

SKILL BLENDING: Connecting (shouldering) two independent skills and expressing them with so little time in between that the skills appear as one.

SKILL CONTINUUM: The reliance upon previous skill foundations to progress to the next level.

SKILL GAP: An underdeveloped skill that creates consistent execution failures during a skill blend, pattern, or sequence.

SKILL PEAK: The process of building the training session/practice to a point. Providing multiple interactions with the skill.

SKILL SEQUENCES: A group of skills utilized in a specific order for competitive advantage.

SKILL VARIABLE CODING: Multiple interactions with a skill. Different order of execution, context, area of the ice, pressure, pairings, and manipulations.

SPIDER HOCKEY: A personal game structure analogy that paints a picture of a spider's web, with the spider in the middle and all strands of the web leading back to the center of the web. In hockey terms, it's a player who positions themselves so well on the ice with such great principles of movement and timing that the puck appears to be following them around. The tactical decisions of the play for their team seem to be going through their hands.

STACK THE DECK: When the skill development activity favors one player over another through space, movement, quality of competition. One player is given a clear upper hand.

SUCCESS EQUATION: A mental map that depicts an acquisition strategy the player can follow.

TACTICAL CONNECTION: The depth of understanding the player has in how skills can be applied for competitive advantage.

TRANSFER TRACKING: Video analysis of the player's games after development and tracking opportunity for transfer recognition and execution.

TRANSLATABLE SKILL: A skill that remains effective when utilized from the level the player is currently to the NHL.

TRANSPORTER SKILL: A skill that can take the player into a new set of skills previously unavailable to them.

TRIPLE HELIX: The interconnected nature of background knowledge, depth of skill, and awareness as a player development methodology.

UNDERCURRENT: A rep-building technique whereby a single skill becomes a mainstay in every drill performed in a given ice session.